002384874

D1564887

The Challenge of Congressional Representation

The Challenge of
Congressional Representation

Richard F. Fenno

Harvard University Press

Cambridge, Massachusetts

London, England

2013

Library of Congress Cataloging-in-Publication Data
Fenno, Richard F., 1926–
The challenge of congressional representation / Richard F. Fenno.
pages cm
Includes bibliographical references and index.
ISBN 978-0-674-07269-5 (alk. paper)
1. United States. Congress. House. 2. Legislators—United States—Case studies.
3. Representative government and representation—United States. I. Title.
JK1319.F428 2013
328.73'0734—dc23   2012033728

Contents

The Challenge of Congressional Representation

Introduction

There are numerous reasons why political scientists might be interested in the individual, as well as the collective, activities of our elected politicians. Whatever the reasons might be—theoretical or practical—our interest in their collective behavior patterns has dominated contemporary political science research. In our work on Congress, studies involving career patterns, roll call vote patterns, committee activity patterns, and partisan voting patterns—both cross-sectional and over time—have been dominant. And individual politicians have usually ended up as integers destined for burial in large data collections. Except for the occasional biographical reference, the activities of particular individuals have not become central objects of political science research.

In the constituency-centered study that follows, however, the activities of five US House members are singled out for sustained inspection, with the intention of strengthening the scholarly case for close-up representation-centered studies in American national politics. And, specifically, to jump-start that endeavor by examining the political activities of several US Representatives in their home constituencies.

Congressional Representation is a study of representation in single-member districts, with plurality-wins-all systems of vote counting. As with the author's earlier study, *Home Style,* the constituency focus and the individual level of analysis have been maintained.[1] But, in this study, the protective anonymity of the elected individuals has been eliminated—all with the express intention of encouraging further research.

As "more of the same," this study is an indulgence. But it keeps afloat an important question for students of the United States Congress. What, if anything, are we doing at the present time to study the subject, and the activity, of congressional representation? Have we done enough? Have we done our best? And how, in particular, might we undertake some further analysis of the constituency-centric world in which, for a good part of their careers, all members of the US House of Representatives live, work, and undergo scrutiny.

Previous studies of House members in their home territories have not, to date, generated a recognizable research effort or an active, collaborative research community among students of Congress. Political scientist John Hibbing, in a thorough and appreciative introduction to a 2004 edition of the author's *Home Style,* discusses several reasons why an "up close and personal" approach to representation remains outside of the scientific mainstream.[2] More recently, the same point was conveyed in the pages of *The Chronicle of Higher Education.* Next to a colorful picture of the *Home Style* cover, the book is described as "a classic study of 18 members of Congress on their home turf." To which the author of the article adds, "The book has become a minor classic—but it has not had many offspring." After which, a fellow political scientist is quoted: "Everyone cites Fenno but very few people do that kind of work. There was remarkably little follow through."[3]

The present study can be viewed as the author's own "follow through." It is the last in a line of one person's explorations into the local political lives of our elected members of Congress. It is driven by the hope that students of American politics might recognize an unfinished and a wide-open research agenda. And, that some of them might respond actively to one last "nudge" toward collaboration in that direction.

The House members portrayed in this study span a half-century of research. The first acquaintance was made in 1964; and the last was made in 2000. In sequence, there are research travels in five very different locations—Upstate New York, North-Central Florida, Downstate Illinois, Eastern Pennsylvania, and Northern California. Three visits were with men; two were with women. Three were Democrats; two were Republicans. Importantly, they shared a respect for scholarship. They are in no sense a statistical—or a "representative"—sample. They are flavorful vehicles through which to make an argument in support of constituency-centric research on the United States Congress.

The timing of constituency visits varied widely over the various campaign cycles. So, too, did the amount of time spent per House member, per visit. While many of the same questions were used in all five cases, no common, written questionnaire was ever prescribed for the research. Constituency variety and personal preference drove questions and conversations in hard-to-compare directions. The usefulness of these preliminary pairwise comparisons can be judged by the reader.

Representation is a large political idea and a consuming political activity. Neither the idea nor the activity is likely to disappear from our politics or from our political science agenda any day soon. Representational relationships promote—and depend on—continuous negotiation. And there will be a lot of negotiation-centered, constituency-based storytelling in the pages ahead. The hope is that storytelling will be a helpful—perhaps even a necessary—preparation for the production of some more definitive and more cooperative representation-centered studies of the United States Congress.

— 1 —

Constituencies, Connections, and Representation

A Research Focus

> "It's hard to tell the depth of the well by the length of the pump handle."
>
> (OKLAHOMA POLITICAL WISDOM)

Politics, Places, and Patterns

The United States Congress is both a representative and a legislative institution. Its members are elected individually; and they legislate collectively. By conceptualizing, packaging, and studying vote strategies and vote patterns inside Congress, political scientists have gained remarkable explanatory purchase in studying the organizing and decision-making activities of our elected representatives—when, that is, House members (and senators) calculate and act inside the legislature. At the same time, however, we have been remarkably slow to study the connecting- and support-building activities of our elected representatives when they calculate and act outside the legislature. The result is a marked inside/outside political science research mismatch.

Policy-making activity in Washington is, of course, the accepted business of Congress. On the other hand, representational activity outside of Washington is the accepted strength of Congress.

At present, however, the study of legislation tends to overshadow, or to drive out, the study of representation. The study of representation—and of representational strength—opens up for scrutiny the political world outside of Congress. It begins with ambition and ends with accountability. And it is especially inviting territory for political scientists.

The US House of Representatives is our most representative national political institution. Its members lead complicated political lives moving between Washington and their single member-constituencies. As

4

yet, however, political scientists have not paid much close-up attention to House member activity patterns in their home places. And certainly not in comparison to our interest in political maneuver and policy outcomes inside the legislature in Washington.

Our literature overflows with studies of legislator preference patterns, partisan governing coalitions, individual voting strategies, and substantive policy outcomes. But we do not yet have a robust constituency-centric scholarship. Given an apparent disciplinary mismatch it will be argued here that we ought to pay more close-up attention than we presently do to House member activity in their constituencies. And, in so doing, that we direct more of our research to the representational underpinnings of our national legislature.

In the 1960s and 1970s, students of American politics discovered Capitol Hill. In steadily increasing numbers we journeyed there. And we collected a treasure trove of information and ideas about the legislative activity of House members and senators in that central meeting place. Since then, we have developed numerous theoretical formulations and measurement techniques to put our years of institution-centered research to good use.

We have, for example, strengthened our working knowledge: of chamber rules, of procedural tactics, of member vote strategies, of partisan and issue-centric vote patterns, of committee and party decision-making activities, of organizational adaptations, and of shifting policy outcomes.

The result is a voluminous, fast-growing, theory-rich, statistically sophisticated, and notably cumulative body of knowledge—about legislator preference patterns, partisan governing activities, voting strategies, and substantive policy outcomes. Our discipline-wide research record—probing, explaining, debating, and theorizing about decision making inside the House and Senate—has been pathbreaking. And to our great benefit, a large proportion of it has been both collaborative and cumulative.

Viewed comparatively, however, that impressive body of work stands also as a measure of how much less data gathering, how much less analytic precision, how much less collaboration, and how much less theorizing has been devoted to the study of House member constituency connections. To the study, that is, of House member support-seeking and support-building activities and patterns in their home places outside of Congress. In a nutshell, we know a lot more about the vote patterns of our "legislators" inside their Washington chambers than we know about the connection patterns of our "representatives" in their home constituencies.

Our analytic interests and our research capabilities in the study of legislative politics inside Congress have outpaced our interest, our work product, and our collaborative ingenuity in thinking about representational politics outside of Congress.

The elementary study that follows focuses on five members of the House of Representatives. And it examines congressional connection politics in each of their five constituencies. It can be read as one small-step effort to help redress a research imbalance. It is not an argument for any less attention to political activity on Capitol Hill. It is, instead, an argument in favor of more attention to the constituency lives and activities of our elected House members. And to the varied "home places" in which those lives are rooted.

Every member of Congress lives a separate and distinctive constituency life in a separate and distinctive congressional district. At present, however, we know a lot more about their voting patterns inside their legislature in Washington than we know about the connection patterns that carried them, and kept them, there. Hopefully, this study will begin to redress that imbalance as manifested in the House of Representatives. Hopefully, too, the study of representation will open up, for increased inspection, the political world outside of the legislature.

We know, of course, where to find members of the House when they are not in Washington. They are at home in their own single member districts. And we know what they are doing there. They are at work on their separate and distinctive playing fields—assessing and strengthening constituent support and constituent trust. Those member-constituent relationships are not "given." Every supportive constituency "fit" is a negotiated fit.

In a diversity of places, within accepted boundaries and through a variety of channels, 435 House members are negotiating positive and sustainable connections with a diversity of constituents. It is very largely a home place negotiation. It is related to, but it is very different from, the Capitol Hill activities of organizing and legislating. On the available scholarly evidence, House member inside vote patterns have been easier to aggregate and to analyze than House member outside connection patterns have been. And therein lies a research challenge. To date, the 435 home place connections have remained largely beyond the observations and the contemplations of the political science community.

Standing alone, our research—examining and explaining congressional politics inside the institution—has been path-breaking. Viewed comparatively, however, that same body of research stands as a measure of how much less data gathering, how much less analytic precision, how much less collaboration, and how much less theorizing have been devoted to member/constituency connections, and to member support-building patterns within their home places outside of Congress. Our analytic interest and research capabilities in the study of legislative politics inside the Congress have outstripped our interest, our work product, and our collaborative activity in analyzing representational politics outside of Congress.

The Challenge of Congressional Representation argues for increased attention to political activity in the countryside beyond. It aims to encourage more scholarly attention to the bedrock, constituency-centric strengths of the nation's most representative political institution.

On disparate home place "playing fields" and at varying distances from Washington, DC, House members can be found building and/or protecting connections with their constituents, one by one and in groups. They are working to win, strengthen, and protect constituent support and to build constituent trust.

Representing begins with the election of an ambitious politician. And it ends with the politician's accountability to the people in his or her constituency. Representing is related to—but it is very different from—organizing and legislating on Capitol Hill. Vote patterns among House members inside Congress are easier to describe, aggregate, compute, and manipulate than are House member connection patterns outside Congress.

The representational practices of our House members open up for us 435 separate research windows on 435 political worlds beyond the national legislature. "Out there" "on the ground," in a home constituency, we can locate and match a person to a party and to a place. Indeed, we know them and we "tag" them broadly in that way: as (D-NY) or

(R-TX). Once tagged, we can then begin to describe each representative's connections and relationships in his or her home place.

"All politics is local" has long been a popular aphorism. But it has yet to stimulate a locally driven body of research on Congress. As a discipline, we have produced very little self-conscious "member-in-the-district" research, much less a comparative cross district literature. And we have yet to develop a set of guidelines—much less a metric—to help us observe, compare, and generalize across the variety of representational motivations, practices, and patterns of House members.

Representing a constituency requires work by each elected politician in identifying problems and in negotiating relationships that are attentive to, and supportive of, constituent habits, expectations, and preferences. House member negotiating activities of this sort point our scholarship toward the considerable diversity of constituency preference patterns and playing fields beyond Capitol Hill. On playing fields in different parts of the country, a considerably variety of House member activities can be observed, examined, and explained.

In sum, to our path breaking studies of House member vote decisions and vote patterns in Congress, students of American politics can usefully add studies of House member connection decisions and connection patterns in their home districts. This book suggests, by example, how such observation-based studies, when undertaken at the point of member-constituent contact, might proceed and enlighten.

A Cautionary Proviso

A member's vote inside the House is, we assume, partly a representational activity. As such, his or her vote can be—and typically is—viewed as a response to the preferences of a home constituency. We might, therefore, be tempted at the outset to draw inferences about member voting connections at home directly from our studies of member voting behavior in Washington. That would be a mistake. It would tempt us to ignore the "Oklahoma wisdom" of "the pump handle" and "the well."

Vote patterns organized and sustained inside the House cannot serve as reliable indicators of connection patterns organized and sustained outside of the House. A member's vote can be viewed as a forward-looking effort to build or retain support in the home constituency. But, inferences about constituency preference patterns drawn indirectly from House member votes—in committee or on the House floor—are not a valid substitute for direct, in-the-constituency research. Political scientists cannot talk constructively about constituency-centered politics without some of us "going there" to observe and to inquire for ourselves. As with the "pump handle" and "the well," there are no shortcuts.

Constituency Politics: Politicians and Playing Fields

Constituency politics is connection politics. And the logic of this study begins with connections in the constituency. To each constituency, the researcher brings House member-constituency connection questions that will help to elicit connection patterns. Our path of inquiry begins outside of the House, not the other way around. This study is in no way dependent on any prior analysis of legislative vote patterns. As argued elsewhere: "Getting connected is not simply a matter of getting elected. Negotiating a constituency fit is a different process, and it requires a separate scrutiny."[1]

The study of individual House member activities in their home districts centers on "connection politics." Member vote patterns in Washington are matters of public knowledge and are available to anyone outside of Washington. But House member connection patterns with their constituents at home are not matters of public knowledge. Home connections, it will be argued here, cannot be inspected, known, and fully understood without some hands-on personal investigative experience in and around some specific, identifiable congressional constituencies.

For now, and to begin with, personal observation is the basic research prescription. The assumption is that representational activities observed and examined in a few home constituencies will give substance and shape to a growing research base. And that several firsthand, point-of-contact reports might persuade—or at least acclimate—other political scientists to a stronger research notion: that political connections which develop in home constituencies outside of Washington can be, and should be, observed and examined on the home ground where they occur. And, further still, that collaborative efforts among political scientists to observe and to study such clusters of representational activity can be imagined and should be encouraged.

House member vote patterns in Washington are matters of public knowledge. They are readily available for study by anyone outside of Washington. But House member connection patterns with their constituents at home are not matters of public knowledge. The study of individual House members at work in their respective home districts centers on connection politics. And connection politics cannot be identified, inspected, and fully understood without some personal investigative experience in and around some congressional constituencies. Or, so it will be argued in the research reports to follow.

The Challenge of Congressional Representation begins with a couple of general questions about our elected members of Congress. What are they like? And what are their ambitions, their preferences, and their connections? Other questions follow naturally about the constituency from which each House member has been elected. How does each member characterize his/her home place? Or, how does each member connect with the people who live there? To pose these questions and to search for answers is very likely to expose the parlous state of political science research on congressional representation.

What, for example, do we political scientists presently know about congressional constituencies as active political places? Where would we go to find the relevant political science research? How, to date, have we gone about observing, examining, sorting, and codifying the constituency connection patterns of diverse individual representatives in their own home territories? How have we conceptualized, and where have we examined empirically, the varieties of constituency connections—either cross-sectional or over time? Where can inquiring students go, at present, to find a disciplinary overview of representation-centered, constituency-based investigations? Where can students go to find—or to develop—a sampling frame to expedite multimember, cross constituency analysis? Where, in short, is our constituency-centered body of literature?

These baseline questions do not yet have useful answers. And for good reason. Congressional constituencies and member-constituency relationships have yet to attract concentrated and sustained scholarly attention from students of congressional politics. From the constituency-centric viewpoint adopted here, there can be no adequate answers until more political scientists embrace the idea that home place activity matters in thinking about congressional activity. And not until students embrace the value of undertaking on-the-scene research from inside a variety of constituencies. And finally, not until a few students of constituency politics find ways of sharing, debating, and actively collaborating with one another on the subject.

The basic argument for "going there" rests on the simple assumption that place is—and places are—central to the representational side of American politics. And further, that it might be possible to describe, for every elected House member, a home place—a constituency playing field. And to describe, further still, a set of connective activities and relationships that have been developed in and around that particular home place. And finally, to convince multiple investigators to collaborate with one another in mapping, collecting, collating, and theorizing about their home place research.

In each home place, the operative question will be: How, and with what effect, does this representative connect with these sorts of people in this sort of constituency? And ultimately perhaps, how do these types of representatives connect with these types of constituents in these types of constituencies?

It is a tall order. And to the degree that scholars become interested in answering representational questions, the message of this study is that they should begin by spending more start-up time learning about congressional constituencies as distinctive playing fields. And, most important, that they should learn by going to those playing fields—to think about the ways in which, the extent to which, and with what effect each representative connects with his or her constituents. After (or during) which activity, it will be important for our discipline that scholars begin to compare and cooperate, and that they devise common, workable interview schedules that can be shared and applied to a range of connection patterns on a range of playing fields.

From a national perspective, congressional constituencies are among the most important testing and proving grounds of American political life. At present, however, they draw scholarly attention only when their boundaries are being set and reset—that is, when redistricting activity is contemplated or actually takes place and, of course, when election time is drawing attention to the home stretch once every two years. But not, it seems, when ongoing and patterned back-and-forth House member/constituency activity is taking place.

The argument being made here treats member-constituency activity as deserving enough and complicated enough to be researched more often, more widely and analyzed more systematically by political scientists. With experience, plus a few guidelines, scholarly collaboration might be envisioned, fostered, and achieved. And from that, we might expand our ability to generalize.

The large argument of this study is simply that more political scientists should take a firsthand look at our House members at work in the home places from which they have been elected. And that we should pay more direct attention to what our representatives do, what they say, and what they worry about when they are at work in these separate and distinctive home places. "Going there" means watching, listening, talking, testing, and accumulating information and ideas about the connection patterns of this House member with these goals, in this place at this time, amid this confluence of events. Measurement and generalization are likely to grow slowly in proportion to the commonly accepted and common use of constituency-centered research questions and to their acceptance by interested scholars. Eventually we may be able to replace this member's goals, time, place, and activities with a more general set of the times, places, and activities of "these" members.

To all such research questions, the answer must involve comparison. Where, we might ask, can we now find comparative analyses of House member-constituency activity to guide our inquiry? To ask is to recognize the extent to which each of us remains on his or her own.

There are, of course, some accessible and reliable compendia to canvas when thinking about immersion in a constituency. *The Almanac of American Politics,*—a truly revolutionary compendium—is the indispensable best.[2] *Politics in America* is close behind.[3] Both are directed primarily toward the study of entire geographical constituencies, not the smaller and active "reelection" or "primary" constituencies. And they describe mostly the "objective," statistically—defined, constituency not the constituency as the representative experiences it.

Both compendia, however, do contain helpful standardized information, including biographies, election results, roll call voting records, and miscellaneous district-wide descriptions. Occasionally, they provide helpful hints about the local political setting. And sometimes a scrap of constituency activity will be mentioned. In that way, too, local newspaper reporting can be of preparatory help. These random accounts can best be evaluated only when and if the scholar already has accumulated some contributory firsthand knowledge.

In sum, any temptation to think of available compendia and a few sentences of local reporting as research tools for measuring "the depth of the well" would be misplaced.

For comparing and for planning, the two currently indispensable on-the-spot, intraconstituency activities are watching and listening. As research prescriptions, these "skills" are neither widely taught nor widely practiced in contemporary studies of congressional politics. An initial goal of any further study is simply to convince political scientists to learn by listening to—and by questioning—a few representatives when they are at home talking about what they are doing and why. The guiding purpose would be to become familiar with a working/learning context under circumstances when the politician is at home, and not preoccupied with the next vote, or the next committee meeting, or some other demanding Capitol Hill activity.

Built-in difficulties facing such constituency-based, connection-centered research are not hard to identify. Data collection, for example, centers on firsthand observation. But, data collection via observation inside a constituency is necessarily piecemeal, intermittent, and difficult to replicate. And until appropriate measurement methods and workable interview schedules are devised, agreed upon, and implemented, results will continue to rely heavily on conversation. And conversation is inevitably imprecise. Ultimately, its value depends heavily upon personal, one on one political scientist-politician interaction—the conditions of which can hardly be "held constant." Interview plans and promising protocols must be adjusted to fit changing opportunities. Testing the boundaries of each personal relationship and factoring in the reliability of information will be a constant preoccupation.

In the very long run, perhaps, we might be able to elevate our understanding of House member outside "connection patterns" to the level of our current understanding of House member inside "governing patterns." But, given the imprecision of member connection activities—as compared to member votes—a more reasonable, near-term disciplinary goal might be simply to use additional on-site observation to develop a working inventory of connection questions and connection patterns for use by fellow researchers. After which, a collaborative scholarly enterprise might be envisioned—of which there are various disciplinary models—to muster sufficient interest and leverage to move our scholarship from exploration toward explanation.

That discussion, however, belongs at the end of this study rather than the beginning. If, as and when a few political scientists could be persuaded to undertake a joint enterprise of this sort (and more about that later), we might work toward an increase in conceptual clarity and in the standardization of data collection. In the meantime, the explanation at hand is put forward as an acceptable holding action. Taken together, the five "travel and talk" studies may begin to develop a research focus and a set of researchable questions to underpin, guide, and broaden our studies of the US Congress as a representative institution.

— 2 —

Barber Conable

Local Boy

House Member and Home Place

In November 1964, Republican Barber B. Conable Jr. was elected to Congress from my Upstate New York district. Two weeks later—prodded by a commission from the *New York Times Magazine*—we met and talked over lunch at the University of Rochester.[1] I had interviewed many House members in Washington, but this was my very first interview with a member of Congress in the member's home constituency. Getting acquainted with Barber Conable was preparation for a planned two-day visit with him in Washington. There was, at the time, no idea whatever of doing research inside Barber Conable's—or anyone else's—home district. Political science research, and my own, had long focused on House member activity in Washington—not on their activities at home.

Barber Conable was a small-town lawyer from west of Rochester. He had been educated at Cornell University and its Law School. He had served in the Marines in the South Pacific in World War II. When we met, he was at the end of his first term in the New York State Senate. After a couple of hours of conversation, my strongest impression was that he loved to talk and to explain, and that he was exceptionally skilled at both. He had keen political sensibilities. His small-town attachments were strong and deep. And in that context he set high performance standards for himself.

The dominant theme of our interview concerned his new political posture. He was, of course, thinking about Washington. And he was relying heavily on his previous experience as a one-term state representative. On the legislative side, his dominant ideas were that he had no preconceptions about his new job, and that he had always followed a policy of no precommitments in legislative matters. "All my ideas," he said, "come from my experience in the state senate."

> I have no preconceptions about the job. Maybe I should have, but I don't. It's just like it was when I was elected to the state senate. I had never even seen the New York Senate chamber. I went there and I asked the attendant, "Is this the senate?" He said, it was; and I asked him if I could go in and look around. "I'm a senator," I said. And, that's the way it is with Congress. I have no preconceptions.

In a similar vein, he continued,

> I have an abhorrence of getting myself precommitted. Fortunately, my opponent in the campaign didn't force me to get precommitted. I don't go around looking for chances to commit myself if I can avoid it . . . People always want to know how you stand, not how you think. But if you use a yardstick instead of your brain, you won't get anything done. I think you have an obligation to your constituents to make your vote as effective as you can. And if you commit yourself to a group before you know what they stand for, you lose that bargaining power.

In the state senate, he said, his colleagues often wanted "a pledge or a declaration of war . . . . And sometimes when I told them what they wanted to hear, I regretted it afterward. When the vote came, the situation had changed, and I had to vote against my better judgment or my word."

He catalogued his upcoming choices in Washington—choosing sides in a tight Republican Party leadership contest, securing his committee assignments, and forming informal alliances. "I don't want to join any group until I know what they want to do," he said. "The time will come when you have to make common cause with the fellows you agree with, but I do not want to precommit myself." He intended to be a representative who thought for himself. His early strategic emphasis carried with it the intent of making a career inside Congress.

A House Republican conference had been scheduled in Washington, he told me; but he had decided, instead, to go back to Albany for a special session of the state senate. "I know where it's most important for me to be—in Albany. It's more important for me to look after the western counties and reapportionment than it is to attend the Republican Conference." It was the broadest description of his home playing field.

Everything he knew about what was going on in Washington, he said, he had learned from "a long chat" and "a couple of phone calls" with a nearby Western New Yorker, two-term Congressman Charles Goodell. "I don't know anyone I'd rather join up with than Charlie," he said. "But I don't want to join any group until I know who they are and what they want to do." Again, "I don't want to precommit myself."

On the representational side of our early talk, he communicated a strong sense of identification with a distinctive home place—the rural, small-town part of his district. For two generations, his locally prominent family had lived there; he had been born and raised in a small town there; he had established his law practice in nearby Batavia, a town of 18,000 people. At the time, he was still representing that area in the New York State Senate. Politically, his congressional district could be divided into three fairly equal parts—rural/small town, suburban, and urban. The rural/small-town part covered four counties. The other two parts came from a single large county—half of it suburban and half of it urban.

In the recent election, he had carried his rural/small town base overwhelmingly, thus offsetting a standoff in the suburbs and a loss in the city of Rochester. "This should be a safe district," he said. "If those people think that with their slick city ways they could go out into Mrs. O'Leary's cow pasture and throw out the local boy, they're crazy." And I noted, "several times, he called himself 'a country boy.'" He was a two-diploma Cornell University graduate and president of the University's prestigious Telluride Honor Society. But, his scholarly distinctions never dominated his local boy/country boy self-description.

When he generalized about his constituency, he sometimes folded it into a larger place with which he also strongly identified, that is, Western New York. "We're all decentralists up here," he said, "We don't trust the big cities and the impersonal government way off somewhere. We like our own local institutions." Western New York Democrats, he added, "are pretty conservative, too."

He was a conservative and a Republican, but he eschewed doctrinaire politics. He had recently read a book by Cornell historian Clinton

Rossiter on the "isms," he said. And he had keynoted a recent speech with an attack on the "tyranny of labels." He would later describe himself to political scientist Jim Fleming as "a moderate Republican," who prided himself on "an independence which my friends in Western New York know is bred in the bone."[2]

A third interview theme was his concentration on "establishing good relationships with my constituents. For a couple of years anyway, I'll postpone my statesmanship . . . . I'm not going down to catch the thunderbolts as they go by." The immediate key, he said, was to keep his predecessor's two top Washington staffers. "They've got what I don't have. My predecessor had the knack of being able to grab hold of just the right handle in helping people. That comes with experience. The staff has it; I don't. I don't want too much of a wrench with the past. I want people to feel they can come to me and get all the help they got in the past." He added that when he had met his predecessor's Washington staff, "I think I made quite a splash in their quiet millpond." And he concluded, "I won't get any political advice from them."

In a sharp break from the past, he had determined that his top DC staffer "will not write my newsletter." It was his opportunity, he said, "to bring government home to people instead of having government be a distant thing." The idea was that he represented not only himself to his constituents, but that he also represented the government to the citizenry. And he wanted to tell his constituents what was going on in Washington. "I was appalled when I saw my predecessor's mailing list. It looked like it was made up of his wife's 'Eastern Star' buddies. Now is the time to get that in shape." He identified Democrats and the Jaycees as early targets.

Finally, he talked discursively about "politics." Several times, he said, "I had no ambition to be a congressman."

> One night my wife asked me if I thought I'd be a state senator for the rest of my life. "Wouldn't you like to be in Congress?" I said, "that's not possible and there's no point in thinking about it. If Harold Ostertag retires, it will be six or eight years. By that time, I'll have seniority in the [state] senate and will have settled into a niche there and will be more valuable to Western New York there than I would be in Congress. Besides, what's wrong with the state senate? Why try to attain the unattainable? That was my attitude.

When, however, the incumbent, Harold Ostertag, announced his retirement, Conable's rural/small-town county leaders immediately supported their incumbent state senator. Whereupon the Republican leader of adjacent urban/suburban Monroe County—in order to avoid an intraparty contest there—announced his support, too, for the neighboring incumbent. "I had no ambition to be a congressman. But when it was offered to me [by the Monroe County leader] under those circumstances . . . I accepted."

With respect to his congressional campaign—managed by his wife, Charlotte—he made special note of his adjustment to the pivotal suburbs, where he had been completely ignored by the local politicos. I was a "submerged personality," he said. So he followed the practice of his winning state senate primary campaign—by organizing groups of women volunteers. Women, too, he said were "submerged personalities" in local politics.

A week later, taking me home for dinner in Washington, he said, "You'll learn more about me from my wife, Charlotte, my most penetrating critic. She ran my campaign. All I did was keep on the dead run." He would always refer to his state senate campaign as his most difficult and his most exemplary electoral effort. He was never seriously threatened thereafter.

A final political note in our conversation involved his relationship with the next-door second-term Republican congressman who represented the other half of Rochester and other adjacent suburbs. The two men had run totally separate campaigns. But afterwards, Conable reported, his Rochester area colleague had made two comments. First, he had informed the newcomer that he, as the more senior representative, was entitled to the larger of the two constituency offices set aside in the downtown Rochester Federal Building. Second, he had advised Conable, "You've got to get a liberal image if you want to run statewide."

Conable reacted negatively. "A Western New York congressman has to accept the fact that the way our state is set up, you can't run statewide. He should content himself with serving his district and not chase some will-o-the-wisp. That's plenty to take care of, too. Being a congressman is more than I ever thought I would achieve in life." It was a view he never changed.

A few weeks later, we met in Washington to talk about his adjustments to the work there. And six years later I decided to undertake some extensive research in Representative Conable's home constituency.

Research Travels; Early Learning

From June 1970 until his reelection in 1974, we drove around together on nine separate occasions. During those years, we occasionally talked about his life in Washington. All writing about our talks and our travels, however, remained subject to the basic ground rule of anonymity. It was only upon Barber Conable's death in 2003 that I felt free to revisit my travel notes, drop the anonymity precaution, and engage in some full-scale reminiscing.

We now know a great deal about Barber Conable because we have available to us one of the very finest full-length congressional biographies of our time—*Window on Congress: A Congressional Biography of Barber B. Conable, Jr.*, written in 2004 by a fellow political scientist and friend, Professor James Fleming.[3] He has written the complete, authoritative Barber Conable story. It is, however, a story researched and written in its entirety after Barber Conable had left Congress.

My remembrances cover a short period (primarily 1964–1974) while Conable was actually serving in Congress. They come from my own intermittent observations and conversations with him during that time. They can be read as sharpened, "on-the-scene" supplements to Fleming's complete biography. They are presented here because they shaped my own thinking about places, connections, and constituency-centered studies of our elected members of Congress.

When we traveled together "on the road" in the spring of 1970, Representative Conable's constituency connections were well established. His first comment reflected that condition. "I don't have time to speak to constituents who are uncommitted," he said.

I'm so badgered by people to whom I'm obligated politically that I spend most of my time performing ceremonially before the people who already agree with me. The ground is very fallow for confronting people who don't have a strong policy position or for converting the enemy. . . .

> Sometimes I do my talking to the same people over and over. But they
> talk to others. And my newsletter [to 30,000 people] has helped.

It was a useful introduction to his weekend schedule: a breakfast with
hometown cronies, two Republican dinners, a meeting with federal
employees, and talks at three small-town celebratory events—a centen-
nial "homecoming," a town hall dedication, and a Flag Day ceremony.
When it was over, he bundled these events together.

> It's been a pretty typical weekend. . . . You can't say I accomplished any-
> thing really, but I didn't unaccomplish anything either. . . . If I didn't
> come to functions like these, people who are for me would be weaned
> away. They expect me to be here. So, I've maintained my contacts, met
> people and remained visible. . . . This sort of thing is a terribly important
> part of what I do. It maintains my reputation for being available, for get-
> ting up and speaking low key . . . . I guess you'd say I'm on display . . . .
> Now they can say, "We saw the congressman and he's OK." That gives
> them an identification with government. I do that just by being here.
> Don't knock it!

I didn't. Indeed, his presentational pattern made so much sense that
I drew even broader conclusions from my visit than he did. From the
time we spent driving throughout the district during that first visit,
I picked up something more basic and more permanent—his attachments to a place—and to the values and the practices of that place. Very
early, I thought, I had found his strongest representational roots. He
was a local boy.

Our first full day began at breakfast with a group of his oldest friends
and community leaders in the town of Batavia, where he had practiced
law. There was a retired judge, a past president of the city council, a
hardware store owner, a retired science teacher, and a retired bank manager. They rehashed old stories, joked, and gossiped about local events.
Conable had begun his law practice in nearby Buffalo, where his city
colleagues had prepared a career-long niche for him as a tax attorney.
But he had left, he said, because he preferred a general practice. His Buffalo colleagues had predicted that he'd "bury" himself in Batavia and
never be heard from again. His Batavia breakfast cronies were among
those who had helped him launch his small-town career—getting him

settled in his law office, and engineering his election to the prestigious Batavia Rotary Club.

As we left the group, he said,

> I guess you can see what an institution this is. You have no idea how invaluable these meetings are for me. They keep me in touch with my home base. If you don't keep your home base, you don't have anything. I'm still considered a local community leader, and though I don't like to get into community affairs too deeply, I have to know what's going on. I have to be aware of what decisions are being made. They've just decided to fire the county historian; and that will cause a greater stir than a lot of national questions. I'll say "it's a local decision," but I have to know what the decisions are. I'm expected to.

The "breakfast group" gossip had such a strong effect on me that it became the exemplary case of a very distinctive kind of constituency connection—the connection between a politician and his or her very closest, very smallest ring of especially supportive individuals. In my later *Home Style* study, it was labeled "the personal constituency."[4] The New York congressman had breakfast with his buddies nearly every Saturday morning when he was in the district.

His chummy get-together in the countryside was followed by a chilly meeting with the New York Federation of Federal Employees in the city. Driving from Batavia to Rochester, he fretted over his connections—or lack of them—with organized labor, his largest, most recognizable group of nonsupporters.

> I've never worked for union support, so I'm not going to do very well here. . . . I'm on the wrong side of most of their formulas. I don't seek meetings like this. I didn't seek this one. But I won't run away either. Right now, I'm getting the heat for my stand in opposition to [import] quotas. The other day, the Amalgamated [Clothing Workers] took me right out of the committee . . . and wanted me to support them . . . I said "Let's talk about it." They said they didn't want to talk about it, they wanted to know what I was going to do. . . . I said I was going to keep an open mind till after the hearings . . . getting precommitted and cast in brass is something that bothers me more than anything in legislative life. I hate to go to the vote with any encumbrance.

The postal workers, he said, "throw my newsletter in the Genesee River. They have me stamped for extinction because I voted against their pay raise."

As for the auto workers and the electrical workers, he added, "I have no contact with them. They oppose me, but they don't go after me. They just identify me as an 'enemy of the people' and leave me alone."

As he anticipated this meeting, he elaborated a difference between himself and his adjacent Republican House colleague. "He will do much better than I will before this union group. He's a bright fella and he won't drop the ball the way I will. He's a formula politician and he keeps a coalition of groups like this supporting him. You push this button and you get the support of this group, you push that button and you get the support of that group. It's a quid pro quo formula. . . . I'd rather use my own judgment than follow a sterile formula." I thought his meeting with the federal employees was adversarial, but civil, and that the group seemed appreciative that he had come. From the beginning to the end of my visits, union leaders would remain, in his eyes, the irreducible hard core of his political opposition.

As we rode back to his home territory, he talked about some ideas he had taken from John Gardner, the president of Common Cause— a liberal-leaning reformist organization. He had fastened particularly on Gardner's advocacy of a "middle course" between "unloving critics" and "uncritical lovers" of the United States. He would use these ideas in his remarks at the three small-town celebratory events that lay ahead. More than once in our travels, he would say that he "treasured" Gardner's upbeat moderation. And in reformist matters such as the public financing of elections, he would follow Gardner's lead.

Our drive back from the city, through the suburbs and into the countryside, produced one of the most memorable moments of our long association. And it was all about the pull of place. I wrote,

> his comment to me about his identification with the rural people of his district was almost poetic in nature, because it came just as we left the four-lane super highway . . . and turned onto the two-lane road to (small town) Byron. . . . Suddenly, he said, "It must be terrible to be without roots, without a place to call home. I have a profound sense of identification with these rural people. My wife still worries about me a little bit in

this respect—that I'm still too much of a country boy. But life's too short to play a role or strike a pose. This will be fun this afternoon. I'm really going to enjoy myself—not like this morning. I worry about the rootlessness of our people, about the changes that are taking place in our values which were, after all, pretty durable." Soon, he brightened and said, "It won't be long now. Here are the Byron suburbs! Those are Gerald Pritts's beets growing over there. He grows 3 percent of all the edible beets in the United States."

The representative was about to connect in familiar territory. And what dominated was his sense for the stability of the place. His appreciation of continuity was a necessary condition for his kind of connections to the people who lived there.

Soon he was knee-deep in people, beginning with his trademark greeting: "How's things?" He reached naturally for all kinds of connections via families and counties, artifacts, work, and history. It was, he kept saying, "just like old home week." He was at home in conversation about their 1880's costumes, about their 1920's automobiles, and about various local contingents in the parade. His short talk began with his connections to local families and his personal memories of the area; and it ended with a celebration of small-town life, of neighborliness, of tradition and stability. "The values of America," he told them, "are rooted in small towns." The special obligation of his listeners, he said, was to keep the nation strong and united.

His next two events proceeded a bit more formally, but with equally strong small-town connectedness. Speaking of the people at the town hall dedication, he said later, "Those are great people, the salt of the earth. I have a strong sentimental attachment to the people of these small towns. I guess you can see that. Gosh, wouldn't it be wonderful if my whole constituency was made up of small towns like this one. Then it would be, 'Anything you say, Barber' instead of 'Conable, you bastard'."

For the rest of the day, he elaborated on his myriad connections to local places and people. He drove from event to event, through the rural parts of his district, weaving from paved roads to back roads, where he kicked up dust at speeds up to 70 mph. And all the time in the car, he talked nonstop from an inexhaustible fund of knowledge.

He pointed out landmarks—prehistorical and colonial. He recapitulated the rivalries and alliances, strategies and battles, victories and defeats among the Iroquois, Senecas, and the Neutrals. He traced the course of the Genesee River as it affected tribal boundaries. At relevant places, he described the varied relationships between the French and the British. As we moved about, he would describe a great Indian leader of each area, along with noteworthy white settlers. He told me how he dug arrowheads as a boy, put on Indian dances as an Eagle Scout, and, as a young man, lectured to Rotary Clubs on the prehistory of the area. "I can still give a pretty good talk on the prehistory of the area," he said later. (Throughout his public career, he would maintain the strongest of ties to the keepers of local history.) All in all, it was a remarkable and enthusiastic tour de force—a commanding combination of knowledge, memory, and tale-telling. It centered on a place and on the depth of his connectedness to that place.

When we got to his home in the tiny town of Alexander (a suburb of Batavia!), his focus changed, but his attachments to place, and his knowledge of place, was still on display.

> We walked around his land. There isn't any doubt about the man's enormous love of the land—his feeling for the land. He owns over a hundred acres. Every spring, he and his three daughters come here and plant dozens of trees on his multi-acre back lot . . . We walked briskly around the land, looking at every single sapling—there must have been a few hundred. He described every sapling; he knew every tree . . . what kind of leaves it had, how it grew, what soil it needed, where the rabbits ate the bark, which trees had survived the earlier spring planting. He kept saying "I love trees." He pointed out every tree and bush . . . the differences between one spruce and another, one kind of fir and another, between hemlock and spruce, tulip and catalpa, and the varieties of locust, oak, and walnut.

He took me inside his house—built in 1830—an exact replica of one that Thomas Jefferson had planned for his daughter, a home that now sits in Williamsburg, Virginia. "The house itself reeked of history," I noted. We walked through the house, and he showed me tables that once belonged to US President Millard Fillmore (of Buffalo). There were pictures of Abraham Lincoln on the wall, along with a collection of old prints of the US Capitol. There were pieces of old furniture that he had bought from Batavia hotels when they were torn down.[5] "I have a great deal of feeling for that house," he said later. "It's my emotional anchor to windward."

In summing up, I noted that an "open honesty" and "a matter of fact-ness" about him had "led me to believe that this was a genuine person." And I added, "I had the feeling that somehow or other, from the events of the Byron celebration, the tremendous erudition concerning the pre-history of his area, and his love of this very old home and the land on which it stands—[that] I had more or less come to find the essential per-son behind the congressman. It was a very revealing experience for me."

Although I did not try to pin it down for over thirty years, the idea of "a genuine person" or "the essential person" was the idea of authentic-ity. What was Barber Conable really like? He was, I decided, very much a "local boy." That is what he called himself or, similarly, "country boy."

He was an authentic "local boy" or "country boy" because he shared experiences and values with his rural, small-town constituents. He had no alter ego, no reserve persona which he put on or took off whenever circumstances presented themselves. There was a strong sense of stabil-ity—of the individual and of his values. From his actions and from my observations, I believed—as he did—that his supportive constituents desired, above all, face-to-face relationships which allowed them—if they wished—to judge the personal qualities of their representatives. Key personal qualities might include: integrity, self-reliance, commu-nity-mindedness, and moderation. In judging their political leaders, I concluded, rural and small-town residents put a high value on acces-sibility and on down-to-earth presentations of self. From my observa-tions, Conable qualified. He was gregarious and approachable. He was not flamboyant—not even exciting. He was not ideological. He was not the spokesperson for any political group or movement. If he was sell-ing something, it was low-key salesmanship. He wanted to connect as a whole person. And he wanted constituents to think of him as "one of us." From that personal sense of identification would come constituent trust. And trust was the ultimate representational connection.

He came home, as he put it, to provide his constituents with reas-surance "that I'm still the same old Barber and will still come around and talk with them. The most important thing is that you don't seem too big for your britches. You don't want people to say, 'What happened to Barber? Why doesn't he come around anymore?'" Even though he had spoken to many of them before, he took the view that "the people I speak to will talk favorably about me. They tell others that 'old Barber' is always accessible and available. And I get a reputation that way. That's how I succeed in this kind of district. People think of me as a nice guy, one of the boys, and they make presumptions in my favor because I'm a nice guy."

So important was his accessibility that he kept a careful count of each trip home. And, he located each event with a pin on a huge Washington office wall map of the district. "I have never come home less than forty times a year," he said during my first visit. And he repeated that statement during every one of our subsequent visits. It was all about connectedness. It was his mantra.

Though I could not know it at the time, during my first visit Conable displayed another personal behavior pattern that distinguished him from every elective politician I would ever know. It was a distinctiveness related partly to shared rural, small-town values/expectations and partly to his self-confidence in connecting with his constituents. Not once in all our time together did a staff person accompany us—not in the car and not at any event.

By contrast, every single one of the other forty-odd House members (and senators) with whom I traveled had, at one time or another, a staff member along—riding in the car and/or helping out at the event, sometimes driving, sometimes not. As a consequence, with two other people in the car, I would be relegated to the back seat. Not so with Barber Conable. Once, we spent a day with a *New York Times* reporter. Otherwise, it was always just the two of us chatting. Sometimes, I would pick him up at the airport and drive. At home, he was a "one-man band." And when I called him that, he agreed, adding, "That's what makes my visibility so important."

His pattern reflected a comfortable self-confidence in his constituency relationships. It demonstrated his preference—like theirs—for one-on-one connections, no trappings, no intermediaries, just "the same old Barber." In all respects, personal and behavioral, he was remarkably self-sufficient.

When he came home, he said, he typically spent two days there and gave "at least two speeches each day." He let people see him, and he talked. As I learned during our first luncheon, he loved to talk. And he was very good at it. Morever, when he talked, he opened up an important side of himself—an intellectual side—his Cornell-Telluride Honor Society side. He was an introspective person—one who kept a journal in which he recorded and reflected upon his actions. He was unusually knowledgeable, analytical, and articulate. He was a broad analyst and a gifted speaker; and he touched people with an easy-going erudition.

When he talked to or wrote to his constituents, he liked best of all to explain. "I have always tried to educate people when I speak," he said.

> It's a terrible feeling to have know-nothings dominate the environment. So, when people ask me a question, I give them an explanation of the problem, not just the answer. They used to say of Justice Cardozo's decisions that not only were they good decisions, but that the opinions he wrote supporting the decisions were educational opinions. You always learned something about the law by his reasoning. That's what I have always tried to do. Maybe it's a liability. People may only want the answer. . . . But what they get from me is an answer within an answer within an answer. That's the way I've always been.

On his explanatory side, he was not "one of the boys," or "just plain old Barber." He was a representative who often referred to his constituents as "my people." And he wanted to tell them something, teach them something—not listen to them. Patient listening was definitely not one of his trademark strengths. And while he might, on occasion, talk past people, he always talked earnestly. I never heard him talk condescendingly to anyone.

He would spend extra time when he met new, unfamiliar constituents—in the hope that they would get to know him by listening to him. After one such informal, overtime visit with people he had never met before, he said, "That was very useful. I really cast my bread upon the waters. They were so interested that I gave them a lot of the inside [Washington] stuff. I want them to feel a sense of personal identification with me. And so I stayed and gave them much more of myself than I ordinarily would. Every one of those people there now feels he or she knows me and has a personal relationship with me." As "the same old Barber," he won constituent trust. As a teacher, he won constituent respect.

"A trip home," he said,

> gives me a feel for things. I'm not sure what it gives me a feel for, but I do it because I feel like doing it. It comes naturally to me . . . it gives my constituents a chance to judge me, to size me up, to test me for comfortableness, to see whether I'm the type of person they want to represent them. And it gives them the opportunity to size up and pass judgment on the system, too. When they judge me, they judge the government. I'm the only government official they have contact with; and I have a tremendous responsibility to the system to make it seem right to them. So when they look at me, they are asking whether the system is a matter of "us" and "them" or whether there are "some of us" in there, too. That's a terribly important part of the political process—representing the government to my constituents.

This idea—that he was their connection to their government—had spawned his especially strong and perhaps unique devotion to his weekly newsletter. On those pages he worked to give constituents a sense of connection to their government. In so doing, he would bind them to him. It was an idea he articulated in our first interview. It was an idea that his newsletter was explicitly designed to reflect and implement.[6]

When he couldn't talk to people personally, he talked to them through the newsletter. "I have always based my political survival on the enthusiasm of a few people rather than recognition by the many," he generalized. "That may not be good politics. But I'd rather rely on people who have some personal involvement with me and not on name recognition. That's why my newsletter is so important to me."

Through it, he could touch people with his analysis and his explanations. "I have a very comfortable relationship with my constituency," he said. "Even the ones who come up and chew on me say, 'We don't blame you.' My newsletter is my greatest asset there. I'd rather have 30,000 people feel close to me and know me than have name recognition with two or three times that number. Maybe I'm wrong. But that's my approach."[7] His heavy reliance on his newsletter as a representational spearhead remained unique throughout my experience.

He said that he had once considered giving it up, but found that he didn't know exactly what he thought about an issue until he thought it out for himself and explained it to others in the newsletter. "It makes me sit down and think through my position on the issues. And I feel much surer about what I think when I have finished." The analyses and explanations of his newsletter, he believed, won him a respectful and loyal constituency—a lot of it bipartisan. He spoke personally and directly to his constituents through the newsletter—educating them through the printed word as well as the spoken word. In his constituency relationships, Representative Conable wanted no interlocutors. It was his way.

Somehow, by a process difficult to describe, his varied appeals came together.

> Now, in a vacuum, people may not have a choice in the election, and they may have to vote for me. But their judgment of me can have a great deal to do with a primary or with whether the Democrats are serious about running against me. If they think I'm popular, they may say it's too expensive and not worthwhile to run seriously against me. People talk to each other all the time—Republicans and Democrats—and word gets around about how I'm doing.

As I listened to him, I concluded that whereas he related to his rural area importantly as a person, he related to the rest of the district importantly through his weekly newsletter. Both types of connections, however, gave him leeway in making his decisions in Washington.

When it came to voting in Congress, he said, "You have to start in every case with the assumption that you cannot know what your constituents want you to do. But I was born in my district, and I grew up in my district, and I have a very close identification with the people in it. I know what their values are." When he generalized about his constituents, his habit was to call them "my people." And that wording bespoke a protective relationship as well as a responsive one.

The congressman was a reader; and he loved the written word. He developed friendships across party lines with politicians who shared that love—Pat Moynihan and Paul Simon, for example. When he spoke, he was aided by a near photographic memory—"an ashcan memory" he sometimes said.

On occasion, he would launch into a lengthy poetry recitation. As the after-dinner speaker at a suburban Lions Club anniversary celebration in 1971, he presented the group of about one hundred with a startling proposition: "I'll give you a choice. I'll talk for thirty minutes on 'what's going on in Washington,' or I'll recite poetry for thirty minutes. What shall it be?" Then, to a silent, bewildered audience, he said, "Let's take a show of hands. How many want me to recite poetry?" (10–20 percent "yes"). How many want a speech?" (30–40 percent "yes"). Forty to sixty percent remained bewildered. "Okay," said Conable. "I really want to recite poetry. But I'll talk about politics in Washington." Which he did. But I knew from his travel chatter that he could have handled Keats, Wordsworth, and Coleridge just as easily had the vote gone his way.

His strong connections with rural/small-town constituents anchored his district-wide electoral strength. In a Republican primary, his four-county "base" contained one-half of the votes. So his home base protected him from any intraparty opponent. The Republican Party in the city, he said, "might think I'm too independent for them. They flirt with labor, and they want me to protect situs picketing. But I go my own way. I think they'll avoid a confrontation at all costs. They won't dare take me on." He was content to take whatever Republican support was there for him in the city—in a few "good Republican wards."

He attended party functions at their request and did what they asked. At his initial city ward dinner, he recalled,

[The leader] drew me aside and said, "I'll tell you what to say—no speeches. Just say what I tell you." So I said, "Well, what do you want me to say?" He said, "I'm the candidate for Congress. I promise to follow the traditions of Jimmy Pecora and to give the personal service that Harold Ostertag did." So I said it. . . . I didn't have any idea who Jimmy Pecora was or what his traditions were, and I still don't. It was the first and only speech I made in that ward. . . . The Republicans always carry it and every Republican wins by the same amount!

We attended a card party, a dance and a couple of dinners in the city; and "he showed the flag" with a sentence or two. Never was there a whiff of an issue. He always seemed to be breaking into someone else's good time. While people there thought it was fine that he came, he never seemed able to join in or to connect in any emotional sense. His efforts at being "one of the boys" in urban contexts were stiff and awkward.

He made the comparison this way, "In the urban area, I'm a captive of the party. I go to rallies, stand up, and make platitudinal, pro-party, solidarity statements. I'm not allowed to be independent, to be myself. People in the rural areas wouldn't be satisfied with this. They expect whole relationships with people—not fragmentary relationships, like city people do. I like whole relationships, and that's why I do so much better in the rural area than in the urban area." It was a country boy's calculation—by an especially thoughtful country boy.

Between the rural area to which he was strongly attached and the city to which he was weakly attached were numerous suburbs—in which his connections were mixed and loose. Where voting in Congress was concerned, this mixture gave him independence. "Because my district is so diverse," he said,

> I can find support somewhere for almost any position I take. That means I can start by deciding how I want to vote and not how I must vote. If I want to vote for an urban program, I can do it, and the people in the rural area will say, "He does have an urban constituency and he has to help them, too." And they will vote for me so long as they think I'm a nice fella. But if I had no urban constituents—if I had all countryside—and I voted for an urban program, people in the rural area would say, "He must be running for governor. He's forgotten who his friends are." And they would hold it against me. The same is true in the urban area. They know I'm a country boy and that I have a lot of rural area. So they say, "He gives us a vote once in a while. So he's probably all right!"

A similar question brought into focus his relations with the economic giant of his district—Eastman Kodak. I asked him whether any one vote would kill him in his district. "No," he answered, "not in my district. My district is too diverse—it's not all urban ghetto or Idaho potato farmers. That gives me a chance to balance my votes. There really aren't any dominant interests. . . . Eastman Kodak is the biggest, and they don't give a damn. They don't give me any trouble [on his pro-free- trade views, with which they disagreed]. I help them with their tax problems; but they're so big that the only people who know about what I do are in the tax department."

More than that, when he could have used their help, they refused to provide it. His case in point came after he saved Kodak employees "millions of dollars" from an added tax on their pensions—and had done so in hand-to-hand combat with the Secretary of the Treasury. "I was the only person who could have done what I did." Kodak's "management," however, despite many entreaties, refused to print any mention of his legislative accomplishment in their in-house newspaper. Their intransigence explained why, in 1974, he and I and a small group stood in the pouring rain at 6:45 A.M. handing out explanatory leaflets at a Kodak plant gate. His district had this very large business; but it was no help to the Republican congressman. In the 1971 redistricting, his House colleague succeeded in taking Kodak's huge downtown office building, plus others, from Conable's district into his own. "He screwed me in the redistricting," reported Conable afterward.

In a close election, the suburbs would be a battleground. "In this district, the suburbs hold the balance of power . . . . I do most of my hard campaigning in the suburbs . . . particularly in the schools and in shopping centers. If I were in trouble, I wouldn't go to party rallies. I'd go to the shopping centers. What I love is shopping center campaigning. I'll do that every time I get a spare moment."

His model campaign and "the highlight of" his "political career" had been his state senate primary election against a prominent small-town Republican opponent. "I ran my legs off down to the knees. Whenever I saw two people together, I would jump out of my car and shake hands. At the end, I was so exhausted I couldn't get out of bed. That is the way I got a reputation as a tough campaigner—in my state senate campaign." And he did it, he said, "entirely with volunteers." The Republican Party was not helpful in the general election. "The organization gives you a peg to hang your coat on. But the candidate has to take all the initiative in promoting himself. They won't do a thing."

Thinking about his suburbs, he commented, "The average age of the people in my district is four years lower than the state average. They are people on mortgage row—young, trying to make it, and on their way up. My next-door colleague has the more mature, affluent suburbs. When people 'make it,' they move from my district to his district. . . . His is an upper-middle-class district. . . . Mine is a lower-middle-class district. I represent the bowlers."

In his largest suburban town, Conable always worked outside the party organization because it was consumed by internecine warfare. In 1971, he said,

> I still haven't met the town supervisor yet—unbelievable, but true. I stay as far away from that situation as I can—and that's why I run so well there. If I got involved, I would only lose. I send my newsletter in there as quietly as I can. My biggest town is my biggest headache. I don't go there any more than I have to. They want you to commit yourself all the time. It's sheep and goats. The supervisor is very ambitious and he loves confrontation. . . . You can't make any nickels in that situation.

"A congressman," he generalized, "has to make a conscious choice whether he wants to be a local political leader, to be a big cheese in local politics, or whether he wants to tend to business in Washington and do what the local leaders ask of him in local politics. I deliberately chose the second course."

When the 1971 redistricting reshuffled him into an unfamiliar suburb, he commented,

> I'm a little nervous about it, because it's new to my district. But I'm glad to have it because it's the one town on the south side of the city that's most like the towns I already represent. All my suburbs are lower middle class. I don't represent any wealthy people. So, in terms of keeping my district catalogue-able, I was blessed to get the new town. These are all mortgage row people, mostly young. They work for corporations, but they haven't made it yet. It's a district with a lot of young people . . . and that means a lot of children—many Catholics, too.

Earlier, he had described his (and my) district as "50 percent Catholic."

I went with him when he met the supervisor of this new suburb for the first time. I noted,

> It was stiff in the sense that Barber rattled off (relevant) federal programs; and sometimes he wouldn't let the supervisor get a word in edgewise—as if he were nervous and trying to impress people. . . . There was no relaxed banter of any sort, of the kind you get with friends. Clearly, he was not "at home." Indeed, he talked over and past a man he was meeting for the first time.

When I asked the supervisor how he liked changing congressmen, he said, "The birth pangs are hard for both sides—while we build up rapport. Barber Conable will measure up, I'm sure. I like him. I don't understand what he's saying half the time; but I like him"—whereupon he praised the previous representative at length for setting up helpful meetings for town officials in Washington. There was a hint, here, of a difference in the representational styles of Conable and his adjacent colleague.

A related stylistic contrast came alive during a joint meeting—in his colleague's next-door district—with some distressed New York apple growers in the rich fruit-growing area along Lake Ontario. Both representatives sat on the platform alongside several farmers. I noted,

> Conable tears into the export/import problems with technical language, etc. His colleague says that he has talked personally with the Secretary of Agriculture and that he has already put one of his growers on the phone with the secretary. His aide keeps running up to him with notes; and the congressman keeps saying what he had done for them. He called each individual grower by name.

One representative's constituency connection was solitary and policy-centered; his colleague's constituency connection was personal, staff-assisted, and service-centered.

Conable had occasion to make a similar distinction when he ruminated, later, about his constituency connections.

> One thing I think is unusual about me is that I have never distinguished myself from my constituents. I have always been considered a reserved, aloof fella. But I've always felt as though I was a part of the group—even when I can't clue in on people as well as I used to. When my colleague comes to a function, he always comes in late, so he can make a special entrance. And he usually comes in with two or three staff people. If you're sitting in the room, you can feel everyone at your table stiffen— "Here he comes." You feel the excitement of the entrance. I have tried not to differentiate myself. . . . If he and I are at a Republican dinner, he will be down working the tables. I don't do that. . . . I don't want to go stick my hand in someone's face while he's eating lunch. I don't feel as if I have any special status that has to be maintained. I think I still have good rapport . . . the same relationship, qualitatively, as when I first started.

The visibly close participation of his colleague's district staff—at the apple grower's meeting, and in this assessment—helps to highlight, again, Conable's distinctive self-sufficiency in his representational relationships. "I guess there just isn't any group I go to for advice," he said.

Not only did he not take staff with him during his district activities, he had purposely chosen to hire only one full-time staff member in the district. And he had closeted that person in the Federal Office Building in downtown Rochester. Other than an old friend to whom he delegated campaign publicity, one staff person handled his everyday constituency affairs. All personal contact he reserved for himself. Most of it was steered to Washington. Politically, he was a "one-man band."

He explained, at length, this most unusual staffing decision.

I wanted to submerge the district function. If you have a big district staff, you create expectations, you encourage people to come to you, and you get a huge caseload. I would rather have the people who really want help—and who need help—have to work a little bit to get it. I want to screen out the nuts. That is why I don't have a lot of office hours quite frankly. So, I deliberately wanted to underplay the district activity.

Secondly, I wanted to have the image that "Barber does it all himself!" If people know that Olga [his lone staffer] is just a conduit, they will feel that the decision is made in Washington, and it is made by me. Once in a while, I get a complaint that I didn't send a representative to a [local] meeting. But I don't want anybody else speaking for me.

Thirdly, I wanted the casework done in the Washington office so I would be better informed on what our office is doing, who we are helping, and how. If there's anything I hate, it's having someone come up to talk about something the office is doing and my not knowing what it's all about.

Also, a little contrapuntal contrast with [his neighboring colleague] doesn't hurt me—in my opinion. He plays up district services and has much more identification as the local [Rochester] congressman than I do. They think of me as coming from [next door] Genesee county. No matter what I did, I could never achieve the magnificent local identification that he has. I would always stand in his shadow. He has created expectations that people don't have of me. He leaves Washington every Thursday night; I leave on Friday nights—usually I'm busy with (my committee) or writing my newsletter. I'm trying to gain identification in a different way. So, put it all together, it spells "Olga."[8]

"Who knows whether it's the right way," he added. Or, as he often quoted from Kierkegaard, "Each representative has his own formula, 'a truth that is true for him.'"

The widely noted and broadly beneficial hallmark of Conable's election campaigns was his ironclad rule to accept no more than $50 from any one contributor—person or group. It was an unusual, if not unique, rule for any representative—and passing strange for a member of a political cash cow, the Ways and Means Committee. Colleagues would remind him of the largesse he could raise from special interests—to no avail. Indeed, "I started it when I went on the Ways and Means Committee." He returned many a large contribution to a flabbergasted individual or organization. This practice, he believed, protected his own sense of independence while it enhanced his trustworthiness in the eyes of his constituents.

Fifty dollars was an amount that allowed large numbers of ordinary citizens to make a tangible and durable connection—and one that built, therefore, an especially supportive base. Its core was his list of people who received his weekly newsletter. That list of 30,000 would be given to "a group of friends who would solicit each one for a $10 contribution." In combination, the newsletter and the contribution limit set highly visible standards—and they connected him to a loyal, respectful support base.

A bottom line, of course, was that he did not need a lot of money. In 1970, he spent $16,000; in 1972 he spent $24,000. In 1974, his only competitive campaign, he spent $76,000. That year, for the first and only time of his career, he held a public fund-raiser in Rochester from which, at $35 a ticket, he netted $17,500. It was the spending scale of a politically secure local boy.

A personal prescription also underpinned what he called "my puritanical position on public financing."

I'm in trouble with a lot of my friends because I support public financing. But I carry such a burden of corporate guilt. I worry about our institutions. And this method of raising money is scandalous. Besides, public financing is consistent with the way I have always run my own campaigns—with not more than $50 for a contribution. I could raise half a million dollars just like that because of my position, my reputation, and the myths about me. But I think that can be a terribly corrupting process.

In this matter, as in the matter of committee power inside the House, he was a strong political reform advocate. Given the dominance of his rural small-town connections, we might assume that his policy preferences were strongly conservative. In the national Republican Party spectrum, however, he was a self-proclaimed "moderate." He was pro-civil rights; and pro-women's rights—in that he refused to sign discharge petitions moving antibusing and right-to-life legislation to the House floor. He regularly drew a conservative, pro-life opponent in the Republican primary. He was a committed economic free trader. He was a mainstream fiscal conservative and a decentralist in his opposition to the regulatory activity of big national government. Until Watergate, his voting record marked him as one of President Richard Nixon's most reliable legislative supporters.

He was not a movement politician or a cause-oriented politician. He did not think in organizational or ideological terms—only in issue-by-issue terms. Whatever the issue, he remained aloof from interest group commitments. He was slow to commit and slow to shut down policy options while he thought them through. Often, he described himself as Hamlet "sicklied o'er with the pale cast of thought."

He resisted—subject to party leadership necessities—all opportunities for entangling alliances. He wanted to explain his own policy preferences in his own way. His policy connections with his constituents, he liked to say, carried inescapably, "the burden of explanation."

To a group of students, he said,

We have a saying in Congress that "if you have to explain something, you're in trouble." It means you should go along, keep your head down, and accept the protective coloration of the group. That's an indication of the low estate to which Congress has fallen. I think we have to take on the burden of explanation more than we do. We have to have the will to govern and then explain to our people what we have done.

It was an educational prescription and a practice that infused his weekly newsletter—and burnished his reputation as a teacher both at home and in Washington.

In 1970, he stated his baseline electoral status this way: "I have a safe district. I don't see how I can lose it. Maybe I should be superstitious and not say things like that. But I could only lose if there is a Republican disaster. Goldwater got 30 percent in my district, and I got 53.9 percent that year. It can't get worse than that. . . . [This year] I should get between 55 percent and 60 percent of the vote. That's pretty solid—even if the economy stays bad. So I'm not going to push the panic button. I'm going to spend $20,000."

Campaign Trail: 1974

In 1974, Representative Conable faced the only competitive election of his House career. He won by "only" 57 percent of the vote—eight to ten points below his normal figure. In a year of historic Watergate-driven election gains for House Democrats, however, Conable's solid margin demonstrated more strength than weakness at the polls.

He always believed he would win. "My opponent [Rochester Mayor Midge Costanza] is getting around to the same people who have always voted against me," he said early on. "She has those people all psyched up and talking to each other as they never have before. And their activity is throwing my supporters into a tizzy. Our biggest problem is morale. So I'm running around trying to jerk up morale by making myself as visible as possible." It was his way. His only concern was that Watergate and its effects might dampen Republican turnout. "I'm running against apathy and disillusionment as much as I am against my opponent. The Republicans are going to have to be dragged kicking and screaming to the polls. If it's a big vote, I'll be alright; if it's a small vote, I may not be." "I get no sense at all," I noted, "that he is running scared."

One big difference between constituency connections "as usual" and constituency connections "during a campaign" is the special need for coordination and organization during a campaign. For a "one-man band" candidate, organization is a major problem. When we bantered later about my "get up here" phone call, he said, "You know damned well that I wouldn't have come home to do organizational work." And I did. His representational connections had never depended on organization. They depended on one man's talents and his presentation of self.

"Barber Conable," I noted at one point, "has less organizational interest, and less of an organization, than any candidate I have traveled with."
Some examples from my notes:

1. Concerning one of his two planned campaign headquarters: "On Sunday, he was supposed to have gone to the opening of his Greece headquarters. He didn't even have it on his schedule! Forty-five people came and waited for two hours for him to show up. He didn't."

2. Regarding the second of his two planned headquarters: "We went to look at it. It was a corner of a big barn-like warehouse. . . . They didn't know how they were going to heat it. There were no telephone facilities, no tables, no chairs, or even any light! Barber said they would have four phones in there. There are no restrooms in sight! I sat in the corner and almost laughed out loud. Here, on October 14th, Conable was at the stage that another one of my House members had been at when I was with him on June 15th."

3. "When we went to pass out literature at Southtown Plaza on Monday, five women were waiting for us without any materials. We were late. They had been standing around looking at each other for forty-five minutes."

4. "When he talked to the Leroy Women's Club . . . the president of the club and the program chair, both young women, asked him afterward if they could help him. He didn't know what to do with them. He had no one to send them to, no organization to plug them into. "Tomorrow," he said, "I'm going to do a little organization work out in the country."

My reflections continued,

There is in this lack of organizational interest, a reverse side—a kind of self-confidence in his ability to run a one-man band. Part of this assumption—that he can handle these problems himself—is a confidence in his ability. Part of it, too, I think, is the notion that he ought not to have to do very hard organizational work because he is so obviously better qualified than his opponent that people will see that and vote for him. . . . He feels that he *shouldn't really have to* [italics in original] spend all that much time on organization and, therefore, he doesn't. He takes the burden on himself because he thinks he can handle it, and because he sees elective office as very much a matter of *personal quality* [italics in original]. . . . (It is) a rural-personal stance rather than an urban-symbolic stance.

In any case, despite having been put under some extra pressure, he had remained every bit the self-sufficient, confident local/country boy.

His preference for personal relationships was reflected, interestingly, in his refusal to ask anyone to vote for him. Other campaigners with whom I traveled routinely asked for votes. "I'd appreciate your vote on Election Day." "Don't forget to vote for me on Election Day." Not once did I hear Barber Conable make such a request—not even in shopping centers when he handed out his wife's recipe books. He presented himself to them and he talked with them; but he never asked them. The idea seemed to be that if he let them take the full measure of him personally, there was no need to solicit votes point blank. That was the rationale behind his weekly newsletter. If they had no chance to listen to him, they would get to know him by reading what he thought about and wrote about.

It was a country boy's straightforward attitude that support came to him from interpersonal respect and trust. If any request for "a vote" were to be made, it would have to be made by his supporters, not by him.

He campaigned at election time just as he campaigned between elections with talk and explanation, with what he called "dialogue." "I love dialogue. I love to answer questions." What he meant was that he loved to talk, to connect to his constituency with exposition and explanation. For him, "dialogue" was a verb, that is, to dialogue." But it was a one-way process—from him to them, not them to him.

In his rural area, for example, he connected with a local historical society by describing its current location on an old Iroquois campground "at the big bend of the Tonawanda River. . . . I think people who live by a stream are lucky," he told them. "They can look at the stream and know that it comes from somewhere and it goes somewhere. It gives us a sense of continuity. We know we are not isolated. We have a perspective—just as the stream of history gives us a perspective." Listening to him, I noted, "his sense of place and of history is a key to the fact that he remains relatively placid and confident while some of his supporters are [he says] 'panicky.' He simply has a longer view of things than his followers."

Later that same day, he charged into a suburban church group saying, "Dialogue is the name of the game. I came to answer your questions!" To a policy question, he ended his answer with the comment,

"I'm inclined to favor anything that's decentralized; it's a good Western New York attitude." To a question about his job, he gave them this piece of his thinking.

> Early in our history, people were successful in some other occupation and went to Washington for only three months a year. Then they came back to their homes, plugged into local values, and recharged their batteries. And they gave an accounting to their constituents. They were not professional representatives. They were somebody's neighbor. It was the highest act of citizen participation. Now I'm very worried that we have become professional representatives, skilled in the art of political survival—particularly in the manipulation of the media.

The next day he turned down an invitation to attend a large Columbus Day luncheon in the crucial Italian-American community—because "I would just be sitting over in the corner somewhere and get a chance to stand up and wave"—in favor of an invitation to speak to a small Rochester sales executive luncheon group. "Besides," he said, "I wanted to create a contrast between myself and my opponent. . . . I don't believe she could have given a speech like that." And he repeated his desire for "whole relationships." "I have always based my political survival on the enthusiasm of a few people, rather than recognition by the many." His campaign illustrated, once more, what he was "good at."

Running against a popular Italian woman in a strongly Italian district, his activity in that context seemed strikingly untutored. His private reaction when he learned she might run was: "I'm afraid my district isn't ready for an Italian woman. The district is probably 30 percent Italian. But Italians are patriarchal, not matriarchal as the blacks are. I'm afraid they will resent her because she is a woman." Later, "I won't call her Midge (her nickname); I'll call her Margaret. I find her a very attractive girl—intelligent, articulate. . . . But labor is just using her." She was, after all, a leader in his main city. And these private responses seemed simplistic and patronizing. She attacked him, broadly, as arrogant and aloof. And, certainly, where her ethnic ties were concerned, she had a point.

Representative Conable worked easily with individuals of Italian heritage. The manager of his first campaign and major lifetime political advisor was one such. But when it came to the Italian community, he seemed remarkably tone deaf and awkward. On our way to a dinner to honor the Republican supervisor of a populous suburb, he tested a pointedly pro-Italian joke on me. And I had to tell him not to use it because his joke was, at the same time, subtly anti-Irish, and the town had nearly as large an Irish population.

On another occasion, I suggested that he solicit a personal endorsement from Joe Altobelli, arguably the most popular resident of his district—as a former major league baseball player and, at the time, the manager of the Rochester Red Wings baseball team. Conable replied, "I've never heard of him." Then, when I told him who Altobelli was, he added, "I've never been in Red Wing Stadium in my life." Some politicians live or die by tending ethnic sensitivities and interests. The "local boy's" clumsiness in connecting with his Italian community was noteworthy. But it was not electorally consequential.

In the end, Conable's strongest supporters—the ones he had cultivated and appealed to from the beginning—easily carried the day. Money (limited to $50 per) poured in; and volunteers appeared in large numbers. He predicted an 18,000 vote margin, and his winning margin was 27,000 votes. His remaining four elections were virtually uncontested. In time, my acquaintance with Representative Conable would become the most continuous, intensive, and long-lived of my constituency travels and relationships. And we stayed in touch to the end of his twenty years there.

Shortly before the 1974 campaign, Representative Conable had expressed a developing tension between his work in the constituency and his work in Washington—a tension between connecting at home and governing in the House. "I'm beginning to be a little concerned about my political future," he began.

> I can feel myself getting into what I guess is a natural and inevitable condition—the gradual erosion of my local orientation. I'm not as enthused about tending my constituency relations as I used to be; and I'm not paying them the attention I should be. I'm beginning to pay the price, I think, for my growing interest in government. There's a natural tension between being a good representative and taking an interest in government. I'm getting into some heady things in Washington; and I want to

make an input into government. It's making me a poorer representative than I used to be.

I find myself avoiding the personal collisions that arise in the constituency—turning away from that "one last handshake," not bothering to go to that "one last meeting." I find myself forgetting people's names. And I find myself caring less about it. Right now, it's just a feeling I have. In eight years, I have still to come home less than forty weekends a year. This is my thirty-sixth trip this year.

What was it Arthur Rubenstein said? "If I miss one practice, I notice it. If I miss two practices, my teacher notices it. If I miss three practices, the audience notices it." I'm at stage one now—or maybe between stage one and stage two. But I'm beginning to feel that I could be defeated before long. Some bright, young Republican could come along and wallop me in a primary. And I'm not going to change. I don't want the status. I want to contribute to government.

It was an instructive intellectual wrestle.

He was reminding himself, and his listener, of the flow of time and of the unending conflict between constituency and Capitol Hill demands.

Postscript

In 1974, Barber Conable became the top-ranking Republican member of the House Ways and Means Committee. He held that coveted position as leader of the committee's minority party members until his retirement, ten years later. In that final year, 1984, his House colleagues—of both parties—voted him "the most respected member of the US House of Representatives."[9] For a minority member, it was unusually high praise.

Two years later, President George Bush chose the New Yorker to be president of the World Bank—a position that kept him in Washington for five more years. At which point, the Conables retired to "the farm" in Upstate New York.

— 3 —

Glenn Poshard

Textbook Representative

Home Place: Southern Illinois, 1996

Glenn Poshard, Democrat of Illinois, served in the US House of Representatives from the late 1980s to the late 1990s. When we met, in the spring of 1996, he was fifty years old and campaigning for a fifth term. He had been born, raised, educated, and made his living in his spacious Southern Illinois congressional district. Only once had he left home—to serve in the US Army in Korea. After which he returned—with his GI Bill—to earn BA and PhD degrees from Southern Illinois University (SIU) at Carbondale. During and after college, he lived and worked in his home territory—first, as a high school social studies teacher and later as a regional education administrator.[1] In 1988, after two 2-year terms in the Illinois State Senate, he was elected to Congress.

Glenn Poshard was not only from Illinois's Nineteenth District, he was of the Nineteenth District. He was every inch the local boy who made good. The bonds of his home place, together with his choice of representational practices, had kept him maximally close to his constituents. He shared with Barber Conable the notably strong and enduring sense that his constituency was home.

My trip to his district came from an out-of-the-blue suggestion of two professional acquaintances at SIU; and we dined together on the evening of my arrival in 1996. As his friends and supporters, they described Representative Poshard as a smart, thoughtful, conscientious, idealistic, constituency-oriented, and independent-minded Democrat. On domestic economic matters, he was devotedly pro-labor union and pro-economic development. But he was also known as an equally strong-minded, stay-within-your-means, pay-as-you-go budget balancer. On the controversial social and cultural issues of his time and place: he was pro-life on religious grounds, he opposed the anti-flag-burning amendment on civil libertarian grounds, and he opposed gun control on cultural grounds.

He described himself always as "a moderate Democrat" or "a centrist Democrat." He viewed congressional politics from a position in the middle range of his party's policy spectrum. By a standard liberal/conservative voting measure (Poole-Rosenthal), three-quarters of his fellow House Democrats were more liberal than he.[2] He was, his friends emphasized, very much his own man. And while they did not always agree with him, they talked about him with equal parts affection and respect.

Their dinnertime discussion of his geographical constituency was especially helpful. They talked about it as a distinctive and durable place—especially so before it had been altered by the statewide redistricting decisions of 1992. Prior to that date, they emphasized, the Nineteenth Congressional District was not only in Southern Illinois, it was Southern Illinois. And Glenn Poshard was, in every sense, the Southern Illinois representative.

Bordering, as it did, the Ohio River, Southern Indiana, and Kentucky, the district had originally been heavily settled by southerners. It was situated as far from Chicago as one could get in the state. To reach it, you flew into St. Louis and drove southward for two and a half hours—first across flat prairie and then into coal, oil, forest, and Ohio River country. St. Louis was said to be the district's favorite city. And the St. Louis Cardinals were said to be its favorite baseball team—not the Chicago Cubs. Similarly, the *St. Louis Post-Dispatch* seemed to be more attuned to Poshard's territory than was the *Chicago Tribune*.

This sense of place was unusually strong. When the congressman's chief of staff called Rochester to report on my reservations at Rend Lake—and, again, when he called upon my arrival there—he emphasized how pleased they were that they had found this particular place for me to stay. Both times, he told me, "It's in the district; and that pleases us even more." "In Rochester," I wrote in my notebook, "who would ever say, 'We got you a room at the Downtown Hyatt—and it pleases us because it's in the district?' Unthinkable!" Almost immediately I had found a sense of community in striking contrast to the total absence of same during my earlier trip to Florida. Glenn Poshard's district was not "nowhere." He represented a distinctive, describable home place—and aggressively so.

The special integrity of Illinois' Nineteenth Congressional District, my dinner companions said, had been underwritten by the longevity, the achievements, and the reputations of the two previous Democrats it had sent to Congress. Ken Gray, a legendary pork barreller—four billion dollars for 1,000 new programs and projects, by his own reckoning—had served for twenty-two years.[3] Paul Simon, a statesmanlike newspaper editor (and later US Senator), had served for ten years. Glenn Poshard, they said, "is half Ken Gray and half Paul Simon. He tends the district like Gray and he's an idealist like Simon." The pre-1992 Nineteenth Congressional District, they added, "was a separate culture and Glenn fit that culture perfectly."

For as long as his friends could recall, the northern boundary of "the historic southern Illinois district" had sliced horizontally across the southernmost part of the state. In 1992, however, the character of the district had been substantially altered by the decennial redistricting process. Representative Poshard's district had been sliced in half vertically—scattering eleven of his counties to the west and north. Nine of his southeastern counties remained, to which eleven new ones had been added to the east and north. His new district—of 11,000 square miles—was Illinois's largest.

The redistricting posed hard questions for the incumbent. "Should I run," and, "if I do run, which piece of my old district should I choose to run in?" Whichever piece he chose, he would be thrown into a contest with a fellow Democratic congressman. When he tested the strength of a colleague to the west and north, he said that the people he approached "slammed down the phone on me. I met a total stonewall. They have a machine up there around East St. Louis. If you waver (in loyalty), you lose your job."[4] His only realistic possibility, therefore, was the eastern side of his old district, plus a string of unfamiliar counties running northward.

The new twenty-five-county district would contain a city larger than anything he had known, plus a richer agricultural area than he had ever represented. And, most important, in the northeast section of the reshaped district, a fellow House Democratic colleague, two-term Representative Terry Bruce—described as "a natural politician . . . who has shown his mastery of the political game"—would be waiting to fight him for the job.[5]

Representative Poshard's initial reaction was to remain undecided. My dinner companions described their friend's lengthy "should I run" indecision as characteristic. He was, they said, not only "very thoughtful," but almost "too thoughtful." "He takes issues to heart." "He agonizes over votes." "Paul Simon could give and take in town meetings and then forget about it. Glenn can't." His office manager in Marion said that when she saw him the very night before his decision deadline, he still had not made up his mind. Only at the very last moment, at 4 P.M. the next afternoon, she said, did Representative Poshard acknowledge his intention to run for reelection.

His friends and his Marion office manager alike detected a familiar religious component in his drawn-out decision making. At dinner, one friend described him as "extremely religious. When he retired from Congress, I would not be surprised if he became a minister."[6] His office manager commented similarly that his hesitation about running for reelection may have involved this competing attraction. "God is in him," she said. "If he had decided not to run because he felt called to a ministry, I would have supported him . . . even though he has done so much for people that we need him." In time, I would learn for myself that Glenn Poshard was an uncommonly contemplative—and empathetic—individual.

His dinner-time friends touched briefly on the congressman's prior legislative performance at the State Capital [in Springfield. They recalled, particularly, his work there as chairman of the Senate Labor and Commerce Committee. When he came to Congress, the *Congressional Quarterly* had described him as "a prolific legislator in Springfield" and as one who "had used his expertise to establish a record on education issues . . . (on) the overhaul of Workman's Compensation . . . (on) rural health care and on 'clean coal' technology." In doing so, "he caught the eye of the Democratic leadership," so much so that they had chosen him to be the "Keynote Speaker of the 1986 Democratic State Convention."[7] He had been tagged, my friends said, "as a rising star" in the Illinois State Legislature.

At the same time, they expressed wonderment and some disappointment that he had not achieved a similar visibility and reputation in the House of Representatives. They speculated that he might have chosen unwisely when he decided, in his second term in Congress, to seek membership on the House Committee on Public Works and Transportation.[8] His rationale, they assumed, was to follow his predecessor Ken Gray's example and put himself in a position to bring construction and road money into a needy district. But that choice, his friends felt, had wasted his very considerable talents and had kept him invisible inside a large and undistinguished congressional committee.

A 1994 appraisal from inside his committee was that "he is bright, involved and appears to do his homework. But he is not . . . a force to be reckoned with."[9] My companions believed that Glenn Poshard was equipped by intellect and political skill to follow Paul Simon's example of an outward looking and distinguished public career. I would soon find, however, that he expressed—and he operated with—a very different conception of his job than his two friends had hoped for.

My forty-mile drive to dinner that first evening hinted at a marked governmental presence and a correspondingly weak local economy. I drove past two large, federally financed lakes: Rend Lake, identified as a creation of the Corps of Engineers, and Crab Orchard Lake, identified as an earlier New Deal construction project. Further along the way, there were signs pointing to a federal penitentiary in Marion. "This district is dotted with prisons," a friend said at dinner. "It's sad, but true. We'll take all the prisons we can get. Nobody else wants them. Chicago sends us all their criminals. . . . You haven't seen anything. There's a big one in Frankfort—you drove right by the turn. And they're building an even bigger prison in _____." When we met, the congressman agreed. "It's sad but true. I have more prisons in my district than community colleges." "When other parts of the state thumbed their noses at the prisons," he told an interviewer, "we took all we could get. It is an important industry in Southern Illinois."[10]

It was no surprise, therefore, to read his related comment that "my district is the poorest district in the state."[11] Or, to learn further that the great bulk of the district's high 15–16 percent unemployment figures came from the hard-hit coal and oil producing parts of the area I had traversed on the way down.[12] My first day was spent in his central Marion district office reading the representative's key speeches on the House floor and his press clips. His Marion staffers seemed experienced and devoted. At lunch, they talked about a close relationship. "It's impossible for us to separate the congressman from the friend." "He's into everything—doesn't miss a thing." "We're like family."

The next morning two people came to the Marion office to ask his help with employment problems. A dietician's VA job had been put in jeopardy; a coal miner wanted a shift change so he could take better care of his family. In the front room, the office manager swapped stories with the waiting coal miner. "All in my family worked in the mines," she told him.

> My grandfather was killed in the mine. My father was buried under once, but he got out all right. I was home when the mine office called and said he was in the hospital. I had to go tell my mother. She was playing Bingo. As soon as she saw me, she knew it was my dad. "Is he alive?" she asked me. We went to the hospital. He was alive; but they had to saw off his arm—without anesthesia. He went back to work, but he suffered black lung all his life. My husband got an ear torn off and lost two fingers. He's a roofer. That's the most dangerous job in the mine. He got laid off when the mine closed. He says he won't go back to the mines. But he's too young to get his benefits, and he'll have to work in some mine till he's 55 to get his benefits. The wages were good; but it's an awful way to make a living. We didn't know anything else.

In a very matter-of-fact manner, she had put a human face on a needy constituency.

When he arrived, the congressman took me straightaway to sit inside his office. He listened attentively and sympathetically to their personal problems. (I supplied the dietician with a tissue when she began to weep.) He agreed to try. "Are you going to be okay?" "Is everything going to be alright?" He had a country doctor's bedside manner—accessible and compassionate.

In that spirit, he had created six additional satellite district offices to make face-to-face service available to his constituents. The staff arrangement was my first clue to his extraordinary attentiveness to constituents. His total of seven district offices placed him "off the charts" in my own calculations in the 1970s. And everything else confirmed it. A staff of seven people worked in the main office in Marion. And seven more staffers were scattered throughout the district in six satellite offices—one staffer per office, and two in Decatur. This unusually large district staff of fourteen people was, of course, related to his unusually large district. But it also reflected his personal priorities—since he kept an unusually small staff of five people in Washington.

In the DC office, the congressman's chief of staff doubled as his press secretary—a job that kept the Washington office in constant contact with everything that happened at home. It was he who had called from Washington to welcome me to the district. I soon learned that he, too, shuttled back and forth from Washington to Illinois. In addition to which, he also helped organize and produce the congressman's 1996 media campaign. Glenn Poshard's overall staffing arrangement was the most district-centered of any I ever encountered.

It illustrated the priority he gave to the representational part of the job. He shared a deep constituency rootedness with Barber Conable. For the New Yorker, however, the connection was exclusively personal. And, as such, it called for the barest minimum of one full-time staffer in his district.

District Travel: South to North

Our first event, on a Saturday morning, took us to the nearby town of Benton to participate in "the 25th Annual Rend Lake Water Festival Parade." On the way, the congressman articulated themes that would become familiar. "It's a neat district," he began,

> because it forces you to shift gears on the different issues. But I hate parades. The round of parades and party meetings are hard. I'm tired; but it's the politics that wear you out, not the issues. There's more partisanship in Congress today than I've ever seen. Democracy is [about] the middle ground bringing philosophical notions together, closing the door, and sledge-hammering an issue until you get it done. But we spend hours and hours in Congress listening to the extremes. And the people in the middle are down on the politicians.

He was still absorbing the aftershock of the Republicans' post-1994 electoral takeover—which had ended forty uninterrupted years of Democratic control of the House.

Partisanship levels were high; and political scientists were pinpointing the disappearance of legislators from the bipartisan ideological "middle." And worrying, too, about the consequent danger of political gridlock.[13] From his position near the center of the ideological spectrum, Glenn Poshard would complain, to the end of my visits, about the wastefulness and unpleasantness of excessive partisanship inside the institution. But in May 1996, we were a very long way from Washington; and his exceptionally strong constituency attachments were the realities we would experience together.

Riding in the parade, the congressman stood in the back of a red, white, and blue decorated truck, waving and throwing bubble gum to the spectators, while his loudspeaker blared Bruce Springsteen's "I'm Glad to Be an American." I rode up front with owner/driver Louis Seaton and wife Ethel. The parade route took us down the main street of Benton, where families with children sat waiting on the curb.

Afterward, the congressman's wife, Jo, joined us, and we headed north to his largest city, Decatur—175 miles away. In the car, he said to her, "You know what I saw today. I saw poverty. Those little kids—hardly dressed, shivering in the cold, with their mothers wrapping blankets around them. Coal country is hurting bad." That evening when I reread his comment, I added, "And that's what I saw, too. Downtown Benton was largely boarded up. The signs were still on the windows indicating the kind of store they were; but they were boarded up. Coal wages were said to be pretty good: $35,000 to $40,000 a year. But the Clean Air Act (over Glenn's opposition) had nearly killed the industry.[14] They mine high sulfur coal here; and the 'scrubbers' to clean it up cost $300 to $400,000 apiece." "My coal counties," the congressman repeated later, "are hurting like hell."

As the three of us began the long drive to Decatur, he commented helpfully on the size and the complexity of his post-1992 district.

> I used to be in the middle of my district. Now I'm at one end of a district that is 265 miles long. Communication was easy. I was within driving distance of everywhere. The three major networks, ABC, NBC, and CBS were concentrated here in Williamson County. The major newspaper (*The Southern Illinoisan*) was here. Now, I have to think of two more TV stations in Decatur to touch the northern part of the district, two more in Terre Haute and two in Vincennes to touch the eastern part of

the district. We aren't able to buy all that media. And we always have to borrow money to run.

"Every fifty miles," he continued,

> the issues change. Starting from the southern tip of the district, the issues are about river commerce, locks, and dams. The next fifty miles, the issues are environmentalism and logging in the Shawnee National Forest. Fifty miles more brings you into coal country; and the next fifty miles is oil country. Fifty miles more and you're in the area where 65 percent of the [new] district's population lives. The first fifty miles there, the issue is abortion—that's all there is. And for the last fifty you get to Decatur with agribusiness—Staley and ADM [Archer Daniels Midland].

At journey's end in Decatur, and in surrounding Macon County, we were light years from coal-country Benton. "Here is the bread basket of America—with the richest, blackest, most productive soil in the world," he said. "The first time I heard the farmers in Macon County complaining about $1.92 bushel corn, I couldn't believe it. I can remember trying to plant through red clay, trying to break up rough brick and drive fence posts on our land to get $.62 bushel corn. And here I was listening to farmers complaining about $1.92 bushel corn." From coal to corn, from poverty to plenty, I had seen two worlds in one district.

The post-1994 redistricting had brought him north to the richer agricultural territory, and with it, to Decatur's huge international agribusiness, Archer Daniels Midland (ADM). Taken together, the corn-growing countryside plus ADM spelled ethanol—a corn-based fuel additive. Ethanol was in ever-growing demand in the energy market—and in ever-growing favor with the surrounding farm country. At the same time, these new interests set the northern part of his district against the strongly independent oil and gas producers in its southern part. "Oil and ethanol interests don't always coincide, but I'll have to work on both," he had commented. "Just about all the oil Illinois produces (the eleventh largest US producer) comes from my district . . . but the independents are shutting down, and it has created big job losses. We've also got to pin down the ethanol issue. For my district, in terms of the economy, it's a huge issue. . . . One [coal] doesn't necessarily support the other, but both are job producers."[15]

In his campaign kickoff he promised to (1) "support the domestic oil and gas industry," (2) "promote the future of family farms through ethanol," and (3) "make infrastructure improvements such as waste and sewer systems, road improvements and other facilities which help attract new jobs."[16] It was one more description of his needy district. And he was determined to help all of it.

In Decatur, the congressman received an award from the nationally prominent Concord Coalition—a leading bipartisan budget watchdog group. In their calculations, his cautious voting record on budgetary and fiscal legislation ranked second highest in the twenty member Illinois delegation.[17] The coalition's rankings, their presentation, and a media interview (in the *Decatur Star Herald,* the district's other regional paper) authenticated his moderate Democratic reputation on fiscal matters ("compassionate and balanced," he said). And he deemed it worth the long trip. Every newspaper article outlining his campaign platform, it seemed, had highlighted his devotion to a balanced budget.[18] He was a career-long advocate of budget reform. And six months later, he would spend more of our campaign day together talking about the federal budget—priorities and balance—than any other subject.

On the way home, when we stopped to deliver a check to a YMCA dinner dance in a second northern (but not new) county, he commented about yet another configuration of interests. "This county is a microcosm of what's been happening here. It's a Catholic, strongly Democratic county. But in 1994, I won it by (only) 100 votes; and every other Democrat lost. It's a pro-life county and that is the only issue. Nothing else matters. The Christian Coalition and the Catholics have joined forces on this one issue."

Since he was strongly pro-life, he speculated that his vote fall-off was attributable to the contagion effects on his Catholic voters from their alliance with the strongly antiwelfare Protestant groups. "I'm about as conservative a Democrat as you'll find outside of the South," he said, "but the goal of these people up here is to attack the government." No member of Congress, in my experience, expressed a more protective attitude toward "the government" than he did. The left-behind, struggling parts of his district depended on it.

"Is this an easy district to represent?" I asked later. "No," he said, "it's a very difficult district to represent. The issues change every fifty miles and you are always embroiled in some argument. There has never been a time when we could sit back at the end of the day and say, 'Well, everything went well today.' It is exhausting. You never bring closure on anything." To which his chief of staff later added, "(the job) is like the hamster and the wheel. When Glenn comes back from the district, the problems come tumbling out. We'll work on them till 1:30 in the morning and start again at 7:30."[19] The congressman appeared to tend the connective underpinnings of his representational relationships as conscientiously as any legislator I had met. Nearly everything I had learned marked him as a person with super-strong representational priorities and practices.

The 1992 Redistricting Story

Glenn Poshard was a born storyteller. And the story that dominated our first day's trip northward was the post-1990 Illinois redistricting plan, his arduous 1992 primary campaign that followed, and his election victory in that intraparty preliminary contest.

As we drove through the county-seat town of Salem, he introduced the sore subject of the 1992 redistricting.

> I've driven this street a hundred times. It was in the old district; and I enjoyed working with the people here. I hated to lose this town. At the time I was redistricted, I had $32 million in highway money on the books ready to spend here and in my district. When I got the new district, I had only three million of it left. All of it was slated for the old district. I lost all my political capital. You have to start your whole political life over again. You have to get to know a whole new group of people, and you have to start from scratch in assessing the needs of the new district and starting to fulfill them. You have no political capital. Do you think it makes any sense to take towns like Salem and Centralia away from my district? It was totally absurd.

The 1992 territorial line-drawing had cost him the tangible political benefits of six years of work inside his Committee on Public Works and Transportation.

This comment, however, only hinted at his major redistricting difficulty. As he told the story: When it became clear that redistricting would cost Illinois two congressional districts, the south-of-Chicago Democrats (he, among them) banded together, hired a lawyer, and agreed to work together to protect each of their districts. Some time later, out of the blue in Washington, a reporter informed Poshard that his district had been slated for elimination. "I was in shock," the congressman recalled. "I knew absolutely nothing about it. I thought we had taken a blood oath to protect all the Southern Illinois districts, and that we had spent $35,000 on a lawyer for that purpose." As it turned out, however, "there had been 'meetings,' in Chicago, between Republicans and Democrats—meetings I knew nothing about."

When he went to the House floor and asked two south-of-Chicago Republicans what had happened, "They mumbled and said something like, 'Oh, don't get upset, Glenn'." When he approached a group of his Southern Illinois Democratic colleagues, he continued, "They just walked away. Not one guy gave me an answer. I said to Terry Bruce, 'You and I are friends. Did you know about this meeting? Were you there?' He walked away. I followed him off the [House] floor; and still he would not speak to me." And so it went.

"They had cut up my district into three separate pieces. . . . [And eventually forced him to change his residence in the process.] Each of the other Democrats boosted his base at my expense. The main purpose was to shore up and save a district for (fellow House Democrat) Terry Bruce. I was angry, very angry. I felt betrayed. But I did not know what to do. For a while, I wanted to go around and knock everybody, hold a press conference, and tell all. . . . That's when one of your SIU friends helped keep the lid on me. He told me to think it over, that I had a bright future in politics."

When he called a meeting of ten Democratic county chairmen in the eastern and northern counties, nine out of the ten urged Poshard not to run. "They said, 'Don't hurt Bruce's chances,' and 'you can't win.' Their advice to me was 'be patient.'" But he had heard that advice before.

> I said to them, "I tended my precinct for years, I kept track of every voter, I took them to the polls; I scraped the sidewalk for the elderly. My precinct had the best record in the county—and you guys kept saying to me, 'be patient.' Well, I was patient and nothing happened. Finally, I decided to run for the state senate. I ran, got my ass whipped, ran again and won. If I had taken your advice, I never would have won."

> I felt I had been betrayed by my friends. I had not been treated fairly. They had cut up my district behind my back. Bruce had $800,000. I had no money. I had never had money. We are not wealthy. We've borrowed money for every campaign. Most I ever made was $34,000 a year. But I knew that if I backed down and didn't run, I'd never forgive myself.

"It turns out," he summed up, "that where turf is involved in politics, politicians will sell each other down the river every time."

The success of his 1994 primary campaign, as the Poshards described it during our ride, depended on Glenn's performance in his new Macon County area—that is, Decatur (pop. 84,000) and its environs. Voters there would now be casting 40 percent of the total district vote. Representative Bruce, who already lived much closer to that county than Poshard, had left his home county immediately and moved to Decatur. ("I have the newspaper headline in my scrapbook," offered Jo: "Bruce Moves Residence into Decatur.")

Representative Poshard set up an office in Decatur, and designated his thirty-something son, Dennis, as his campaign manager—in charge of all the new northern counties. Glenn and Jo rehearsed the campaign, with Glenn carrying the theme, and with Jo ("I'm his biggest fan") adding to it at every step—how she felt, how she thought other people felt, and how Glenn felt.

Dennis Poshard held down a job in the capital city of Springfield throughout. And his performance was the centerpiece of his father's story. "We rented a motel room in Decatur," Glenn began,

> and opened a tiny headquarters. I knew nobody in Decatur. I don't think I had ever been to Decatur in my life. We stayed up there and went to talk to every county official and every Democratic committee member. We would be out all night, sometimes with flashlights, trying to find the right house of some precinct committee member. We talked to every single one, face-to-face, told them we were running and did not ask for any pledges. . . . Some nights, I would drive Dennis to the parking lot at the end of the evening. And he would get into his old car and drive back to Springfield. Dennis spent a lot of time talking to them, having a beer, explaining my ideas. . . .
>
> One month before the election, Dennis called me and said, "Come up to Decatur. The Macon County officials are going to have a press

conference." I said, "Don't push them." And Dennis said, "No, they want to have a press conference and they want to endorse you." And they did—the whole group—right under Terry Bruce's nose. Dennis had done it by talking with them over and over. . . . That was the turning point. When the folks down here saw that I had the support of the Macon County officials, they became energized. They said, "This guy has a chance." "He could win!" And they took off.

Tears welled up in his eyes as he spoke; and he dabbed at them with his handkerchief. "I don't know why I get so emotional about that campaign. I think it's because of what Dennis did, and how proud I was when he was at his best. We did it together." And they had done it in the same manner that he had cultivated the rest of his district—with heavily personal grassroots campaigning. Whatever caused his tears, the conspirators had certainly underestimated the sheer doggedness of their designated victim.

"Glenn and Jo savored the memory of that victory," I noted. "They replayed election night—especially the returns that exceeded their expectations in each county—area by area." "We thought that if we could get 35 percent in the northern counties, 75 percent in my old counties, and 44 percent in the others, we could win. We got 90 percent in my old counties, 45 percent in the northern counties (and in Decatur), and 50 percent in the in-between counties." He was endorsed, they said, by "all the newspapers."[20] "That was some night," the congressman summarized. Their pleasure was undoubtedly made sweeter by the contrast in expenditure totals. Estimates varied, but the huge disparity did not. One widely used report put Poshard's spending totals at $150,000 to Bruce's $740,000.[21]

Their own thumbnail explanations centered on comparative job performance—that Glenn Poshard was a better working representative at home than Terry Bruce. "People expect to see their congressman," said Jo. "Glenn comes home every weekend and goes wherever he's asked." In a later comment, the congressman added that the defining issue was his support for President Clinton's 1990 budget compromise calling for gasoline tax increases and Medicare cuts. "Terry made that vote the overriding issue in the campaign. They mailed thousands of slick brochures tying me to (Former Republican President George H. W.)

Bush. I spent all my time explaining my position on deficit reduction and entitlements. In the end, people showed they were more scared of the debt."[22] Also, "When (Bruce) ran those negative ads, day after day, I think people began to say, 'Wait a minute, we've known Glenn Poshard for ten years, and we haven't seen that at all.'"[23]

Six months later, as we traveled the district, a reminder of the 1992 betrayal popped up out of nowhere—like a recurrent nightmare. "They took four of my five largest counties away from me and took half of the other one away," he exclaimed suddenly. "And they placed my home 400 yards outside the half they left for me. They not only took my voting base, but also my fund-raising base. I always raised one-third of my money in Jackson County [home of SIU]. They did everything they could to destroy me. . . . They put me in such a political corner and created such a challenge for me that I had to run or spend the rest of my life wondering."[24]

Constituency Roots

On my second day in the district—Mother's Day—the Poshards drove to his childhood environs to take his elderly widowed mother to visit her brother in the countryside, and to take her to lunch in town afterward. Their invitation, to a person they had just met, was an unusually trusting gesture.

As we drove the constantly curving road from Marion to Harrisburg, he talked about his work in the House. "This is a road that I'm real proud of," he began.

> It used to be the most dangerous road in the district—a narrow, winding road. More people were killed on this road than any other. For decades, people had tried to get the money to make it a four-lane highway. I got the money. We've just completed half of it, and we'll start work on the other half this summer.
>
> I know I talk a lot about projects. But I spend most of my time on projects like this. This is a poor district and it needs help. . . . I take pride in the fact that I never miss a committee meeting that deals with projects in my district. In our first staff meeting every year, we write down all the

needs of the district; and we draw up a chart so that we can follow them day by day as each one moves along. There may be six things in committee for my district.

Some people say this isn't an appropriate thing for a congressman to do. It is for me. I'm for cutting government. But I'm going to work like hell to get all there is to get from what's left in the pot.

In committee, he worked hard to win his fair share.

But that was it. He did not come across as an inside player or a wheeler-dealer. And he never expressed any leadership aspirations or career expectations inside the House. Indeed, the previous comment about his committee performance was the longest one he would ever make concerning his committee life—or, indeed, about his ambitions for influence inside the institution. He had none. Looking ahead, Glenn Poshard exemplified a very different blend of representative and legislative activity from that of Karen Thurman—more tightly tied to his home place and less participatory in the House. As we rode along, the Poshards filled me in on his family. "Jo likes the city. She'd be happy living in a city," he commented. "I wouldn't. I'm more of a rural person. I like to live in rural areas." Together, they taught me a little about Glenn's early rural life. His father had a third-grade education. One of his arms had been shot off in a boyhood accident; and Glenn demonstrated in detail how his father rolled cigarettes with one hand. He made a living in part by netting fish and trapping animals along several nearby rivers. Both stories put high value on self-reliance—a quality often in evidence during his son's career.

The father taught his son something, too, about conservative, pay-as-you-go budgeting. "When I was growing up," the congressman told another interviewer, "every Friday night my Dad would put the check on one side of the table, the bills on the other side of the table . . . we figured what we had, what we had to pay out, and the difference was what we went into town with and traded."[25] And he added, "The principle was: you do not spend what you do not have. Period. You just don't do it."[26]

"Two things I got from my father," he said. "One was a love of politics. The other was that he never complained. He took what he was given and made the best of it." More than once, he said, he had returned to his father's words to help him resist the strong temptation to strike back at the Illinois Democratic colleagues who had betrayed him. "My father taught me a lot about party loyalty. He was a Roosevelt/Truman Democrat and proud of it. He grew up in the WPA, CCC days and believed in being loyal to your party. My father loved Harry Truman. . . . As hard as it is sometimes, I believe you should . . . never besmirch your party." In this spirit, he added, he had publicly supported even the colleagues who had "betrayed" him.

We collected his mother at her retirement rooms in Carmi and drove into the hills to her brother's house. She had lived near him most of her life, even after her husband died, said Jo, "living a very simple life—never went anywhere. . . . Her little church and her religion were her support. . . . She's almost childlike. She has had so little experience with the world. She has no idea what Glenn does, and no understanding of politics." At that, Glenn piped up: "When I won my first election, I called her up. I said, 'Mom, I won the election.' She said, 'You did?' I said, 'I'm going to Washington, Mom.' She said, 'How are you going to get there?'" When he was in the state senate, he laughed, "She asked me one day, 'Are you still living in that big house up there?'"

She and her brother, "Uncle Pete," could not remember when they had seen each other last. And they swapped stories in his living room. Afterwards, we drove back to a pleasant restaurant in town. She was a very sweet lady whose conversation "repeated itself over and over." She would turn to me every little while—in the car, at Uncle Pete's, and at the restaurant—and say, "You're from New York. That's a real big city." When we left her, she gave me a big hug and said, "I'm glad I met you."

The visit to Uncle Pete's very small home in the community of Herald produced two insights—one about the representative and one about the constituency. We paused at the two-room Herald Elementary School where he had spent eight years—"four grades in one room, and four grades in the other." It was no longer in use. Paint had peeled and windows were broken. "Sometimes," he said, "I go in there and just stand. I have great memories." He walked to school two miles each way—often with cardboard covering the holes in his shoes. We drove the length of his route. "There were fifteen kids and we'd pick 'em up along the way and walk together. I loved the creeks and the hills and the trees. I made friends for life." Jo added, "He lived in real poverty, but they didn't know it because everyone else was poor."

When he went to high school "in town" he was known as one of "the hill people." But he studied, graduated, joined the Army, and ended up in Korea. It was his ticket to the larger world. "I loved the service. The service was what gave poor boys a chance—a career. All my friends and I gravitated to the service. Every member of my family was in the service." Glenn Poshard was every bit a self-made man.

At Uncle Pete's, I had an unforgettable look at the wages of industrial rapaciousness in his rural home place. Directly across the road from the front door was hilly farmland, dotted with numerous "stripper" wells pumping rhythmically to salvage oil from deep beneath. (There were two stripper wells, too, pumping outside my Rend Lake apartment!) "My grandpaw," said Glenn, "bought those 120 acres in the 1940s." Later, Standard Oil came to test whether or not there might be oil underneath the property. And they assured Glenn's "grandpaw" that there was none. They offered him $2,000 in exchange for the full title to the land and anything under the land. "They made tens of millions off the oil under his property," said Glenn. "If we had had the Legal Services Agency, he would have had a lawyer and gotten a fair shake for his land. But he was a poor immigrant farmer; $2,000 was a lot of money to him. What did he know." The sense of injustice was palpable. It brought to life Harry Caudill's book, *Night Comes to the Cumberlands*.[27] That story, too, helped me understand the depth of Glenn Poshard's devotion to organized labor as the indispensable weapon in fighting corporate dominance.

As we turned away from his "home" territory, he suddenly exclaimed, "Do you have any idea what a triumph it is for me to be a United States Congressman? Never in my wildest dreams did I ever think I would have such an honor and a privilege. When I walk on to the House floor, I think it is incredible that I'm there." "Many a night," he added, "when I leave the office at 10:30, I will walk down to the Jefferson Memorial and just sit there on the steps." Where he reflected, I assumed, on his journey from the backwoods of White County, Illinois. Once, on the floor of the House, he told of a springtime trip to the Memorial to wrestle with his conscience ("Glenn" "Yes" "It's God" "Yes?" "Still struggling?" "Yes") on a particularly gut-wrenching vote.[28] He had never lost, it seemed, a sense of wonderment at how far he had come in the world or a lively devotion to the political system that made it possible. Glenn Poshard—not Barber Conable—was an authentic "country boy"!

And a bit of evidence was just around the corner. We left his mother's home to drive to a human catastrophe two counties away at the tiny, unincorporated community of Birds. All of its fifty-eight homes had been devastated by a flood two days before. "Driving in," I noted,

> You could see piles and piles of rugs, appliances, furniture, etcetera in front of the homes waiting to be hauled away. And the people told us that they had already been hauling stuff away for two days. They had no insurance because they lived on a flood plain and weren't eligible. It was a poor, blue-collar citizenry living in mobile homes and real modest wooden homes. All fifty-eight homes were damaged, two mobile homes were destroyed, and twenty-eight other homes had "major damage." The Red Cross was there providing food and blankets and shelter for the hardest hit.

Glenn had come to preside over a public meeting "to give the people some hope," he said. We found about one hundred people jammed into their one community church. "There is not anyone in this room that hasn't felt hardship," he told them. "When you live in Southern Illinois, it seems like hardship is part of what we are. We have overcome and we will overcome."

A nearby refinery, he noted, "had just closed, costing the area 400 jobs." The atmosphere was one of despair. A young woman in tears said it all. "We don't have nothing. We lost our home. We got no money. We ain't got nowhere to go. What are we supposed to do?" The one tangible hope the congressman held out was that the federal government would declare it a disaster area. But the hitch was that the entire county (Lawrence) would have to be included for Birds to receive any aid.

He seemed very much at home in that tiny, tucked-away constituency corner. Like the "family doctor" persona I had seen during his office hours, he empathized with the group and with their plight. His ground-level familiarity was particularly striking. "It became clear to me," I noted,

> that no one could do what he was doing and do it well without knowing where the rivers flow and what the problems are all along the (complex of) rivers. When questions about dredging, silt pileup, log jams, and bridge problems come up, Glenn knows. And he had examples of other

flooded areas to help his explanations and his conjectures. It was the tiniest bit of his district's territory. But he knew it.

Driving away, he expressed disapproval of the local elected official who had ducked the obvious problems by blaming "the government." He admitted that he had felt pretty helpless, but that he had tried not to give people false hopes. "Tomorrow morning first thing," he added, "I'll start making calls to see what I can do to help."

On the drive home, the sight of a Walmart store revived his earlier theme of unjust corporate behavior. "It's a profitable company," he said. "But they pay their employees just above the minimum wage; and they provide no benefits. . . . There ought to be a more equitable distribution. . . . I'm a big union man." In a similar vein, "I voted against NAFTA (North American Free Trade Act). It split my district between farm country and labor country. I always thought it was more of a marketing device; (more) an export program than a job producing program." Jobs were his constant bottom-line constituency concern.

By the end of my first trip, I had come to think of the congressman as an especially compassionate and down-to-earth individual with strong attachments—personal and policy—to the workaday people of his district. He felt uncomfortable, he once said, sitting in the reception room of the Archer Daniels Midland Company waiting to be called up to "take my turn" in the executive suite. He wore his heart on his sleeve; and his relationships with others were markedly transparent. With this member of Congress, it seemed especially true that "what you see is what you get."

Citizen Representative

In conversation and in the newspapers, the word most commonly associated with Glenn Poshard was "integrity." It was fitting, therefore, to find that a personal encounter with a stunning lack of integrity had propelled him into elective politics in the first place. In his role as a local educational administrator, he had pushed actively for passage of a particular measure in the Illinois State Senate. And he had won a commitment of support from his own state senator. When the bill came to a vote, however—and with Poshard and fellow supporters watching from the gallery—the senator voted against the measure. Whereupon, as Poshard told the story, "he looked up at me in the gallery and laughed. . . . I came home and said to Jo, 'He's a rascal. And I'm going to run against him in the primary.'" And he did so. "I worked hard, but I lost," he recalled. "I announced my full support for him and went to work for the party. When he died near the end of his term, the party chairman appointed me to the state senate seat for three months." He then ran for the seat against a Republican state representative. And, "I beat him in every county."

As a member of Congress, Glenn Poshard expressed a remarkably dutiful, textbook true-good-citizenship view of what being a "United States Representative" meant. His determination to provide his constituents with exemplary representation dominated our conversation. Indeed, his strongly held, and often expressed, ideas about representation drove out of our conversation whatever substantive legislative ambitions he might have otherwise entertained or expressed. As a result, the subject matter of our visits would contrast most sharply to my subsequent conversations with his legislatively oriented colleague, Karen Thurman, in Florida.

For starters, there was his devotion to the procedures of the House. Early on, I learned from his staff that he came home every weekend (schoolteacher Jo Poshard stayed home), yet never until the last roll call vote had been recorded. The routine was sacred. "He doesn't want to miss votes," one explained, "and he has not missed one vote since his first term—when he missed three or four." He told questioners, "it's something that I take a lot of pride in, that I'm there."[29]

Each week, he waited at the Capitol till the last scheduled vote. On Friday (occasionally Thursday) afternoon, he would rush to catch a plane to St. Louis—usually the 2:20 flight—then drive two-and-a-half hours from there to the district. After a weekend spent driving up, down, and around the district, his staffers continued, he got up at 3:20 A.M. Monday morning (sometimes Tuesday) to catch the 7:30 flight from St. Louis to DC. His goal was to get to the House floor by noon to answer the opening roll call vote on the reading of the House Journal.

When we met, he had just completed a year without missing a single roll call vote—and had maintained a career-long attendance record of

99 percent.[30] Small wonder that several times during my visits, he would say "I'm tired." Or, "This district beats you down." So why keep such a demanding commuting schedule, I asked. "It's my job," he replied. And that was that. The morning after his late-night primary victory over Terry Bruce, he flew back to Washington, arrived "shortly after noontime," and went directly from the airport to a committee meeting. Why? "Because that's what's important," he explained.[31] He was a self-described "workaholic."

It was a second element of his textbook representational credo that while he might have to shortchange his constituents on occasional House work days, he deliberately refrained from flooding the district with compensatory advertising. He answered his constituency mail religiously. But he did not send newsletters or any other self-advertising—direct or indirect—to the home folks. As a matter of pride and of record, he returned a high percentage of his expense allowance to the US Treasury. In a 1992 *Chicago Tribune* accounting, he spent only 9 percent of his House member office expense allowance—less than any other Illinois representative and less than 93 percent (i.e., 403) of his House colleagues.[32]

In 1993 and 1994, the Capitol Hill newspaper, *Roll Call*, examined his overall performance and named him to the "Obscure Caucus" of five House Democrats and four House Republicans "who shun the spotlight, who rarely hold news conferences, who can't be counted on to deliver pithy sound bites."[33] He reacted with a self-effacing comment.

> I know what my role has been here—it's to concentrate on my district and do the best I can to help with just basic things. I think I've been just a basic congressman. They portrayed me pretty much as I see myself. I don't go on the floor often. I don't speak on a lot of issues. But I never miss a vote. I never miss a committee (meeting). I do my homework. That's pretty much what I came here to do.[34]

At home, he turned the designation into a political plus. His flagship 1994 and 1996 newspaper campaign ad carried the headline in large print: "*Roll Call*, the Capitol Hill Newspaper, Has Selected Glenn Poshard for Its List of 10 Members Who Are "Workhorses, Not Showhorses" [underlining in the original]. He defined himself—and he was defined by others—in terms of his sturdy constituency ties, and in terms of his sense of obligation to strengthen them.

These dutiful job choices resulted in less attention being paid to floor debate than was the case with other House members. It was Poshard's habit, whenever he deemed an issue of importance to himself and/or to the district, to deliver a lengthy speech on the House floor. There, he would lay out his thinking and his position with care and in detail. It was not intended to influence debate, but rather to clarify his vote decision for himself and for anyone back home who might be interested.

On my first day in the district, I was handed a small packet of seven such speeches. They were a profile of the large issues that he cared about: "First Flag Speech" (6/20/90), "Second Flag Speech" (6/26/95), "Abortion Speech" (11/1/95), "Balanced Budget Amendment Speech" (1/26/95), "Budget Speech" (1/3/96), "Tax Speech" (4/23/96), "Welfare Speech" (3/23/95).

As position-taking pronouncements, they are carefully constructed and well argued. He cared deeply about all of them. And his position in each case would be of considerable interest to some set of constituents at home. But they were not intended to influence the legislative process on the House floor. And they did not signal any personal legislative involvement. He came to the floor; he delivered his speech; and he left. When it came to his personal priorities of time, effort, and reputation, a concern for the practice of good representation dominated Glenn Poshard's public life. "I didn't come here to be an authority on everything in the world. I came here to help my people."[35]

Among his basic tenets of constituency representation, none became more noteworthy at home than his refusal—after his first election—to accept PAC or corporate contributions. Taken together with his limit of $500 on individual contributions, it was another decision based on his idea of what good citizenship prescribed for elected representatives.

In his first 1988 campaign, he recalled, he had taken money from numerous PACs. "I spent three interview days at a time signing for PAC money. There was some union group, I forget which." But when their key vote came up, he disagreed with their position.

> I was sitting in my office with a big knot in my stomach. I didn't agree
> with their position on the issue. But I had signed their statement and

taken their money. I hadn't made up my mind when the bells went off. I waited to the last ten seconds and then I voted the way I had told them I would. I didn't want to be called a liar. I went back to the office and told the staff, "I can't do this again. I can't go to war with myself every time I vote. The only way is not to take their money." And I told them "that's a keeper!" For me, it's the best decision. I've never tried to tell others how it should be done.

In his first campaign for reelection he said, "Among those who came in with me, I was the only one who declined PAC money."

The capstone of his textbook prescriptions governing the practice of representation—and the one with the greatest effect on his political career—was his devotion to term limits. "I believe in remaining a citizen legislator. I taught kids in my classroom that our forefathers believed in that."[36] "They clearly meant for a person to train themselves in a profession, leave the profession for a time, serve in the national assembly, and then to go back, allow someone else the chance to share their experience in this body."[37] Before the national term limits craze of the mid 1990s, Glenn Poshard had pledged to serve no more than five terms (i.e., ten years) in the House of Representatives. Characteristically, he made no case for the idea as a general public policy prescription. It was for him a personal preference—a way of inoculating himself against any suspicion that he might be in politics for personal gain.

He recognized that several of his "citizen legislator" decisions might be costly. But he stuck to them. His anti-PAC decision had been particularly costly, he admitted, because it multiplied his fund-raising tasks. "Sometimes I'm not sure it was a good thing," he said. "It put the family under a lot of pressure. In 1992, we had to borrow $100,000 to run in the new district. We don't have much money; and we have to borrow every election. It's hard. Terry Bruce had all that PAC money." Indeed, one early look at the 1992 campaign found Bruce with a war chest of $699,000 and Poshard with $20,000.[38] But he held to his "no PAC money" position to the end. As he did with respect to his position on term limits.

He never mentioned the relationship of his term limits decision to his post-gerrymandering, intradelegation political fight of 1992. My own guess, however, is that the two were very closely related. As suggestive evidence, consider his list of the Illinois congressmen he approached on the House floor, on the day he learned of the decision. The Republicans were Robert Michel (House Minority Leader) and Dennis Hastert (future Republican House Speaker). The Democrats included Dan Rostenkowski (Ways and Means Committee chairman), Richard Durbin (future US Senator and future Senate Democratic Whip), Jerry Costello (then, and now, the East St. Louis area Democratic leader). It would be hard to find, in any state and at any time, a more impressive concentration of career politicians than these five. Is it any wonder that when these men faced the 1992 redistricting problem, they would combine to protect and extend their careers at the expense of their term-limited colleague? This huge mismatch of ambitions seems persuasive. In a life-and-death negotiation among insiders, the textbook good citizen congressman was the obvious sacrificial lamb.

When I asked him point-blank whether term-limiting himself "had any effect on your career," he said it had not. To the contrary,

> You have a greater sense of freedom to do what you want to do—and a certain sense of security. You don't have to worry about going up the ladder. I have never had a desire to do that. I have had more independence in making judgments than the ordinary party member. . . . I have always believed that the experience you bring to Congress is more important than the experience you get while you are there. We need new ways of looking at problems; and we don't get that from career legislators.

I never sensed the slightest bit of regret over his early decision. Near the end of my second visit, he said, "I'm going to do all I can to win. But if I lose, I'm not going to grieve over it. I have a sense of 'okay-ness' about that. I'm not sure I could handle defeat if I had a career."

Explanatory Politics

"When you grapple and struggle and agonize over an issue and never get to explain—that's the frustration of the job." This was the standard Glenn Poshard used in evaluating his election campaigns as they affected his constituency relationships.

"My first (1988) race for Congress was my best race," he explained.

> It was a classic—the kind that every race should be. I ran against a sharp law professor from SIU. We had some of the greatest debates. We went

to every community college and debated the district's issues—no poison pills. The gyms were filled with enthusiasm and noise; and it got you really pumped up. I got so I considered him a friend. We were free of personal rancor, and it freed us for a spirited debate. We accomplished what candidates should be able to do. He was a moderate, staunch Republican. There was nothing personal. It was a fair display of the difference between the parties—no extremes. It was the high-water mark of my congressional campaigns.

It was also an easy victory. But his evaluation focused less on the outcome than on the explanatory process.

Win/lose calculations did not dominate his description of the following (1990) campaign either. Even though that campaign produced his most lopsided victory, he described it as "the low-water mark" of his reelection efforts. It was a single-issue campaign that centered on a single vote—his vote against the proposed constitutional amendment prohibiting the desecration of the American flag.

"My opponent got into the race after my vote on the flag. Every meeting, every forum, every minute of the campaign it was nothing but 'he burned the flag.' He was a one-issue candidate. There was no discussion of any of the other issues facing the district. In my sleep, I still hear that one speech of his which ended, 'and he burned the flag.'" To soften the memory, the congressman followed with a humorous sketch of his opponent, standing alone, on a windswept Colorado mountaintop attacking his vote on the flag. "You hope," he concluded, "that the public will judge you on balance—that they will judge you on your whole record, not just one vote."

That "one vote," however, was the most difficult, soul-searching vote of his entire career in the House. His friends mentioned it at our early dinner, because he had called them for advice. He had favored the amendment at first, they said, but had changed his mind after thinking about it and praying on it. "As a veteran," Poshard said,

> The flag meant everything to me. I read everything I could get my hands on. I knew I could come to grips with the constitutional issue. The question was: could I come to terms with the deeper issue. For the veterans, symbol is substance. I had to go back to my faith before I understood it . . . my faith made me see that you must not limit dissent. . . . It ensures democracy.

"I had to understand it in my heart," he said, "before I could understand it in my head."

He gave two introspective change-of-heart speeches on the House floor—in which he rehearsed his arguments and his doubts. He reconstructed imaginary dialogues with God, with his father, and with Thomas Jefferson. The latter is illustrative.

> "Glenn?" "Yes?" "It's Thomas." "Yes?" "You walked over to my memorial last night." "Yes." "Why?" "Because I'm struggling with a decision on a constitutional amendment to alter the Bill of Rights, and I needed some help." "What's the problem?" "Some people burned our flag and the country's upset. The president and several members of Congress want to forbid the practice." "What do you want to do?" "I don't know. I'm torn. I'm a history teacher. I've taught the Bill of Rights and the Constitution to hundreds of people. I've emphasized the importance of the freedoms that you and others penned in that precious document. But now we have this issue with the flag. I love the flag . . . couldn't we just make this one an exception . . . (and) forbid just this one way of dissent?" "You mean the symbol has become greater in the minds of the people than the substance behind the symbol?" "Well, what do I do now?" "Maybe you should start teaching again, as a congressman. And trust the people to understand . . . and leave your children no less freedom than we left you."[39]

He voted against the amendment. It passed the House 310–114.

He won election easily. But his "flag vote" carried a political cost. "The veterans will never forgive me," he said.

> I've tried to explain my vote in dozens of Legion and VFW halls—where I am welcome. But I don't think they'll ever know why I did what I did. That will hurt me in places where they don't know me. The Legion and the VFW halls are major social clubs. In these small towns, anybody who is anybody belongs. They are in the forefront of everything. I'll never forget the Fourth of July following the vote. I was already scheduled at Steelville and Cairo. I'll never forget it—Steelville especially—the booing, the yelling, the screaming. It was rude and it was awful.

In the 1988 campaign, his most prominent, all-purpose newspaper ad carried an endorsement (among others) by the district's veterans' groups. But in his otherwise identical 1990 newspaper advertisement, the veterans' endorsement had been removed.

A second independent-minded vote also brought him political grief—with the important (and overlapping) anti-gun-control groups in his rural, pro-gun constituency. Historically, he had fought beside them against all restrictive provisions. And when President Clinton's gun-control legislation first came to the floor, Poshard resisted. Twice he voted to remove an assault weapons ban from the legislation. But when he lost that pivotal fight, he supported the crime bill on final passage. "I can't recall any vote I made in the past where I have been forced into a position I have in this bill, where voting for things to fight crime came along with a gun-control measure."[40] And that one last vote brought him a ton of grief from his all-or-nothing pro-gun supporters. It brought threats of violence. And it cost him National Rifle Association support in the next election.[41]

"I didn't have one minute's hesitation over the crime bill," he explained afterward. "It was a good bill, and I knew I was going to vote for it. I tried to protect Second Amendment rights to the very end. But once the assault weapons ban was put in the crime bill, I never had any doubt about what I was going to do." "No one has been more supportive of Second Amendment rights than I have. I grew up with guns. I know how gun owners feel. . . . I've voted to protect their rights a hundred times." But, invoking the presence of gang warfare in Decatur, he said that the final bill simply had too many crime-fighting benefits.[42]

"The whole point of our job—if we have the opportunity," he generalized,

> is to talk in-depth so people will understand why we did what we did. Agreeing is not the bottom line. It never bothered me if people disagreed with me. What bothers me is not having the chance to explain—being bashed by thirty-second commercials. That's my only fear in this business—my only sadness. I don't care if 100 percent disagree with me as long as people understand why I did it. I want my shot. If they throw me out after that—that's great—so long as they understand. I know that maybe only 5 percent will ever hear me. The rest have no chance.

To which he added, "That's why I do so many town meetings."

"Town meetings are my job," he said. And explanation via town meetings was his most structured representational activity at home. Press releases were devoted to announcing the time and place of his town meetings and (sometimes) a subject matter schedule as well. There were twelve meetings, for example, in June 1993 on southern area problems and ten budget seminars in April 1996. Local newspapers printed a schedule, too, of his district-wide town meetings, to explain and discuss current legislative issues.[43] When he returned from a trip to Bosnia to examine the American military activity there, he scheduled town meetings to explain why the trip had changed his mind from opposition to support for our interventionist policy.[44] His constituents "gave me the benefit of the doubt," he said. And he described those meetings as "the most gratifying town meetings I've ever had."[45] The attitudes that underpinned all of his citizen legislator practices and preferences were markedly upbeat. They emphasized tolerance and openness in dealing with opposing views, plus optimism about the influence of explanation and dialogue.

He capped these views with overarching support for the legislative system. "Can you imagine the cynicism people feel toward government? The only thing that makes me fear for our government is the terrible public cynicism." Or, "I have never seen as much partisanship as there is in the House (post 1994) today. The extremes are so strong, there is no middle ground." The public attitudes that worried him most were those reflecting nonparticipation and extremism. "I may suggest reforms, but I would never demean the institution the way some people do."

He had set this upbeat, protective tone from the first moment we met. He had remarked then that despite the destructive partisanship in the House, he wanted to give an upbeat one-minute speech on the House floor—"to say that some things are going pretty dad-gummed well." He openly criticized and, at the same time, openly cherished the representative institution. From my particular vantage point, "up close and personal," he was distinctively not among that majority of House members I had previously observed "running for Congress by running against Congress."[46]

Campaign Day: November 1996

Three days before the 1996 election, I rejoined the congressman for a long November day (8 A.M.–9:45 P.M.) electioneering in the southern heartland of his district. He began by circling a county courthouse with a loud speaker at 9 A.M.; and he ended indoors by riding in a donkey basketball game at 9 P.M. We rode all day (in) a friend's truck, with a huge "Elect Poshard" sign in the back. And we visited twelve of his longtime county-seat towns.

Using a microphone and loudspeaker, he would call out in each town: "Folks, this is Congressman Poshard. I'd appreciate your help at the polls next Tuesday. Thanks for all your help in the past. Thank you very much." "He'd sing out whether he saw anyone or not," I noted. "People were not plentiful as we circled each courthouse. But some waved, some waved from passing cars, and some took no notice." My earlier companions, Lewis and Ethel, were there with their truck— and Bruce Springsteen! They stayed with us all day—as did two or three other cars. Others joined and left as we went along. In two counties, he went indoors—once to talk to a large group and once to participate in a party rally. He came across as "a down-home guy. His outfit for the drive-around looked like he'd just come from working in the yard."

He expressed a rationale I had heard before. "I don't have to vote the way people want me to, but I do have the obligation to come back and explain what I did and why. When I have done that, I have fulfilled my obligation to the voters." He never expressed the slightest sense of entitlement in connection with his position. He had a job to do. First and foremost, and in every way possible, he formulated and pursued the representational part of that job.

To the question, "Who are your strongest supporters," he answered, "The people who were with me in my first race."

> They are not Johnny-come-latelys. They are the people who still believe in you even though you have failed them—as you always do. There is a cadre of such people in every county—the ones who stay with you because they understand that you are in it for the big picture and not because they think you can do something for them. There are dozens of people who tack on in every campaign because they want something—a job or a benefit of some kind. They may stay. But they are not the activists. The activists know you are in it for the greater good. They are always with you. I have run eight times. You come to it very early that they are the ones that carry you. . . . Ethel and Lewis—they would go anywhere

for me. Lewis is no liberal. He's a blue-collar poster boy Democrat for this district. And he's with me. That's worth a million bucks. There are not many professions where you throw yourself on the mercy of others. You relinquish control and you say to others, "Carry me along man; I can't do it by myself." It's almost a step of faith that politicians make. There is no other way. You can't do it yourself.

Speaking of "what I did," he said, "I think it comes down to a question of leadership. The main interests in my district revolve around coal, oil, and agriculture, and I feel like I have helped out in these areas of greatest need. . . . I just pay a lot of attention to those kinds of basic needs in this big, rural district."[47]

On the day-long trip we sampled his trademark down-to-earth, service-centered activities. "We can drive around . . . and see the tangible results of all our efforts," he explained, "and that is very satisfying. . . . Our pay has nothing to do with a paycheck. It comes when we see a water tower or a road or a levee that we brought to our constituents. People have these wild imaginings about what a congressman does. You know what we do? We build sewers!" Indeed, he told another interviewer that he spent "sixty percent of my time working on sewers . . . literally! I mean literally!"[48] Without sewers, he argued, it would be impossible to coax businesses into the economically struggling places in his district.

"Over there, on the hill," he continued,

> is a school for disabled children that wouldn't be there if we hadn't gotten them some money. There are 200 kids in that school. They won't produce any inventions or do any great things for our society. But they are a world apart now from what they would have been without that school. If we have helped make the quality of those 200 lives better, then that is payday. If, in your old age you can look back and know that 200 people are better off, that you made a dent, that's enough. It's these little things that really matter. And we work at this part of the job every day.

We traveled all day through hilly, woodsy, sometimes picturesque countryside and sometimes near a winding river. We visited what he called "poke and plumb towns"—"you poke your head out the window and you're plumb out of town." Along the way, he talked about his involvements.

Shawnee Community College: "We brought millions in grants to that little community college over there, so that they could have computers, and so our kids—in the poorest part of the district—can know what was going on all over the world and can reach anywhere in the world. They don't have any technical grant writers to peruse the lists of available grants and opportunities. They have one or two faculty members who may help. So we find out what's available and we go down to the Department of Education and we sit there for hours and we make their case. If the college didn't have a congressman as its advocate, it couldn't compete. That's the only way we get our fair share. In areas like this, the congressman has to do that. It's part of the job."

Lock and dam at Olmstead: "Drive down that road there and you will find the first stage of construction for the biggest lock and dam in the world—a project worth one billion, one hundred million over twelve years. It means 500 good jobs. It could have been built at many places up and down the (Ohio) river. But we fought for it and we got it. It will have a tremendous impact on the area. The towboat company in Metropolis tells me their business will increase. The quarries will have all the business they can handle with the roads that must be built. Olmstead will get a boat ramp and a new city park on the river. It's a big deal in the area. And it had a better than two-to-one benefit cost ratio."

He said later that the Army Corps of Engineers had three offices in his district, and that his staff dealt with the Corps "every day."

Cache River Project: "This area is part of the largest wetland between the Ohio and Mississippi Rivers. During the New Deal, the WPA and the CCC worked on it. It has been a very controversial area. The farmers want it to be drained for farming. The Forest Service wanted to harvest the ripe timbers before they rotted. The environmentalists agreed with them, but then found a rare bird and wanted to keep the trees. We got involved, brought the farm and environmental communities together, and created a National Refuge that both would support. It is recognized as one of the ten top wetlands in the world. People come from all over the world to study it. Our job was to mediate and educate. It's an important part of our job."

In several places, he talked not of a single project, but of a single industry that spread over several of his counties. "This is coal country," he said in Franklin County. "The Clean Air Act wiped us out; and we are struggling to diversify and develop new business. It's slow going. We put all our eggs in one basket for all these years. We shouldn't have. But when things are going good, you don't plan."

In adjacent Saline County, he expressed himself again on the state of the industry.

> Three mines closed down last year in this county. We've been devastated by the Clean Air Act. We could have had legislation that would have helped us so much, but we blew it. The Act punished six states that produce high sulphur coal. If the other states had given us one-half of one percent of their increase in electric bills, we could have pooled the money, put in "scrubbers," and kept tens of thousands of miners working. But the guys in the rest of the country said, "Hell no, we're not going to clean up coal." There was no national approach to the issue. My district was devastated. The coal miners lost everything. Whole counties were wiped out and put on welfare. It was as if the country had no conscience for people like coal miners—who lie on their backs chopping low-seam coal out of the earth that shakes six hundred feet down from the blasting. They do this for $35,000 tops per year. And you can watch them come out of the mine and spit black goo. Fifty people were killed every year in the mines. If it hadn't been for John L. Lewis and the United Mine Workers, the local companies would have gotten away with more.

His praise for the United Mine Workers of America was a recurring theme. "Before the UMWA came in," he said, "it was not uncommon for miners to die of black lung before they reached forty. The millionaires back east, who owned the mines, didn't care. The union brought safety regulations and air circulating equipment. Before that, miners were treated like animals." "One of the bloodiest and worst incidents of violence in American history" (between union members and strikebreakers), he said, had occurred in his home county. Now, having failed to stop the Clean Air Legislation, he was pledging to fight for "clean coal technology." Glenn Poshard was the most passionate protrade union advocate I traveled with. Altogether, the day's running commentary on local places, problems, and projects demonstrated his working knowledge of—and his close attention to—the needs of his ailing constituency.

Partisanship and Personality

In a couple of places, our campaign caravan stopped, and he went inside to give a campaign talk to a waiting group. To each audience, he spoke as an ardent Democrat. And on that day, his favorite subject was the federal budget. He was traveling in the neediest part of the district. But his pay-as-you-go, balance-the-budget philosophy was one of his most deeply held ideas. His budget prescription, "compassionate and balanced," was the basis for his reputation as a moderate Democrat.

In his crucial 1992 campaign, for example, Terry Bruce's main argument had been to attack Poshard for his support of a 1990 budget compromise.[49] But Poshard's more moderate position had won him strong editorial support in that career-saving contest. Do not, he would tell his House colleagues, saddle tomorrow's generation with today's debts. Now, in 1996, he was advocating a budget balancing, pay-as-you-go gasoline tax to build roads instead of putting the burden "on the backs of our children." In private, he even blamed his own House Democratic leader, Dick Gephardt, for stoking excessive budget partisanship inside the House.

On "the stump," however, his campaign talks featured a rip-roaring partisan defense of Democratic President Clinton and his budget—and a furious attack on the competing budget of Republican House Speaker Newt Gingrich. Standing on a chair at the juncture of two corridors inside the Hardin County Courthouse, he spoke to fifty to sixty people on "the tale of two budgets." He proposed "a simple side-by-side comparison of the two budgets." He preached to the choir, blistering the Gingrich budget for cutting the earned income tax credit, cutting out all money for clean coal technology, and cutting low-income home energy assistance.

Under President Clinton's initial budget, he shouted, 46,000 low-income constituents (family of four earning less than $26,000 a year) had benefited from the earned income tax credit; but under the Speaker's proposed budget, the amount would be reduced to $1,400.[50] "Those numbers represent the difference in philosophies between the two parties." "Look at the Speaker's budget. For God's sake, look at the Speaker's budget. Fifty-two percent of the Republican tax cut goes to people making over $125,000 a year. Don't tell me not to get angry about those things. When you strip the safety net, watch out America! A lot of people are going to get angry."

He invoked Hubert Humphrey's Democratic mantra, that "the test of a free democracy is the way we treat people in the dawn of their lives and people in the shadow of their lives—children, the elderly, the disabled, the disenfranchised, the depressed." "When did we ever agree in this country to take from people who need it most and give to people who need it least?! Is this justice in this country?" he thundered. "Sixty-five percent of the mines are closed down, and the clean coal technology program is gone in Speaker Gingrich's budget. Where's the justice? You tell me what justice there is in that!"

"More than before," I wrote, "I realize what a terrific public speaker he is—passionate, articulate, strong, emotional, urgent, sincere, a stem-winder, an old-fashioned stump orator—a committed partisan." (The local state senator said he had refused to speak at the party rally "unless they scheduled me before Glenn.") "But," I added, "he is also a compromiser. For all of his pleading with the audience (on the stump), he is (otherwise) a clear-headed educator. His sweaty, hoarse-throated, partisan sermon had shown but one face—the campaign face of a candidate among his strongest supporters."[51]

In the middle of that same day, in the "poke and plumb" town of Golconda, for example, he had taken me up onto the levee to view a peaceful Ohio River panorama. I described the scene as "beautiful," "serene," "awesome," and "pristine"—with only "one tug and a couple of houses" visible, and otherwise, "nothing but wide water in all directions." "When I worked for the school board," he said, "I used to bring my lunch up here, sit on the bench, and just look at the river." His love of solitude was reinforced when he commented, later that evening, "I love to walk alone on a clear November night like this one when the stars are so bright they seem close enough to touch."

His reflections reminded me of his comment during my earlier visit, about returning to "stand alone" in the shell of his old schoolhouse. They reminded me, too, of his trips at night to the Jefferson Memorial—and his particular contemplation there on the eve of his flag vote. A year later, I learned about his occasional visits to a Trappist monastery in nearby Kentucky. "I just zonk myself away for six or seven days a year," he explained, "and try to get things in perspective."[52] In public and on the stump, he could be a flame-throwing orator. But, in private, he was—as I had noted from the start—an unusually contemplative individual.

Last Look

On Sunday, my last day in Illinois, the congressman's private, reflective, and forward-looking demeanor dominated. With workhorse chief of staff/press secretary Dave Stricklin at the wheel, we drove northward to a county seat town in the post-1994 agricultural part of the district. Poshard was scheduled to be "keynote speaker" at an annual multi-county Lutheran Brotherhood Dinner. It was his only event of the day. And it would produce a 180-degree change in performance and message from the day before—from noisy partisanship to quiet reflection.

Because the trip would take us two plus hours each way, I noted my continuing amazement at "how undaunted they are by the distances. They'll hop in the car and drive long distances without thinking." When I wondered aloud why they were traveling so far for a single event, the congressman said simply that it was his job. "If I once started using distance as an excuse," he added, "it would be hard to keep from using it again. Just because I live at one end of the district, and it takes more time to get to the other end, that doesn't change the fact that they are my constituents, and it's my job to be there if they ask me." The two men agreed: "We do this all the time."

"The Christian Coalition handed out their scorecards in church this morning," the congressman said.

> They gave my opponent 100 percent and me 45 percent. All the votes they scored were Republican-sponsored measures—no Democratic proposals. Well, they gotta do what they gotta do. I used to worry about them, but not anymore. It still hurts, though, because their church is the same one I was baptized in—Southern Baptist. I just have a different interpretation of what that means than Pat Robertson and Jerry Falwell. I have met with the coalition in the past. But this year, they canceled

their appointment. They would say to me, "Why can't you be a good Christian?" As I say, they gotta do what they gotta do.

"Glenn is strongly pro-life," I wrote, "but I never did hear him talk about it."[53]

Our trip had been delayed because Glenn and Jo had spent a long time on the phone comforting her terminally ill mother. "When he got in the car," I noted, "he was very absorbed in Jo's mother's problems. . . . [He] talked a lot about faith and the strength that people draw from their faith at such a time. It was very introspective. He talked about a friend who had led a model Christian life and, yet, had shot himself. 'Did that mean he had no faith, or that his faith had failed him?'

"He picked up the subject again in his (after-dinner) talk to the Lutheran group." In his talk, "He went through his own religious experiences in getting to the idea (the theme of his speech) that volunteerism is not only beneficial for others, but is also good for the volunteer. And that the latter consequence is even more important than what the volunteer does for others, because it has to do with a person's relationship to God." "He is," I added, "a person of deep and thoughtful faith; and he gave a sort of 'testimony' to that faith in his talk. It's a side of him I had never heard before, but I knew was there."

These agricultural area constituents looked more prosperous than those I encountered the day before. And they provided me with a unique cultural experience.

> At the meal, Dave and I took empty seats in the middle of three long tables. No one around us initiated any conversation with either of us throughout the entire meal. We talked, had a nice time, and agreed that we didn't feel uncomfortable. They didn't talk much to each other. In my only effort, I asked the lady across the table if more than one church was represented in the group (of about seventy-five). "I'm from Casey," she said, "I don't know." That was it. No one talked to her either, except the man she was with who spoke one or two sentences. Glenn said (afterward) that no one talked much to him either at the head table. He tried and got short replies, but no interest. It was bizarre; but it had the ring of perfect normalcy about it.

"It's very common behavior for German Lutherans," Glenn explained afterward.

They are very much into themselves. Underneath, they are warm and generous. But they will not initiate any interest in you. They are just different. They have an excellent work ethic. They are extremely neat, orderly, and they keep up their property. They help each other tremendously. But they keep to themselves. They are also some of the most prejudiced people in the world. I don't think I have ever been with a group of them when I didn't hear a racial joke or a racial slur. I doubt if there's a black person in the entire county. They're just different.[54]

The area had recently turned Republican, he said; and he was the only Democrat who, despite slipping margins, continued to carry it. He survived, I surmised, because of his strong pro-life position—and his personal attentiveness. At dinner, it was a clear case of "warm guy— cold group."

He had been "at home" amid responsive audiences in his longtime southern territory on Saturday but was much less so in his newly added northern territory on Sunday. Combining Saturday and Sunday, I had seen his down-to-earth empathetic political side and his contemplative, reflective side in both ways. Taken together, they captured a lot about the man I had followed. They were not, in my experience, commonly concentrated among politicians. He was, indeed, an uncommon representative.

Transition

On the ride home, a wholly new subject appeared. He said he'd been getting feelers about—and offers of support for—a run for governor. He added that he didn't know what to say and was not encouraging it. "What I want most," he said, "when I leave Congress is to be at home. I'm tired of traveling to Washington and being away all the time." I commented to the effect that "if being at home was of paramount importance, he couldn't run for governor." On the other hand, he parried, "the Democrats have run out of good candidates." Within a few weeks, an upstate political columnist would write of Poshard's possibilities with the comment that "the people down there would have elected him God."[55]

In the car, a disjointed conversation morphed into problems of scale that would attend any statewide venture—especially the vastly different media requirements. Dave (the staff director) emphasized the degree to which Glenn ran his own campaigns, adding that he would have to turn a gubernatorial campaign over to others." But the congressman demurred. Last time, he said, "Dave did it. We got some pictures and wrote a script. Dave got time at a studio from three to six in the morning and put it together. We did it all ourselves— no high-priced media consultants. . . . The first time I ran, I let the DCCC consultants do it. . . . [Finally] I told them to leave us alone." "Dave is a media person," I noted. "But that doesn't prepare him for the big time."

The idea was briefly intriguing. "He's such a down-home guy," I noted, "that it's hard to picture him as governor. He has the talent, the philosophy, articulateness, vision, ideology," I wrote. "But whether he could put together an organization and preside over it is another question. Is he too local or, perhaps, too moral? He would be a fresh face, for sure—a diamond from the Southern Illinois rough!" The idea was intriguing, but hard for me to take seriously.

In the car, the congressman's interest had already turned to the inevitable scramble for his job.

> As soon as the votes are counted Tuesday night, the fight for my position will be in the open. In this part of the district, there is [sic] one state senator and two representatives. . . . They don't like each other—actually it's venom and hatred! They are all tied up with local politics . . . each wants to be boss. . . . None of them has the slightest idea what it's like to be a congressman . . . going from Springfield to Washington is like going from dark to light. It's that great. People expect leadership from you. They expect problem solving. If you try to be a local boss, you'll get your throat cut. You don't have any time to play that game. I have stayed out of local politics deliberately. I have no interest in controlling jobs. I have stayed out of internal Democratic politics.

Listening to him, I thought that if ever he became governor, he would find it impossible to stay out of "internal Democratic politics."

But all such speculation would be resolved some other day. My time in Illinois was up. And a firsthand political education in that distinctive place with a remarkable political figure had come to a close. I never saw or talked with him again.

Postscript

A year later, he entered and won the statewide Democratic primary; and he became the Democratic Party's nominee for governor of Illinois. In November 1998, he lost the gubernatorial election 52 percent to 48 percent. Not surprisingly, he lost it in the Chicago suburbs. Shortly thereafter, he returned home to become a top-level administrator at Southern Illinois University in Carbondale. In 2000, former US Representative Glenn Poshard, child of southern Illinois, became the seventh president of Southern Illinois University.[56]

— 4 —

Karen Thurman

Promising Legislator

The Representative: Florida, 1994–2002

When we met in Florida, in 1994, US Representative Karen Thurman was a forty-three-year-old Democrat and former schoolteacher who had served for ten years in the Florida State Senate. She had been elected to Congress in 1992, from a newly created district. We met through the good offices of a student of mine who had worked for her at the State Capitol in Tallahassee. We traveled around together in her home district for a total of seven days during three campaign seasons—in the fall of 1994, the summer of 1996, and the fall of 2002. And we visited briefly a couple of times in Washington.

Representative Thurman came to Congress from a west central-north coastal part of the state. As congressional districts go, Florida's Fifth District was one huge puzzle. It was a brand new district created in 1992 as a response to Florida's rapid population growth. It had no history. And its future promised only continuing growth and constant flux. It was, of course, a legal entity. It had clear boundaries, and it contained the requisite number of people. But it was a polyglot conglomeration of nine counties and numerous small places cobbled together and strung out over a 4,600-square-mile area—third largest in the state. It was described by observers as a "rambling," "sprawling," "meandering," "humungous," "geographically imposing" district, embracing "several distinctive regions."[1]

Inside the Florida legislature, State Senator Thurman had played a part in creating the district—by making certain that a sizeable part of her state senatorial territory was included within its boundaries. Her "geographical constituency" had no obvious center of gravity. It encompassed three media markets—marked by the *Tampa Bay Tribune*, the *St. Petersburg Times*, and the *Gainesville Sun*. It was serviced by three airports—Tampa, Gainesville, and Orlando. It had only one smallish city, Gainesville (pop. 68,000). Its dominant character was rural. People never could agree on how to describe its location—calling it "North Florida," "North Central Florida," "North and West Central Florida," "Gulf Coast Florida," and "North Suncoast Florida."

Its boundaries were the outcome of an internal legislative push and pull, plus her "side-payment" negotiations among neighboring incumbents and prospective newcomers. A 1992 campaign description emphasized the district's "wide range of interests." "It mixes university professors from Gainesville with lumbermen from Dixie, miners in Hernando and retirees of West Pasco," wrote the author. And "its diversity leaves (any candidate) without homogeneous district concerns."[2] It was a hard-to-catalogue residual district in an ever-changing, fast-growing part of America.

The district was hard to describe, too, because it was underorganized and underpoliticized. It had no common political past. It had no coherent political, economic, or cultural center of gravity, and few organized interest groups of any size or wealth. She would always be heavily dependent on outside PAC contributions to finance her campaigns. The nation's commerce did not run through the Florida Fifth. It had no describable political culture and no dominating partisan organizations. The area was historically and still—at 55 percent—marginally Democratic. But, with its ever-changing population, Republicans were becoming competitive. In 1992, cranky, independent presidential candidate Ross Perot received a noteworthy 24 percent of the district's votes—four points higher than his national average.[3] Political allegiances were not frozen.

Lacking a core of organized interests, located in a bundle of hard-to-describe places, and unsettled in its political habits, Florida's Fifth District was hard to digest. It was especially vulnerable to external dismemberment and reconstruction. In 1994, for example, when a mid-decade civil-rights-based realignment was ordered by the federal courts, the Fifth District—lacking any protective concentration of interests—lay open to the depredations of several adjacent House members from both parties.[4] Its boundaries were altered and redesigned. And there was no natural, historical, or institutional core with enough "standing" or clout to complain.

If Representative Thurman was going to solidify political support at home and build a legislative career in Washington, she would—more than most—have to conceptualize and put her personal stamp on this new place, both politically and personally. She would have to adopt and care for an orphan constituency. She was very much on her own, in a changing district that she would eventually describe—in a moment of frustration—as "nowhere."

Given a political scientist's interest in the constituency connections of a female member of Congress, it was a helpful circumstance that Karen Thurman had been elected to Congress in 1992, the much-celebrated "Year of the Woman" in American politics. In that year, a record number of eleven women—seven of them Democrats—had entered the House of Representatives. As the 1994 congressional elections—and Thurman's first reelection—approached, however, the national press was predicting trouble for Democratic incumbents. The *Washington Post* headlined, "Are the Democrats Losing It? November Is Looking Better For the Republicans All the Time."[5] In follow-up articles like "Endangered Species," and "On the Inside Now—And Struggling to Stay There," Washington journalists were paying special attention to the fate of first-term Democrats—and especially to the first-term Democratic women.[6] "Unhappy New Year for the 'Year of the Woman'" predicted the *Washington Post*.[7] And *Congressional Quarterly's* predictions headlined, "1994 Elections Are Looking Like the "'Off Year' of the Woman."[8] Both articles put the spotlight on the group of seven first-term Democratic women as endangered incumbents. Karen Thurman was one of them.

Two top *Washington Post* reporters featured the Florida congresswoman in their analyses of the imperiled female Democrats. One argued that Thurman was "in trouble" and was "vulnerable" because the creators of her congressional district had left her without a necessary cushion of liberal African American supporters.[9] A second reporter featured Thurman in a story entitled "The Democrats' Gender and Class Gap: Young Affluent Women in the Suburbs Are Redefining the Party."[10] The Democratic Party, its author argued, would have to rely increasingly on candidates such as Thurman—whom they defined as "women who can win support from Republican and Independent voters concerned with issues such as health care and abortion rights—in an increasingly suburban and college-educated electorate."

These Washington journalists, however, had little or no understanding of Karen Thurman's constituency.[11] She had never needed all of her tiny, 5 percent minority of black residents. And her electorate was certainly not "suburban and college educated." In the subsequent 1994 election, six of the female freshmen—all of whom met the criteria attributed to the up-and-coming women representatives—were swept out of office. Only two of the first-term women survived—Karen Thurman and a New York City colleague. Representative Thurman was reelected with 57 percent of the vote. In this historic pro-Republican election, she was never in trouble.

If the *Post* reporters had gone to Florida to look around, they would have discovered that Representative Thurman was distinctively not a good example of the first-term Democratic women in the House.[12] Her major policy interests were not like theirs. Her district was not like theirs. Her position on some hot button issues was not the same as theirs. It was a reasonable hunch that her relationships with constituents and with colleagues might also be different from theirs.

Consider the contemporary analysis of "women friendly" House districts (1992–2000) by political scientists Barbara Palmer and Dennis Simon.[13] "Female Democratic House members," they conclude, "tend to win election in districts that are more liberal, more urban, more diverse, more educated and much wealthier than those won by male members of the House; they come from much more compact, 'tonier,' upscale districts than their male counterparts."[14] On every one of their criteria, Karen Thurman's district failed to qualify as "women friendly." Her district was not "more liberal," not "more urban," not "more educated," not "wealthier," not "compact," not "tony," and certainly not "upscale."

These familiar female-related factors were of no help to an observer in figuring out what Congresswoman Thurman was "really like." Stereotypes would not work. Her district did not conform to the commonplace categories of political scientists. And neither did she. Both had to be taken on their own terms.

We can get some purchase on the functional makeup of her district by comparing some of its (1994) gross statistics to Florida's other twenty-two districts. Her Fifth District was 95 percent white. It was Florida's third most rural; it had the third lowest median family income; and it had the fifth lowest percentage of residents with a post-high-school education.[15] In terms of makeup, she often described it as "the second oldest and the second poorest district in Florida."[16] In 1994, its 188,000 Social Security recipients ranked in the top two or three districts in the entire United States. And six years later, the recently altered Fifth District would rank number one.[17] This abnormally high population of retirees also contained, reporters commonly said, "the largest population of (military) veterans in the nation."[18]

In conversation, she always spoke of the two sets of constituents possessively as "my seniors" and "my veterans." She never used the common clinical term "casework." The connections were personal.

The district had little or no smokestack industry. But it did have a sizeable agricultural economy—fruits, vegetables, beef. In their 1994 endorsement editorial, the *Tampa Bay Tribune* described Representative Thurman as "a politely liberal former school teacher (and) a Democratic defender of government assistance for the retirees, veterans and even farmers in the district."[19] She represented an especially needy constituency. And she returned to it—and to her husband and two children—every Friday.

The district voted slightly more Democratic than Republican, with the former group tilting conservative and the latter group increasing in size. But it was not an especially gender-sensitive, or suburban-sensitive, or educationally sensitive, or racially sensitive constituency. She had, indeed, been elected in the "Year of the Woman." But she was not a typical first-term female House Democrat. The representative and the district proved to be a good deal less stereotypical and a good deal more challenging than first imagined.

Our initial conversation took place—appropriately enough—in front of a large district map tacked on the wall of her Inverness campaign headquarters. Waving at the map, she divided her constituency into five far-flung "chunks"—four small northern counties, the county containing Gainesville, two coastal counties further south, and one partial county on the far southern rim near Tampa. (A half hour earlier, I had caught my first glimpse of the congresswoman at an early morning meeting with UPS drivers, where she had been peppered with questions about gun control. "I'm a strong believer in Second Amendment rights," she had told the group. "I always have been. That's just the way I am. And that's that.") Pointing, now, to the northern counties on her map—none of which had been in her state senate district—she said, "That's 75,000 people. All they care about is their Second Amendment rights. If you don't support them, you're dead. They won't even look at you. I can't afford to give away 75,000 people."

Pointing southward to her other "chunks," she said,

> The people here (in Gainesville) and the people down there (in exurban Tampa) are both strongly pro-choice. What boggles my mind is that they are pro-choice on constitutional grounds (just as) the others "up there" support Second Amendment rights on constitutional grounds. They both feel strongly because it's a constitutional matter. So why can't the pro-choice people understand why the other group feels so strongly? I keep talking to the pro-choice people trying to educate them to understand the other group. That's why I'm in trouble. That's why I'll always be in trouble in this district.

It was a telling introduction—anti-gun control "up there," and pro-abortion "down there"—to the district's marked lack of coherence. Indeed, when she did characterize her constituency as a whole, she called it "this nine-county district"—most often with the exclamation, "This nine-county district is tough!"

The two subjects she jumped into via her district map—gun control and abortion—would continue to be among her four most troublesome and most highly publicized issues during her career. They were issues that would separate her, too, from the other six women with whom she entered Congress. She remained opposed to major gun-control legislation. She supported a woman's right to choose, but she drew a bright line against federal financial support for abortion.[20] Both stances set her apart from her female classmates of 1992. Shrewdly and firmly, to keep herself from persistent pressure, she had laid down both markers at the very outset of her congressional career.

The Washington media attention being given to Karen Thurman's 1994 reelection campaign was not, however, driven by any desire to illustrate the constituency dilemmas of women representatives. Media interest was driven entirely by the unique celebrity of her 1994 Republican opponent. "Big Daddy" Don Garlits was a world champion drag racer. His celebrity contributed greatly to Republican hopes and to media estimates of Thurman's vulnerability. The GOP targeted her with "scathing radio ads" as early as December 1993 and as late as October 29, 1994.[21] Garlits's one-of-a-kind novelty—as an offbeat celebrity espousing ultraconservative views—explains the unusual national media attention. Journalists seemed not to understand Thurman's point of view or her electoral prospects. They chose their themes because of Garlits. They highlighted his unique appeal, and they labored to locate her weaknesses.

It was a mighty frustration for the first-term incumbent. After our initial map lesson, she handed me two articles. "I'm steamed," she said (by a local Gainesville article), "because they did not mention any of the things I've done. There's nothing in there about our work on water or immigration issues. I talked to that reporter for two hours. Honestly, I don't think they know or care about what I've done. This article isn't about Congress. It's all about celebrity."[22] Turning to the Washington-based article, she continued. "I talked to this guy for thirty minutes. You wouldn't know that from the article, would you? My comments are there, at the very end. It's all about him (Garlits). He's the celebrity. He gets all the publicity."[23] The celebrity attraction and the lopsided coverage only added to the gross misunderstanding of—and the lack of journalistic interest in—her actual constituency relationships. Not to mention her activities and accomplishments in Washington.

The Legislator: 1994

Representative Thurman was able to make sense out of her hard-to-describe district because she had previously represented parts of it for ten years in the Florida State Senate. As chairman of the Senate's Committee on Reapportionment, she had helped to draw the lines of a district that included a part of her home county, all of another county, and most of two others from her existing senate constituency. When criticized as self-serving in that effort, she correctly demurred that the relevant redistricting map had to be approved by a redistricting expert and by the federal courts.[24] True enough. But in an intralegislative battle, which she described as uniquely "mean, nasty, and ugly," she had, in effect, superintended the drawing of a customized congressional district.[25]

It was the mark of an accomplished legislator. And it gave her a head start in connecting with her constituents through personal recognition and through her working knowledge of local issues and preferences. In 1992, she was endorsed in the primary and in the general election by the district's leading newspaper—as "thoughtful and caring" and as "the knowledgeable coalition builder."[26] She had been opposed, however, by the newspaper in her one and only—but new to her—city, Gainesville.[27]

The central event of my 1994 visit was a debate in her only city, Gainesville. It was home to her district's largest enterprise, the University of Florida. "This area is completely different from all the rest," she said as we drove to the debate. "It is young, liberal, and highly educated. All the rest is seniors." It was her most reliably Democratic "chunk." And this time, the local paper supported her. But Gainesville would always be more of a liberal outlier than a constituency bellwether.

In her opening debate statement, she presented herself as a busy legislator. "I ran for Congress just two years ago to make some changes in the way this country was running. And I have to tell you that I think we've done a pretty good job so far in just two years (i.e., deficit down, jobs up, student loans up). Then,

> I've worked on some things individually—things that I've been taught over the last several years, things that I've been involved in at both the local level, and then with the state legislature. The first one would be the illegal immigrants. For the first time, Florida will receive a period of dollars, or a group of dollars, coming back—for the incarceration of illegal aliens. That means that less [sic] dollars have to come out of the state that should be used for education. We also looked at water issues—the future issue of the state, and has been for a long time—and that was to look at alternative sources to find dollars available so that places to the south of us would actually come under the alternative sources being used instead of having to pipe water from the northern counties. Those were issues that we brought from our experience in the state legislature, from our

experience at the local level, and certainly something that needs to be dealt with at the local level.

She presented herself as an earnest, experienced, successful, and con- stituency-centered legislator. She highlighted her current legislative interests and accomplishments—immigration, financial relief, and clean water. And she emphasized her legislative experience. That was the persona she had worked for and wished for—but was not receiv- ing—from the media.

Her opponent came to the debate waving the 1994 Republican campaign document, the famous "Contract With America." He also attacked her for her vote in favor of President Clinton's budget and tax legislation—especially the gasoline tax—as "the biggest tax increase in American history." He attacked her for her vote against "the [Brady] anti-crime bill," and for her support of Democratic President Clinton's "big government" health proposals.[28] She, on the other hand, showed no interest in debating with her opponent. Without ever mentioning the president or her opponent, Thurman retaliated by listing the ben- eficial aspects of these votes—for example, the deficit reduction feature, the protection of "my seniors" in her budget vote, and the benefits to veterans in the health legislation.[29] And she followed by touting, again, her own legislative accomplishments. As a public platform performer, Representative Thurman came across as neither articulate nor artful. But she nonetheless came across positively—as straightforward, ear- nest, and above all, legislatively involved.

"I wanted to walk over and punch him in the nose," she said after- ward. "I had so many chances to zap him, but I didn't. . . . My problem is that I always answer the questions. Maybe I should attack my oppo- nent or just make a speech. But I keep saying to myself, 'Karen, answer the question.' That's the teacher in me. You can't ever get rid of that. I have a desire to educate." Her desire was captured in the opening words of her every comment: "Let me suggest to you . . . ," "I want to tell you . . . ," "I have to tell you. . . ". She took a schoolteacher's stance toward her audience.

She contented herself, afterwards, with a favorite expression: "He ain't got a clue, not a clue." And she vowed to "kick butt" in her upcom- ing campaign ads. The thrust of her presentation, I summarized, "was relentlessly constructive. She never bashed Congress; she never referred to public anger. She kept talking about what she had done, what more might be done, what could be done. She acknowledges problems, but her attitude is 'you keep trying.'" She was practical, not philosophical.

An outsider would soon perceive that Karen Thurman thought of herself, and presented herself to constituents, as a working legislator. She had cut her teeth on the Dunnellon City Council and as mayor. She had served for ten years in the Florida State Senate and had risen to become chairman of the Senate Committee on Agriculture. She took pride in her state senate performance, introducing "between 60 and 80 bills in any one year," and achieving "an 85 percent passage rate."[30] She had been at work, now, for two years in Congress. It was a constant source of frustration that "people have no idea what we've done—water, the environment, immigration." And, she added, "People have to be made to understand that legislation takes time." She was not a talker. On the record, she was a doer. And to the degree that she was not known as an active, productive legislator, she was frustrated.

On water problems, she told a WRZN talk show caller: "I've been working on water (problems) ever since I was on the city council in Dunnellon." And to a reporter: "I'll have to take you back to my work in Dunnellon and in the state legislature. . . . Half the population of this district turns over every two to four years. Most people have no idea of who I am or what I've done. And nobody tells them. . . . I'm in my nineteenth year working on water problems. The newspapers send us reporters who are six months out of school and who haven't a clue. We train them and then if they are any good, they are gone." "Tell me," she pleaded to the *Hernando Today* editorial board, "What can I do to get the story out?" In the state legislature, she noted that "My three water amendments" had led to legislation that protected lakes and private wells against saltwater degradation and had improved wastewater sources for farmers. She prided herself on her stick-to-itiveness. And she wanted, most of all, to be known as a legislative "player."

The success story of her first two terms in Congress was that she had secured a $30 million appropriation to encourage two large nearby urban counties (Tampa, St. Petersburg) to develop water reuse methods that would relieve her counties of water shortages and water pollution.

But this two-stage sequence of benefits, she admitted, was not easy to turn into a political plus. "The money will not come into my district. It goes to people I don't represent and who do not know me. I won't be cutting any ribbons. I'm trying to solve problems. My opponent has no interest in solving problems."

Her featured legislative story was this: that she had personally secured the $30 million appropriation by appealing directly to the relevant Appropriations Subcommittee chairman. "I did not know (Rep.) Lou Stokes," she said later. "I had never had any contact with him. I called him and asked for an appointment. I went to see him. I said, 'Mr. Chairman, I need help.' I told him the problem. He said he didn't have any money. I told him again how much I needed it. He promised me nothing. When the Conference Committee Report came out, there was $30 million dollars!" It was chalked up by this visitor as a very personal, behind-the-scenes accomplishment of a hardworking and effective legislator.

Two other pieces of legislation displayed her ability to work with her fellow representatives. With a California Democratic colleague ("my partner in crime") she tackled another Florida problem. "We put together a coalition from the states most affected by illegal immigration—California, Florida, Texas, and New York—and we pushed an amendment requiring the federal government to reimburse the states for the costs of incarcerating illegal immigrants. . . . We got a good coalition going. We put the senior (subcommittee) member's name on it; and it passed." "I got no credit for it," she said later. "But legislation is problem-solving."

Working across party lines with a Florida Republican colleague, she helped formulate, and pass in the House, a provision requiring that "risk assessment" studies of all proposed regulations be required before any new environmental regulations could be promulgated by EPA. The proposal received favorable editorial notice.[31] Although it passed in the House, it did not in the Senate; but several years later, it became law. "When we proposed it," people said, "you can't do it," Thurman recalled. "But I did it! When the amendment was up (on the House floor) people said to me, 'Karen, you go over and stand by the door. If people know you're for it, they'll vote with us.'" To which she added, "You get things done by blending in, not by sticking out."

"So, how do you 'blend in'?" she was asked.

First, you do it by reaching out. When I went to the Florida legislature, I broke out of my education field and learned new areas—areas
that women aren't supposed to know about, like water and agriculture.
I spent ten years on the Agriculture Committee, and I became the first
woman chairman of that committee in the history of the Florida Senate. I have to be careful about this because I owe a lot to my district. My
district gave me diversity . . . (and) the chance to learn different subjects.

Two other things I learned in the state legislature. One was that my
word is the most valuable thing I own in a legislative body. I had a great
teacher on that, Dempsey Baron. And I learned to give good information. When I tell anyone anything, I make sure it is good information.

She seemed to know her business. And she seemed to be good at it. She
had become a player in the Florida legislature where she had built a
reputation as an astute, active legislator.[32] Her Washington goal was to
do likewise in the House of Representatives.

At the end of her first year there, she told an interviewer, "I like to
think that what I did best in the Florida legislature was build consensus and build bridges, not just between Democrats, but between Democrats and Republicans. I like to think I can do that here, (and) I'm
working on it."[33] She was soon identified by state and national observers as "a skilled politician," "a member to watch," "a skilled political
operator" and as someone who "seems to thrive in the House," "shows
vigor and skills," and has "perfect political pitch."[34] She was on a path
to realize her legislative ambitions. And, given half a chance, she would
talk about them.

In a district with no industrial concentrations, the one economic
interest to which Thurman was strongly attached was agriculture—to
its vegetable and fruit growers and to its cattlemen. The relationship
began with her water improvement and allocation legislation in the
Florida State Senate. It continued when she became the first female to
chair the Senate Agriculture Committee. In Congress, she had chosen to carry her work forward as a member of the House Agriculture
Committee, where she continued to work on drinking water improvements.[35] Her relationship did not produce a lot of campaign money.

Indeed, she was praised at home as "courageous," "gutsy," and daring when she refused to accept any contributions from her district's tobacco growers.[36]

When asked, in 1994, if she wanted to change committees in the upcoming Congress, she said, "No, not this time. The agriculture bill is coming up in the next session; and I have promised the farm people that I will stay on that committee. Florida has always been underrepresented on that committee. So I can help the whole state." "The Ag Committee has been run by midwesterners," she told an interviewer, "and now for the first time, they're starting to understand Florida agriculture . . . beef production, winter vegetables."[37] On that committee, she had become a champion—early and late—of Florida agriculture.

In turn, however, her constituency stance led to one of her most controversial congressional votes. Her strong agriculture-protection preferences produced a high-profile "no" vote on NAFTA (North American Free Trade Agreement).[38] It reflected an agriculture-protection passion which separated her, once again, from her suburban-oriented, free-trade sisters in the 1992 "Year of the Woman" freshman class. President Clinton, Thurman recalled, had lobbied her to change her position—"first in the room next to the Oval Office and then in the Oval Office. There were about twenty of us in there with him. And because he and I had already talked, he looked over at me and he said to his aide, 'forget about her; she's solid.'" She took a legislator's pride in the telling of it.

Strictly Personal

During our lengthy car ride to the Gainesville debate, she discussed her personal background. "My father was in the Army—the regular Army for twenty-four years. He was the tail gunner in a B-52. I grew up in the Army." When he retired, they landed in the small town of Dunnellon, where she graduated from the University of Florida, married, raised two children, and became a 7th- and 8th-grade math teacher. Calling Dunnellon "a small, rural community," she said, "they grew me up. They raised me. They gave me my values. I was a service brat; and this was the first town I settled in. They taught me what a caring community was like." Many other small, "one stoplight towns" in her district seemed to be a lot like Dunnellon.

When her students complained that the Dunnellon City Council had shut down their popular local beach, she entered the public arena. "I didn't know anything about politics; but I told them 'let's see how we can get city council to reconsider.' We found out how they set their agenda; we went to the meeting, and we got the order rescinded. The kids were so happy that a couple of them said I should run for city council. So did my husband. I decided to do it. The kids worked; and we went door to door. We won by five votes." "It was my toughest race," she told a reporter. She was thirty-four.

After ten years—four as mayor—she decided to run for the state senate in a newly reapportioned district. "I knew the issues from my work on city council—water, transportation, agriculture. I had helped to reorganize a hospital. From that work, I had met people throughout the (senate) district. People said, 'What's that little girl doing—running for the state senate. She can't win.' We kicked a little butt."

The congresswoman did not take to the political scientist's first visit with enthusiasm—insisting that I not ride in her car, but follow her instead in my car as she whizzed around her spacious constituency. Which I did—in the beginning and, occasionally, during later visits. A major negotiating hang-up, I learned from the staff, had been her worry that the professor would be bothered by her smoking habit. It was a revealing concern, because it involved—as so much did with her—personal relationships. When I made it clear that I couldn't care less, the trip fell into place. And in time, the sheer awkwardness of her two-car preference worked to undermine her travel restrictions.

Our second-day ride together to her distant Gainesville debate proved to be the turning point in our personal relationship. Sheer logistics dictated that I ride in her car. When she smoked, she puffed out the window. After the debate, the congresswoman, her top aide (a woman), an old political friend (a man), and I enjoyed a couple of beers together. That context put us on common ground. I became a real person—and a bit of a comrade, too. The next day, I overheard her tell a friend that she had been "leery" of my visit. And I heard her explain, "He doesn't mind my smoking; he drinks beer; he can ride with me; he's our kind of person." She seemed relieved. I certainly was.

The Legislator: 1995

For House Democrats, the aftermath of their epic 1994 defeat was trau-
matic. Now in the minority—for the first time in forty years—they had
to relinquish all their leadership positions and squeeze all their committee memberships. When we talked on the telephone in mid-December,
she was immersed in the retrenchment controversies inside the party
Caucus. After thanks for my postelection comments to local reporters,[39] she talked about her second-term nuts-and-bolts career concerns.
    She had become a participating House colleague.

> Everybody was worried about who was going to be elected minority
> leader and whip. We said, "Wait a minute," there are a lot more impor-
> tant things than that. There are rules. There had been no preparation
> by Steering and Policy about committee appointments, who would get
> them, how they would be chosen . . . we think they should have been
> more inclusive. (Rep.) Tim Roemer and I have been talking to CRS,
> looking to what might happen. We stayed up late Tuesday night, but we
> got nothing.
>
>   So the next day, we said, "Wait a minute." What is going to happen
> when people get bumped off exclusive committees? Can they go to any
> other committee where there are vacancies? Do they have a chit to get
> back on these committees if we take control? If they go on a new com-
> mittee, do they take all their seniority with them? How will you protect
> the junior people on committees—and new people?

Her personal worries centered on her Government Operations Committee—on what the Republicans would do to the committee and what
domino effects it might have for her.
    In her first year, she recalled, two of her fellow first-termers

> wanted a rule that said people should be removed from their positions
> if they voted the wrong way on certain issues. They wanted a litmus test
> on people. "How good a Democrat are they?" We said, "wait a minute,"
> you ought not to run Congress this way. We have to vote the way we did.
> You should pick people who will be good members of the committee, not
> on their voting record. Some of us wouldn't have been back if we hadn't
> bucked the system.

She had worked, she said, to keep constituency factors from being ignored.

> You know what I like? I like the idea that now, for the first time, we have a rule that mentions (as one criterion) the word "district."[40] It mentions the people we represent. Imagine that! It's a rule that gives our people their vote back; it gives the vote back to our constituents. That rule of ours was voted in unanimously. But who knows what will happen behind closed doors?

Capitol Hill's *Roll Call* quoted her, too, on the committee appointment process, noting that she "also pushed for some reform proposals in last week's (Democratic) Caucus" on organizational matters.[41] She was behaving like an experienced, ambitious, and institutionally minded legislative insider.

On electoral matters, her postelection concerns were fueled by her belief that had not the party leadership been deaf to people like herself on gun-control issues, the Democrats might not have lost the election.

> We said, "Wait a minute." We felt that if the leadership had listened to us on the gun issue, we might not have lost control. In October, I told the Speaker, I told the majority leader, and I told the majority whip: "you should take the assault weapons ban out of the crime bill and vote on it separately, because if you don't, I'm not going to be able to call you Mr. Speaker, Majority Leader, and Majority Whip any more—because you will lose control of the House."

Her problem was that the president had chosen to bargain with House Republicans for the swing votes instead of accommodating the "gun rights" Democrats like herself.[42]

At the end of our phone conversation, she turned to her own reelection. "The numbers were great. The size of the win surprised me—the best since 1986." She mentioned a few counties as especially "great." But she added, "We haven't done any analysis yet." She was heavily attentive to the legislative here- and-now.

But she had also been "out and about" back home. "Let me tell you a story," she began.

> In Dixie County, one of my smallest counties, there are some fishing communities—mostly they fish for mullet. They are not well off, but they have

been fishing for generations. They were very hard hit by the big winter storm a couple of years ago. I got in there and worked with FEMA so that they would be eligible for disaster aid. It meant upgrading their homes and raising them up off the ground. Now you know that costs money. Those folks didn't have much; and you know how hard it is to change anyhow. So it's one of those cases where you do something and you have no idea how you are going to be perceived. So I was up there a few weeks ago, and I met two of the county commissioners. One of them told me that when he came to the area to campaign last fall, the fishermen said to him, "You're going to support Karen Thurman, aren't you. Because if you aren't, we won't support you." When I looked like I didn't believe him, he called the other commissioner over, and he said it was all true. They are the kind of men who ordinarily would take the attitude that "She's a woman, she can't get anything done." That one conversation made my whole day.

She went on to say that there were about 40,000 people all told in a couple of small, nearby counties and that this favorable attitude toward her would ripple around in the area. Constituency service, she believed, was the backbone of her appeal at home.

Three months later, when we talked in Washington, she was once again absorbed in Capitol Hill politics. First off, she made sure that I stopped in to say hello to my congresswoman. "I told her you were coming," said Thurman. "I like her a lot; and I'd appreciate it if you would give her a call." I had no prior plan to do it; but, of course, I did.

Next, she inquired about my Rochester secretary, "Mary Rose," with whom she had once spoken on the phone. When I replied that "Rosemary" had recently lost her husband, the Florida congresswoman talked at length about her husband's mother, who had passed away recently. "She went on about that at such great length," I noted, "about the illness, the last days, the cemetery, what she thought the woman and her husband would be doing now, that I thought I would never get my interview. It was most unusual for me, since I've dealt mostly with men; and they don't open up at great length about such matters." Later, in the Capitol, she took me to see the suite of rooms that had been set aside exclusively for congressional women. There, she showed me how she had been able to throw a blanket over an exhausted senior colleague resting on the couch. The three experiences, I thought, showed "a woman's touch."

On the main track, however, the Florida representative came across as an active legislator. She had just come from the House floor, where "I was watching over my veterans—one of my major interests, you know." (They were always "my veterans" never "the veterans" or just "veterans"). "Did you get the money (for veterans) restored?" "Yes, but at the expense of the president's national service corps legislation. I tell you, the Republicans are ruining the country. The place is in a turmoil. They are hurting the people we shouldn't be hurting. They haven't a clue, not a clue."

Legislatively, she was, of course, adapting to the sudden and strange minority status of her party. She recalled urging more vigilance on the part of her stunned party leaders. "The Democrats didn't know how to play defense," she said. "I went to the leadership and said, 'Get someone out there on the floor. And every time they (the Republicans) say something, be ready to confront them.'" She knew a thing or two about action on the floor of a legislature.

When she ticked off her own legislative activities, she expressed an educated view of what she might accomplish—quite apart from the new partisan context. It was an educated view that took into account differences in decision-making systems. "For people who came here from state and local office, Congress is very different. In Tallahassee, you could get a lot of big wins. In Congress, you don't get many wins. A big win is unusual. So you have to make a difference in the way bills get passed or amendments passed." On the Government Operations Committee, she said, "We were able to get two amendments in on the line-item veto—one in committee and one on the floor."

About a second bill in her Government Operations Committee, she commented, "The Republicans . . . don't know what's in the bill, and they can't answer questions about it. The chairman admitted he didn't know what some of the provisions meant; but he wanted us to pass it anyway."[43] She compared the new Republican chairman with his Democratic predecessor. "When (Democrat) Jack Brooks took his bill to the floor, he protected the other members. He understood they had responsibilities to their constituencies. He knew what questions they would have to face back home. He took into account their problems. The Republicans don't do that." They were, instead, on a forced march to enact their "Contract With America" policy document in one hundred days.[44]

Her main legislative effort focused on food stamp policy in her Agriculture Committee. As she told it,

> The Agriculture Committee met every day for three weeks on food stamps. Two days a week we met from nine in the morning till five at night. I sat there every minute. Only three or four of us did. I set everything else aside so I could be there. It's important to my district. I asked for membership on the committee. It's my job. The chairman did an excellent job with the witnesses, as good a job as anyone would do. . . . I was able to pick up on a few things and make some points. But when it came to marking up the bill, the marching orders changed. Everything became completely partisan.

Later, she elaborated: "Members from agricultural districts have always worked together regardless of party. We (Democrats) have to because we are in the minority. But the Republicans are driving us apart because (when) they take their orders from the leadership, it is hard for us to work together. It is very sad."

A proposal of particular interest to her was one that reduced food stamps if an unemployed person stopped looking for work after a certain time period.

> I'm very interested in food stamps because I'm afraid we're going to take food away from people who need it. I think of the people in my district. Florida Power and Light laid off 350 people. They are people who have been able to buy a car, take out a home mortgage, feed their families. And now they have no job. What are they going to give up? They may lose their home. They can't lose their car. You know my great big district. There are no bus lines, no subways, no public transportation. If you don't have a car, you can't look for a job. And now the Republicans were going to take away their eligibility for food stamps—even if people could not possibly stay engaged in a job search. I tell you, when you get down to things like this, you can tell who is a Democrat and who is a Republican. On a lot of issues, you can't. But when it comes to taking food away from children, you can tell. Democrats have a heart.

Her work on food stamps landed her on the PBS MacNeil-Lehrer News Hour.[45] She expressed reservations about the interview's lack of focus, but took pleasure at the special recognition.

One cause of the program's lack of focus, she explained, was the complexity of the legislative context. She had worked on food stamps as a member of the Agriculture Committee, which had jurisdiction over that subject. But, eventually, her committee's food stamp provisions would have to be folded into, and made compatible with, the more comprehensive, more politically explosive piece of legislation being designed to reform the nation's welfare system. Indeed, she was already anticipating that final stage. Using her food stamp expertise, she had become involved in the Democrats' alternative welfare proposal. "I'm working with (Rep.) Nathan Deal (Dem.) on a welfare bill that will not hurt the children," she said. And I would pick up on her legislative immersion during the next constituency visit, in 1996.

In 1995, however, she was not the politician I had first met in Florida. In 1994, she had campaigned at home as a faithful representative and as an experienced legislator. She had not campaigned as a party partisan or as a Democrat. She had attacked her opponent, not for being a Republican, but for being a far-out, inexperienced ideologue. But now, here she was, after a few months of legislative experience in the minority—and in the context of a historic Republican takeover—talking like a partisan Democrat.

Evidence of Washington's influence could be found in her reaction to the formation of a conservative/moderate Democratic group—of "Boll Weevils" or "Blue Dogs."[46] For the Karen Thurman I had met during her 1994 campaign, this group should have been her natural home. Now, however, while still calling herself "a moderate Democrat," she had become less interested in joining them. "I started with them," she recalled. "But when it came right down to it, I decided I couldn't join. I am a Democrat! And when I saw the way it was being perceived I said, I can't do it! . . . I may vote with them. But I am not one of them." Her party's electoral defeat seemed to have had positive party-regarding effects on "the gentlewoman from Florida."

The Representive: 1996

Returning to her district, in the late summer of 1996 to catch her reelection campaign, I was welcomed as a friend. She called my motel shortly after my arrival in Inverness; and she wanted to talk. Her first comment:

"One of your friends (Congressman X) came up to me the other day on the House floor and talked about you. He said, 'What have you two got going? He has such a good time.' I told him, 'I put him in the back seat and let him watch me put on my makeup. And I feed him beer.'"

Our conversation centered on her husband's ongoing campaign for reelection to a third six-year term as county judge. The *St. Petersburg Times* had recently written a harshly critical editorial opposing Judge John Thurman. "It threw me for a loop. It made me sick. I couldn't imagine why anyone would do that. I don't know what to do. What can you do? Keep licking and sticking, I guess."[47] She was on her way, she said, to the home of a staffer to help "stick and lick" her husband's 17,500 brochures. She suggested I join her there. "I'm bringing the beer," she said.

We had, indeed, bonded over beer. It was a bond without pledges on either side. But it was a personal bond—one which would help me to get a better picture of her constituency connections and, perhaps, her legislative strengths.

The rest of the evening was spent stuffing envelopes—with the congresswoman and her husband, plus several friends and coworkers of each. Her top aide said to me, "We have to start getting our campaign organized. Up to now, we've spent every waking moment on John's campaign. We've canceled our reservation for the National (Democratic) Convention. . . . It's strange to see Karen so nervous."

In this context, she was a wife worried about her husband, and worried, too, that his sacrifice for her—by staying at home and taking care of their two teenage children—had jeopardized his own career. And, of course, her own race could be affected by his.

John and I are running totally separate races. But people connect the two. One of the reasons I'm worried about John's race, quite frankly, is that if he should lose, that would be taken as a sign of weakness for me, too. If I show strength, they won't want to drop a lot of money into my race. . . . As of now, our understanding is that the Republicans have written off my race. If we show weakness, they may reconsider. That has me very concerned. If—I should say when—John wins, I'll have a normal race.

You asked me what votes I'll have to explain during the election. The only way I'll have to explain any vote is if they put money into the race. No money, no explaining.

As it worked out, John lost his 1996 race and Karen won hers.

During the two years between my visits, the boundaries of her district had been changed as the result of a Justice Department civil rights ruling involving an adjacent Democratic district. While the resulting changes were not radical, they were made by the Florida legislature without her input. And they were not to her liking.

In the Republican-controlled Florida Senate, she explained, two Republican members of Congress from adjacent areas had cut a territorial deal with an incumbent Democrat, who had then come to Thurman saying, "Karen, you've got to sign off on this." "I got very upset and I still am. It's taken me a long time to get over the bitterness. Their plan not only took my home town out of my district, it also reached out to take away an acre where John and I have an option to buy land. I think they intended to give it back, but they had us two Democrats at each other's throats, just as they had planned all along . . . We were completely locked out of the process on the Senate side."

She continued, "So, when the (Florida) House was getting ready to pass its (redistricting) version, John and I packed up and went to Tallahassee. What we ran into there was that the (Democratic) chairman of the powerful Rules Committee wanted to run for Congress. . . . He wanted two of my counties which he represents in the (Florida) House. When I saw what he was doing—and how powerful he was—we packed up again and came home." Her fellow Democrat seized two of her counties. And a deal-cutting Republican congressman wrested most of a third county from her.

To make up for her losses, Thurman was given the rest of the populous and reliably Democratic county containing Gainesville, plus "the most Republican" part of an unfamiliar county. She had been defenseless in trying to hold her "nine-county constituency" together. It was an acute reminder of how lacking her "orphan district" was in any unifying sociocultural rationale or any protective political or economic interests. Because she lacked these organizational bases, she had to "construct" her first constituency by herself. And now, having it "deconstructed" without her input was all the more upsetting.

She drove all day—with her top aide and confidant up front and me in the back seat—to a series of campaign-time connecting activities: a candidate forum, a League of Women Voters debate, a local fair, and two Democratic Party rallies. At the candidate forum, she watched three Republicans compete for the right to oppose her. None of them, however, posed a threat. One sidled over to her to say hello. "He has a sense of humor," she said afterward. "I like him. He's the one I'd like to campaign against. He's a gentleman." (She did not get her choice.)

"I love the job I have campaigning. I really do," she said. "There are so many great people out there—wonderful people. And there are some horses' asses. I talk to them all. When I think back to 1982, when I first ran for the state senate, I think the reason I won was because I talked to everybody. My opponent would only talk to people if he thought they were important." When we stopped for gas, I noted, "Karen hops out, washes her windshield and the back window and talks to the guy at the next pump. She is unbelievably sociable—hugs all the men she knows." "I just got two hugs at that booth," she said at the fair. Her conversations were punctuated with colloquialisms: "Okie dokie," "You're a sweetie," "Hellooo," "Tell me about it." "Out and about" in the district she was connected and enthusiastic.

Between afternoon events, she suddenly called home to tell her two children—ages seventeen and nineteen—that she would be stopping by. "I want the house picked up and cleaned up when I get there. If not, there won't be any money, and you won't be able to do all those wonderful things you do on Saturday night. I love you." After her event, she called them again. "Have you cleaned up the house? I mean have you cleaned it up enough so I can bring a man you've never met into the house? Yes, a man who is writing a book about ME. . . . I love you."

"Her telephone calls were distinctively those of a mother," I noted. "None of the men I traveled with ever made phone calls like those. Taking me to a house full of children was a part of admitting me into her world—in a way that a man would not." Or as none, to my recollection, ever had. In that context, too, she was a natural.

When we arrived, there were eight or nine teenagers hanging out in the TV room. In the car, she had worried, "One problem the kids have around here is that they don't have enough to do. Their idea of fun is burying a truck." "I'd rather have them here than somewhere else," she said later, as she rewarded her son for his cleanup. She showed me around the house; and we stood on a dock out back to watch the Withlacoochie River meander by. (It was the closure of a downriver

Withlacoochie beach that had pushed her into politics.) "The river," I noted, "was the loveliest, cleanest, purest, spring-fed river I've ever seen, drinking water clean, limestone bottom, tons of fish (no fishing allowed) . . . overhanging trees with Spanish Moss, pure Southern picture book."

During our inside house tour, the atmospherics were reversed. The interior was a veritable collage of life on the run. And I wondered what the "cleanup" had accomplished. "She was showing me the way they lived," I noted, "discombobulated, with John as house Mom most of the time, with her on the road or in DC, and with the kids sort of stalled out in adolescence. . . . I suspect it was the real world she lives in and that she sees nothing extraordinary about it—sort of happy, inevitable chaos. It was more trust than most politicians show toward me." At the end of our long day, the congresswoman, her top aide, and I sat down in a Chinese restaurant to enjoy a glass of "the coldest beer in Dunnellon."

Legislator and Representative: 1996

Her 1996 travel talk was heaviest with reflections on her legislative activity in the context of Republican rule. In the Agriculture Committee, she had taken a special interest in food stamp legislation. And she had fought, inside the committee, in favor of certain cost-of-living food stamp protections. She had fought especially hard against folding any food stamp money into block grants—into lump sums that would be given to each state for allocation however and for whatever use the state decided. The committee's Republican leaders shared that view, too, in opposition to their own party leadership.

As a result of her activity and interest, she said, "I became the Democratic point person on food stamps. (So,) when the agriculture bill passed the House, I went to the (Democratic) leadership and asked to be put on the conference committee—naive little me. The Blue Dogs demanded two slots and the rest was by seniority. I was very upset; and I let the leadership know it."

When welfare reform proposals reached the House agenda, "I worked very hard," she said, "on the Democratic welfare bill. And we got all the Democrats to support it, plus two Republicans." It was not

enough. In any case, the Republicans controlled the House agenda.
And, because the food stamp provisions in any welfare legislation had
to come from the Agriculture Committee, she pitched in again. "Xavier
Becerra [D-CA] and I," she said, "put together a Democratic food stamp
amendment that got to the floor and lost. We worked hard on that. I
had a lot of input on it. It was one of my best days in Congress."[48] When
the Republican version passed the House, "I was put on the conference
committee. It was a fascinating experience. I was the (party's) point
person for food stamps." Inside the Democratic party, she was becoming a legislative player.

On the person-to-person aspects of her interparty work, she seemed
to connect easily with her Republican colleagues. She described her
Agriculture Committee chairman Bill Emerson (MO), as "a wonderful
man. . . . He and Pat Roberts (KS) saved food stamps. They kept it from
being 'block granted' in the agriculture section of the welfare bill. Emerson hated to lose; and he told the leadership he would fight them. . . .
And Henry Hyde (IL) is another one. I like Henry Hyde. . . . He opposes
the Republican leadership when he disagrees with them. He's independent—a gentleman." But, she added, "There aren't many of them left. . . .
[party] leadership tells them what to do . . . . They're like a cult."

In the context of the historic Republican takeover of 1994 and their
Contract With America legislative program, she was now expressing—
in 1996—a lot more overall partisanship and using stronger language
than I had heard two years earlier. For example: "I hate this Congress.
I hate what the Republicans are doing to the people of this country. If
they get in again and continue on this path, it will be the beginning of
the downfall of this country. I truly believe that. They have made me
understand, more than ever, why I am a Democrat. . . . The Republicans
did not care what they were doing to their parents and grandparents
with their budget. They did not care. I truly believe that!"

Again, "I was an original Blue Dog. I stayed close to them in the
beginning, but they started to move further away from the party. I
wanted to work within the party. And, as time went on, I became more
comfortable in the party." Finally,

Because of what the Republicans have done, I have become more liberal
than I was. The more they pushed their legislation, the more they pushed

me toward the other side. Maybe that is where my thought processes were taking me anyway. I used to be more in the middle. They have made me more liberal than ever before. And I feel more comfortable where I am now. That's curious, isn't it?

Political scientists have worried about, debated, and tested ideas about the relative strength of constituency influences outside the legislature and party influences inside the legislature in explaining the legislative behavior of our elected representatives. Karen Thurman's behavior illustrated the push and pull of the two influences. It is a particularly good example of the interplay and the equipoise between the pull of constituency when connections are being made at home and the pull of party when decisions are being made in the legislature. For this representative in the immediate legislative context, the pull of party was growing stronger.

In spite of her increased sense of partisanship, however, when she was put to the test inside the conference committee on the welfare bill, she pursued a moderating and ameliorative course. In a later interview, she looked back on her contribution in the conference room. "I knew that there was going to be a piece of legislation passed. I knew I had to be involved to limit the damage. So I couldn't go so far over to either side. I kind of had to maintain that . . . 'main street' kind of thinking. There were times when you couldn't go as far as you would like to. . . . (and) I probably got into a little bit of trouble."[49]

And, in a Rutgers interview:

> Being kind of in this moderate position I'm in (and) since I knew there was a piece of legislation that was going to be passed . . . you should try to be involved . . . to implement things that you think would be good. . . . If you weren't involved, then you're really kind of relying on maybe too far to the right or too far to the left for me. So the only way I knew how to have an impact, and potentially have the opportunity to play in it, was to be involved in it.[50]

Her instinct was to get into the decision-making process whenever and wherever she had a chance—no matter how small or peripheral. She would accept political constraints. And she would legislate constructively and incrementally, if, as, and when she could.

When the conference committee report came back to the House, she voted in favor of the welfare reform bill. It was, she said, "the most difficult vote of my career." Back in the district, however, it stamped her, helpfully, as a "moderate liberal."[51]

Back home, she explained that she owed her conference committee appointment to the intervention of a leadership confidante, Representative Martin Sabo of Minnesota. Then she added, "The way I got to know Marty Sabo was very interesting—bridge! There's a group of us who will go out to the Rayburn Room (off the House floor) when there's a long evening debate and play bridge—Marty Sabo, George Brown, Cal Dooley, and others. When staffers walk by, I say, 'Where's the beer?' One night, they brought me a bottle of wine."

Inside Congress, as well as outside, informally as well as formally, Karen Thurman was a natural at making friends. And notably so with her male colleagues. When a group of them organized a "skeet shoot" in Maryland, she joined them and took part in their activities. "It was their world," she said. "And I was the only woman there. They look at you differently after something like that." On the same wavelength, she loved University of Florida football; and the family kept all home games "sacrosanct."

In a book about women in Congress, a House Democratic leader singled out Florida's Thurman as "a man's woman," and as "one of the boys," as someone who had been notably effective at "fitting in" with male House Democrats. "Just where she sits on the floor," he said, "who she deals with . . . she's developed a rapport with (Dan)Rostenkowski (chairman of the powerful House Ways and Means Committee). She's clearly been a legislator for quite awhile and *has established ties beyond the coterie of women who came (here) together*"[52] (italics added). Her ease in the everyday company of men—of both parties—underscores her strong emphasis on personal relationships—as a habit of her constituency life and as a key to her legislative accomplishments.

It also squares with her out-of-sync profile among her "Year of the Woman" female newcomers–and with her aloofness, for example, within the organized Women's Caucus in the House. On three occasions—1993, 1995, 1997—she was interviewed at Rutgers University's Center for American Women and Politics at the Eagleton Institute. When asked about her activities and relationships with the Congressional Women's

Caucus, Thurman's answers reflected general "sympathy with," but a marked lack of "interest in" or "devotion to" Caucus activities.

For example: "I'm not involved in it yet because I really haven't been in the Caucus for long . . . so I haven't built relationships" (1993).[53] "I probably do not participate as much as some others do. I just don't. There are some issues that I disagree with them on, and it gets me into trouble sometimes. So I'm not as active as I probably should be" (1995).[54] "I am not active in the Women's Caucus. Don't ask me why because I haven't a clue" (1997).[55]

There is, however, a proximate clue—her voting support for legislation prohibiting the federal funding of abortions, that is, the well-known Hyde Amendment. And the underlying rationale can be found in her constituency-centered explanation of her vote. "It is a difficult issue for me," she told an Eagleton interviewer, "and we [I] got blasted by women's groups—in a year that I saw a lot of my women colleagues that I came in with, go down. . . . I was livid with them. I just told them, 'Fine . . . go find out. Who are you going to replace me with?'"[56] "I voted for the Hyde Amendment," she explained, "because I have a very conservative district. When people think of Florida, they don't know the area I represent at all. Gainesville, the most liberal region, is a small part of the district. The rest of it is very rural, in some cases, still left over from the Bible Belt—then a lot of urban sprawl." Furthermore, "I just always believed that government ought not to be involved in reproduction. . . . I'm comfortable. I also know who I am, where I am, because I am very pro-choice."[57]

Overall, she maintained, "When you take polls in your district, and you find what's on women's minds, it's exactly the same as what's on men's minds."[58] Her sense of sorority did not extend to the full range of pro-abortion preferences held by the great majority of her contemporary Women's Caucus colleagues.

What did come through most markedly in her discussion of the Hyde Amendment was her awareness of—and her attachment to—her constituency. In Marjorie Margolies-Mezvinsky's book about Congress, Thurman became the poster child for the broadest idea of representation: "We draw the line," Thurman told Margolies -Mezvinsky,

> and we ask women about these things, but men are in the same situation
> because they are expected to be a certain way and women are expected

to be a certain way. The bottom line is we're representative of people. We are representatives. And we're probably reflective of our districts. We have to be. That's what the House was intended to be . . . to be the pulse of the constituencies. . . . We all have to be aware of those issues that are forced by a constituency. And that means you can't be put into a cubicle or identified or characterized as single issue.[59]

In her Rutgers' interviews, she regularly tilted her views on issues away from questions about women's activity inside the House and toward references to all constituents in her district. For example: "I kind of try to not think in terms of just women's issues. If you're talking about Medicare, that crosses all lines. If you're talking about economic issues, that crosses all lines. . . . I find it very difficult to separate that" (1995).[60] Question: "Why did your vote [on gun control] differ from those of most of the other women in your party?" Answer: "Probably district. It is a big issue for a lot of my folks. They feel pretty strongly about it."[61] On women's issues in general: "I guess . . . the other thing that you have to look at for women, depends on what you think your role is up here. Quite honestly, in the district that I'm in, there are very, very few women's groups. . . . It's not like we have the Hollywood Women . . . you know what I'm saying? We have NOW. But only in two counties and very, very, very limited" (1995).[62]

"On health care, were you associated with work on fighting Medicare cuts?" she was asked. "Probably on Medicare (I was) just trying to hold the line . . . let it not wither on the vine. These are my constituents. That's the second largest senior population in the state of Florida, with the second poorest. I can assure you that mine are very fragile seniors. It is also a very old population" (1997).[63] Questions about her women-related activities nearly always—and very quickly—turned into answers that focused on the congresswoman's representational relationships in her constituency.

In her two post-1996 terms, her constituency agenda continued to focus on legislative and administrative relief directed at the availability, cost, and coverage of prescription drugs for "my seniors" under Medicare.[64] And the same—together with improved health care facilities—for "my veterans."[65] In 2000, she spoke on the subject at the Democratic National Convention.[66] In addition, reaching back to her work in the Florida State Senate, she continued to focus on environmentally sensitive "water improvements." Her long fight for legislation to find alternative sources of drinking water passed the House in 2000.[67]

In 1996, she won a third term with 61 percent of the vote. Editorial judgments from the constituency were highly favorable. The *Tampa Bay Tribune* endorsement called her "an able advocate for her lower income constituents from retirement communities, farms and small towns in the district . . . (she is a) former teacher who usually follows moderate instincts . . . knows her district well and has always been accessible to constituents."[68] The *St. Petersburg Times* endorsement said, "There can be no doubt Thurman has a mind of her own, and that is one of the primary reasons for our support."[69] And the *Times'* chief political writer wrote: "Thurman says she's a moderate, and the record tends to bear her out. Thurman supported the recent welfare bill, which liberals opposed. She is also a staunch supporter of gun rights and opposes federal funding for abortions—two of the hot button issues for the Democratic Party's left wing."[70] The *Tampa Bay Tribune's* second "confident" endorsement echoed that "she has a mind of her own" and "that while she may have voted along party lines, the votes were sympathetic to her constituency."[71]

Those performance judgments—describing her as "moderate," downplaying her partisan sentiments, and emphasizing her "dedication to constituency service"—seemed appropriate to me. They carried her to two more winning margins at the polls—66 percent in 1998 and 64 percent in 2000.[72] During this time, she had risen steadily to a position of inside legislative influence.

After her 1996 reelection, her legislative work habits and her negotiating skills had been recognized and rewarded with membership on the House Committee on Ways and Means, the most powerful committee in the House of Representatives, and, arguably, of the entire Congress. It was the committee on which Barber Conable had built his legislative reputation. From an author's view, she had come to Congress with a legislator's instincts and habits, had been an effective legislative contributor, had been a reliably partisan Democrat, and had won the strong support of well-placed colleagues. She had, in short, become a proven, effective Capitol Hill player. And she had been rewarded with increased responsibilities.

The Committee on Ways and Means—with its influence over taxes, trade, social security, and health legislation—had been her long-shot first choice back in 1992. Chairman Dan Rostenkowski "treated me very courteously," she had recalled, while telling her that he had "other priorities." It could not have been sheer coincidence that, as noted earlier, she could be seen sitting beside him on the House floor! By 1996, however, he was gone. The Republicans had taken control of the House. Charles Rangel of New York was now the senior committee Democrat. And Karen Thurman had renewed her application for membership.

As she told the story, when she met with Democratic Minority Leader Dick Gephardt about changing her committee assignment to Ways and Means, he had offered her the Commerce Committee instead. And she had said she would have to consult with her supporters. Leaving Gephardt's office, however, she had bumped into veteran Ways and Means Committee member Barbara Kennelly going in. Kennelly, who was leaving Congress to run for governor of Connecticut, said to Thurman, "Don't you ever give up. If you give up, you will disappoint all the women in this country. And there won't be a woman on the Committee. Don't you ever give up." "I was stunned," said Thurman, "by what she said. And I said, 'Okay, I got your message.' Then Barbara went in to talk with Gephardt. I don't know what she said, but. . . ." Some years later, Kennelly recalled publicly, "I traded everything I had to get Karen Thurman on Ways and Means."[73]

On decision day in December, Thurman was called to a meeting of the Committee's Democrats. As she recalled it,

> There were all the Democrats on the Committee; and they started drawing their chairs around in a circle. It looked like musical chairs. I had no idea what I was there for or what was going on. I knew I was supposed to keep my big mouth shut. But, finally, with my big mouth, I said "I don't know what I'm doing here; but I'd be happy to be a part of the same circle with the rest of you." Charlie Rangel spoke up and said, "Does anyone want to ask Karen any questions?" Barbara Kennelly spoke up and said what a great member of the committee I would be. John Lewis [Karen's regional advocate] spoke up and went on and on about what a great member I would be. Another member asked me, "Karen, I see you don't have any large winning margins. You don't win by 80 percent, do you?" They were worried that I couldn't take hard votes. I said that I could take hard votes and that I had proved it already—so long as I could explain

them back home—and that I had done just that in 1993 (by supporting Clinton's tax program). I also said, "You will have to give me some votes now and then, too." That was about it. I was dismissed. I had no clue how it worked. I had no idea what the result would be.

Shortly thereafter she received the good news. "Who told you?" I asked. "I can't remember," she said. "I was so excited. The two people who were most important to me were probably Barbara Kennelly and John Lewis." "For my delegation to promote me, for the leadership to select me," she told reporters. "It's a little overwhelming, very humbling." And, "It's great for Florida. It's great for my constituency."[74] In Washington, she was no longer an ordinary legislator.

For a while, she worried about her relationship with top committee Democrat Rangel. "I couldn't figure out whether Charlie didn't like me or whether he was waiting for me to prove myself. I've decided it was the second. . . . I think I'm okay now. Charlie knows I'll take the hard votes. I've proved myself. I think, too, that he thinks I'm a populist. He thinks of himself as a populist, and that helps."[75] She had enough confidence to get up once in Caucus and say, "I know some of you guys win by 65 percent and don't have to worry at election time. But I have the toughest election of any of you, and I'm willing to stand up and take hard votes. You should be too. . . . (Otherwise) I don't say a lot in Caucus. I let the same ones who run their mouths do it."

I asked her to compare her voting record with that of her colleagues. "It depends on the issues," she said. "If it was trade, I'd be with the unions. If it was defense, I'd be closer to the 'Blue Dogs.' If it was guns, I'd be closer to the 'Blue Dogs.' If it was prescription drugs, I'd be over with the liberals. And if it was Social Security, I'd be a Bernie Sanders liberal—as far over as you can get."[76] Her expressed willingness to "take hard votes" had been certified first by her support for the president's budget in 1993, and second by her vote for welfare reform in 1996 ("the hardest vote I've ever taken"). Inside the committee, her "hard votes" were cast in favor of trade liberalization—first on the renewal of GATT (General Agreement on Tariffs and Trade) and then on trade with China.

From an outsider's point of view, Representative Thurman's rise to a position of inside legislative prominence was a personal triumph. Promotion to Ways and Means has often been based on the requirement that certain recognizable economic or political interests be represented on this most powerful policy-making unit. Representative Thurman's congressional district contained no such interests. It was totally without economic or political clout. She had come to legislative prominence in the House because of her proven legislative abilities and her personal collegiality. Given the amorphous, unorganized character of her district, that is the only way it could have been done.

At the time I was not surprised. I had assumed, too, that she was in good shape and that my visits to Florida were over. I was wrong.

Redistricting

After her reelection in 2000, Representative Thurman's district boundaries had been redrawn once again—this time by a Republican State Legislature. The result put the Democratic incumbent in electoral danger at the hands of a prominent Republican state senate leader. A district that had always lacked a center of gravity or protective interests had been, once again, dismembered and re-created. National and local reports quickly highlighted Karen Thurman as an especially endangered incumbent.[77] These dire predictions drew me back to Florida to take a third look at the congresswoman as she connected in her heavily reconstructed district.

Driving north from Tampa to Inverness, after six years, I found stability amid change. As always, two-lane Highway 41 featured an endless, seedy-looking array of automobile and truck advertisements—"auto sales," "auto repairs," "auto parts," "body work," "sell, trade, repairs," "auto salvage," "auto junkyard." "The nearby countryside," I noted, "still looks poor." On the other hand, with the highway being widened, construction delays reflected Florida's relentless population growth. Already the attractive county-seat town of Brooksville, where I had stopped in 1996 to browse in antique shops, had been dead-ended by a new bypass with its accompaniment of roadside stores. Further north, signs reminded travelers that to the west, a new north-south "Suncoast Parkway" would be ready for use in the near future.

Not far from my destination in Inverness, a huge multicolored roadside billboard reminded me of why I was returning. It said: "Elect

Ginny Brown-Waite, Republican." Incumbent Thurman faced a serious challenger—the president pro tem of the Florida State Senate. Under Brown-Waite's watchful eye—the Republican-controlled Florida legislature had redrawn the boundaries of the Fifth District to create what she freely acknowledged was "a predominantly Republican-leaning seat."[78] Party registration, which had been 46 percent Democratic and 36 percent Republican in Thurman's previous district, was now 42 percent Republican and 41 percent Democratic in her current one. In the 2000 presidential election, Democrat Al Gore had carried Thurman's old district by 50 percent to 46 percent. But in the new district, the 2000 result would have been George Bush 53 percent, Al Gore 45 percent.[79] My two-and-a-half days on the road would be spent catching up with the legislator's recent activity in Washington and watching her cope with a new electoral context.

As redesigned on paper, the Fifth District was now a Central Florida district with a projected Republican majority. A succinct description:

> The new district boundaries . . . take Alachua County (Gainesville) and its reliable source of Democratic votes out of Thurman's district. The new lines also would take away west Pasco County, which Thurman has represented for years and substitute east and central Pasco, which is Brown-Waite territory.[80]

A little over half of its constituents would be new to Thurman. The redistricting process that Karen Thurman had once "tweaked," on her own behalf, Ginny Brown-Waite, as a member of the Florida State Senate's redistricting committee, had now "tweaked" in return. Thurman's original "nine-county district," which had already lost two northern counties in 1996, had now lost its largest county and gained two more. A popular incumbent was facing an accomplished challenger in a changed constituency. In public, Representative Thurman's upbeat attitude was: "(Even) if the lines change, the people don't. The issues in Central Florida remain the same."[81]

Her new district was as much of a puzzle as the earlier one. In contrast to the circumstances of her Pennsylvania colleague, impermanence remained the dominant characteristic. Two helpful markers—the city of Gainesville in the north, and the Tampa exurbs in the south—were gone. At both ends, the district had been moved eastward into Central

Florida. It was every bit as polyglot as her old district. But this time, it was a brand new polyglot.

When I started to explain my difficulty in locating and describing her new district, she interrupted me and said sharply, "It's nowhere!" The comment caught me by surprise. But it reinforced my judgment and my difficulties from the start in making sense of her political territory. "There is no center of gravity in her constituency, no focal point," I noted, adding "I think it's a main part of her problem. Politically, she comes from nowhere. And she is now trying to cultivate a redrawn version of nowhere." And that was, for her, an added frustration. She had, of course, taken no part in the new line-drawing adventure.

My first glimpse of her reelection campaign "in the new nowhere" came at a traditional kickoff event, a fund-raising fish fry, on a Sunday in late August, at the American Legion Hall near Dunnellon, in Marion. She was circulating through a crowd of about three hundred people—elderly, white collar and blue collar, middle class to lower-middle class, mostly white—shaking hands and renewing acquaintances. As she came to me, she grabbed my hand, asked, "How are you?" I said, "fine, thanks." She smiled and moved on without any sign of recognition.

Her pep talk began, I noted, "with her usual feistiness."

> There's been some interest in this campaign. For six months, all we've heard is "we're going to take the government back." "We're going to redistrict her." "We're going to get her." They forgot about one thing: people power! [Cheers.] They can change the [district] lines, but we have people—and people talk—people who have lived here for twenty years. You know people in Sumter County, in east and central Pasco [County], and in Lake [County]. Talk to them. Let's make this a grassroots campaign. It's not about money. It's not about TV. It's about you telling people about Karen Thurman. Your word of mouth, your phone calls will make the difference. I love all of you.

She briefly hit on three issues, comparing Bush administration views and activities with her own: health care for veterans, "Bush wants to take us into war, but he won't help the ones we already have"; prescription drugs for seniors, "I think we can win the election on that issue alone"; and opposition to the privatization of Social Security, "It may have looked good two years ago, but it doesn't look so hot two years later." And she ended, "For twenty years, I've had a great time; and I'm looking forward to two more. And you won't see me just at election time. I'll be out and about."

Afterward, her top staffer told me, "I forgot you were coming." Then she reminded the congresswoman who I was. "Wasn't that great," Thurman enthused. Then she told a bystander, "He's from Syracuse." Everything seemed normal!

When asked at the time by a local reporter to describe her campaign, she said, "We are trying to get out and introduce ourselves to about 250,000 new voters, going to service clubs, walking through government buildings, having some fund-raisers that some folks have put on for us. And just enjoying it."[82] That was what she was doing. And that is what I had come to watch.

Near the end of my three-day visit, I asked her to rank in order eight of our campaign stops in terms of personal enjoyment and political importance. She gave her fish fry kickoff the number one ranking in terms of her personal enjoyment. It was, of course, wall-to-wall friends and supporters. But she gave it a more modest third place ranking in terms of its political importance. Why? I asked. "Because half the people there were no longer in my district. And many of them didn't know it." New boundaries—Republican-drawn boundaries—were, of course, her overwhelming obstacle.

After the fish fry, I followed her to an all-candidates outdoor rally in the next county, sponsored by a local church group. It gave me a glimpse of Karen's competent sounding opponent, and a taste of district conservatism.

Shortly after posting and saluting the flag, a church choir's stirring song contained a challenging refrain: "We must take America back; we lost America; it's gone to the dogs. I pray that the Army of God will rise up and take my America back." [Applause.] When Karen's turn came, she said, "The proudest moment in all my public life was the day after September 11, when the members of Congress went out on the steps of the Capitol and sang 'God Bless America.' We were united, and we were strong, and we said we would never let anyone harm America. That was the proudest and most moving moment of my service in Washington." [Applause.] The first anniversary of the 9/11 attack was only a few days away.

"What did you think," Thurman's top staffer asked me afterward. Not wanting to assume a cheerleader role, I said, "She was good." "Just good?" was the reply. "Is that the best you can say?" Then Karen came over and asked, "Not enough oomph?" "Yes," I said. "How did you like my 'God Bless America' comment? I thought it was a most appropriate reply to that song didn't you?" I agreed, "Yes, I did." Later, she ranked the rally dead last in political relevance, but sixth in personal enjoyment. Why? "It's nice when people like the fire chief come up and say they are with you." Her patriotic "reply" was, indeed, the highlight of an otherwise dull rally on a suffocating summer day. Afterward, she and her top staffer went off to an NAACP meeting. "We forgot you were coming," said the staffer, "and we have no extra tickets."

Our second day began in her new Lake County territory, with a luncheon in a gated residential community with twenty or so business men and women, many of them from SPRINT. To punctuate her unfamiliarity, we got completely lost on the way there. (She was, as always, behind the wheel. She never, in my three visits, let anyone else drive.) "She took it all with good humor," I noted. "This is one of the problems when you get a new district," she laughed. "You get lost!" It was, indeed, "nowhere."

"Do you have all of Lake County?" I asked. "Thank God, no," she said. "It's very Republican." She continued,

> this area is what the coastal area looked like before it was built up. As it got crowded, people moved into the area. If you look at it from the air, the whole area is covered with water. It's all lakes. And people have built developments centered around [sic] the lakes—all with golf courses. These developments are now the suburbs of Orlando. They are different from anything I ever had to represent before. I had lots of small towns, but no bedroom communities. And they are younger than I'm used to. When I first drove around in Clermont [Lake County's largest town] I was struck by what I saw—basketball hoops and minivans.

Students of political change highlighted Clermont as an example of the county-wide "empty nester retreat of elderly constituents."[83] It was a new kind of constituency. "They are Republican, but I don't know, maybe . . ." she added hopefully.

A cordial luncheon, plus a Q and A session (testing her views on various issues) took place in the community's clubhouse building overlooking a lake and a golf course. It was, I conjectured, not the most congenial context for her—an affluent retirement setting with a dozen or so corporate people. And the atmosphere could not have been more different than from her homegrown, enthusiastic, and less prosperous looking kickoff rally two days before.

The woman who introduced her said several times, "She's a friend of business" as if that was the main message. But I sensed no special enthusiasm. The six men at my table talked exclusively about University of Florida football. The only mention of politics came during dessert, when one finally took notice of me and said, "I hate Ginny Brown-Waite." I did not know, of course, what was talked about one on one before and after lunch. No doubt they would find a Ways and Means member of some interest to them. And no doubt some contributions were involved. For me, however, the meeting was an indicator that a ton of new time-consuming, person-to-person slogging in unfamiliar environs lay ahead.

In her end-of-my-visit rankings, the congresswoman placed the event fairly high—in third place, both for enjoyment and politics. It was enjoyable because "I met new people." It was helpful because "we made inroads into new territory." Her modest goals and upbeat appraisal only strengthened my dominant impression that she faced a daunting electoral task in her new territory.

Driving away, she mused about her likely problems in her new, nearby Polk County slice of "nowhere":

> I haven't a clue what's there. There's a large swampy area, and everything is just built up around it. That's going to be the hardest part to get into. . . . I don't know how I'm going to get in there. There is no cohesiveness there, no community. There are no Rotary Clubs or Chambers [of Commerce]. It is all rural area around the swamp, plus closed communities. There are 52,000 people, and 31,000 of them are voters. I'll need a lot of help reaching them.

I asked if the balance of issues would be different in these new places. "I don't think so," she said, "all of them will be interested in Social Security and Medicare—the big issues in my district. Of course, I won't know until I start hearing from them." She speculated that water problems, too, would be important to people in areas of new homes, and that her expertise and legislative accomplishments in that policy area would be helpful. So, too, might her teaching experience. "I think I can get into the closed communities through education," she said hopefully.

She had been given a lot of very unfamiliar territory. For a representative who depended heavily on personal relationships, gains in small group rapport, let alone threshold familiarity, promised to be a very hard adjustment slog.

That evening, the *Citrus County Chronicle* held a nonpartisan, all-candidates forum at which all local and national candidates were given a few minutes to make their pitch to a broad audience of about one hundred fifty people—some proportion of which, as usual, were campaign staffers of the candidates. The congresswoman talked about her legislative ideas and the activity of her staff on behalf of senior citizens and veterans—with special emphasis on new clinics for veterans and affordable prescription drugs for all. And she touted her position on the Ways and Means Committee.

> I do all the taxes for the country and all the trade issues for the country. I do Medicare and Social Security and a big part of the budget. Sixty-five percent of the money we spend goes through my committee—75 percent of everything you need, we touch. It's a great position for solving problems. But I don't just come back here at election time. I come home every weekend, and I'm always out and about every weekend in your communities. I like to stay close to people.

In her ranking of events, she placed the forum in fourth place for enjoyment, but in first place for political impact. "Because of the numbers," she said, "and the fact that they were all voters who took the time to come out. And because they are all in my district."

The morning after the forum, she unloaded, privately, on her opponent's performance. "Last night at the forum, she did something that made me mad as hell. She took my program, my proposal, my bipartisan amendment (on prescription drug coverage for Medicare recipients) that I got through the Ways and Means Committee; and she announced it as her proposal. Can you believe it—just stole it and called it her idea." When a reporter asked her the next day whether she, Karen, wasn't moving toward her opponent on the issues and becoming more conservative, Thurman said, "Well, she's taken my solution to the prescription drug problem—all of it—and called it her own. So it looks to me more like she's moving more toward me than I'm moving toward her. Wouldn't you say that?"

The incumbent knew she faced an experienced and resourceful challenger, a person she neither liked nor respected. She described her opponent as a politician who played hardball, kept score, tended to make enemies, and was altogether different from herself in those respects. "A lot of people who know her don't like her. . . . She's not the kind of person you'd want to have in a legislature. You wouldn't want a person like that in Congress. There are too many of these already." They were the judgments of a person-to-person politician and an institutionally oriented legislator. She did not, however, dwell on the subject.

Our last day began poorly for me in the town of Bushnell, county seat of newly added Sumter County. Driving there, I made a wrong turn and arrived as her five-person Kiwanis Club breakfast was breaking up. And I was banned from the sheriff's personal tour of his law enforcement facilities that followed. In her ranking of events, the breakfast was tied for last in political importance, but ranked fifth in personal enjoyment. "I like small groups where you can talk and get to know people." She ranked her time spent with the county sheriff, however, in second place on both counts. "When someone that important takes that much personal interest and everyone takes so much time, it has to be important. All of the law enforcement people were there. He took a lot of pleasure in showing me around. It's an important new county." As we left, she traded quips with the sheriff's helicopter pilot, then said to me, "I thought my comeback was a pretty good one, didn't you? I love to go back and forth with people that way." I had long since been convinced.

Leaving my car in Bushnell for later pick up, we headed for a Kiwanis Club luncheon in newly acquired Dade City. On the way, we dropped in for a quick visit with an old friend, now a judge. "Do you like the job?" he asked. "I love it. I love it," she said. "Of course, there are frustrations. But I'm getting some things done." Dade City is the county seat for Pasco County—home to her biggest chunk of new territory—with 140,000 former Brown-Waite constituents in its central and eastern regions. When asked about this sizeable population, she was upbeat. "Most of that area is still agricultural, and we have strong support in agriculture."[84]

The Dade City luncheon was better attended than breakfast—two tables, ten people each. It did have a little agricultural flavor—I counted ten pick up trucks in the parking lot. She talked as usual about her position on Ways and Means—in language similar to that which she used at her brief forum talk the night before. The Q and A covered a wide range of topics. Many revolved around post-9/11 congressional action—the Patriot Act, homeland security, customs policy, Coast Guard funding—and the looming decision over war in Iraq. The question period took on a conservative tone on spending and a hawkish tone on Iraq. There was a good deal of back and forth about the latter.

"There's no doubt about it," she said afterwards. "Iraq is the main issue now. In my district, two-thirds of them want to 'go get Iraq.'" During the discussion, she reminded the group that her father had spent twenty-four years in the Air Force and had been a tail gunner in a B-52. And afterward, she said, "My strong feeling for the military helps me with people who might otherwise think of me as too liberal, people who just want to bomb Iraq. It gives me credibility with people like those at my table—who think that a woman doesn't know anything about the military or about war." But she did not commit herself.

She asked for my impression of the conversation. I said that I thought the older World War II veteran there had hit the nail on the head when he cautioned that the American people were not prepared for war, that "they have no idea what war is like," and that "they are just playing at war, hoping that it can all be done without casualties." She nodded agreement. "Like a lot of military people who do understand casualties," I noted, "I think she is not gung ho about Iraq," but that "she is in no sense a dove on Iraq." I never did get a clear statement of her thinking or her position. And, of course, she never had to cast a vote in the matter. The luncheon brought fairly low rankings for the visit—sixth in personal enjoyment, seventh in political importance. It was more of an indicator for me than for her.

Driving away from the Kiwanis luncheon, she told a story that exemplified the hopeful side of her campaign ledger. A Farm Bureau leader who had actively opposed Thurman on the issue of estate tax reduction was at the luncheon. He favored total repeal; she favored moderate revision. He was a Republican preparing to vote in the upcoming Republican primary. At her invitation, they had lunch and discussed various compromise positions, to no conclusion. "I also invited him to an event we were having nearby the following week," she continued. "He said 'no'; but much to my surprise, he came. And just before lunch today, he said to me, 'You've got my vote.' Then he asked me, 'Do you know why?' And I couldn't believe it. He said, 'I saw you dancing at the party and I said to myself, I want to vote for a real person for my representative.' He's going to vote for me because I was dancing!"

A local reporter had described her similarly as "the girl next door."[85] And that down-to-earth description—as "a real person"—came close to my own. A female House colleague had once said to me, "I love Karen Thurman. We'll be sitting in her office, and she'll pick up the phone and talk to a constituent. She's so direct and so plain. What you see is what you get. I love her."

In both places—and this is the point—her natural interpersonal skills were foundation stones of her success and of her authenticity in political life. She was liked as a politician and she was respected as a legislator. And she was easy in both roles. Only in public speech-making did she ever seem unnatural or uncomfortable. In her presentation of self to her constituents, she was a neighborly "legislator next door."

Her 2002 preoccupation was, of course, the campaign. During my visit, she worried most—on the surface anyway—about money. When I asked her, "What people would you expect to be your strongest, thick-and-thin, do-or-die supporters?" her answer was more about money than voters. "With or without Gainesville?" she answered.

> With Gainesville [it would be] the university folks. They love me. . . . But without [Gainesville] I don't know. I just don't know. I'd have to think about that. I rely on the PACs; and I don't know whether the PACs would be with me. The health care folks and veterans would be. In Citrus [County] there's a group of contributors. But given that we're the second poorest district in the state, I don't know where the money would come from.

To an unusual degree, she would be financially dependent on political action committees beyond her constituency—and on the Democratic Party, both state and national.

On my last day, we arrived early for a "hob nob" event in a gated community. She pulled into a vacant roadside area and spent an hour and a half making phone calls to various interest groups asking for money. With the primary season not yet over, she was hopeful of landing contributions that would not count against a group's general election totals. I noted,

> While we sat waiting, she called one PAC after another . . . it was grueling. Over and over, she would be frustrated trying to (A) get to the right person—half ended up with callbacks and (B) trying to get them to ante up a little more. Despite some rejections, she kept her good humor. To one inquiry, she answered, "Personally, I'm great. I'm having fun getting out and meeting people. But I hate raising money. I'd take walking up to a stranger's front door any day."

She told these likely contributors that "this is the biggest Republican target in Florida," or "this is the number one targeted district in Florida." "In spite of that," I noted, "she gets no special treatment. And worse, she feels she is being neglected." Again, my picture of an out-of-the-way, indistinct, and benighted district came into play.

"When the DCCC (Democratic Congressional Campaign Committee) had their [fund-raising] event in Miami," she said,

> They didn't even send me one invitation. And when I went anyway, they didn't even introduce me. And I'm the number one targeted district in Florida! Now, Tom Daschle [Senate majority leader] is coming to Miami next week; and all the money will be soaked up in other districts—not mine. I need it the most; and I get the least. It just doesn't make any sense. . . . I'm going back there [to Washington] and kick butt with the DCCC. They don't have a clue about what's going on in Florida.

And she added a most uncharacteristic comment. "If it were [Florida Congressmen] Peter Deutsch or Jim Davis or Alan Boyd, you don't think there would be a problem, do you. I hate to say it, but I think that it has a lot to do with it. I really do."

I noted, "She's very frustrated with the money chase. She rarely pushes the 'woman button.'" It was rare; but so was her sense of financial stress.

The indoor "hob nob" event took us to the second upscale, gated, retirement community of my visit—new territory, once again, for the incumbent legislator. This time, all candidates set up campaign display tables to meet residents informally. In a secret straw vote of the attending residents, she lost by 47–36. She ranked the event third in political importance because, "I made some good connections." But she ranked it dead last in personal enjoyment because "It hurts when you lose." She also expressed displeasure with the work of her staff. "They should have been out talking to people instead of sitting in the booth." The problems of her one-by-one vote quest in these new-style parts of "nowhere" still looked overwhelming.

Driving away, she returned with emotion, to her money problem. "We are doing things we never had to do before—raise $500,000 in soft money. . . . I don't think I can do it [all by myself]. If I have to, I'll try. But if I can't do it, we'll just have to cut back on our plans. I don't know how we can do it; and it makes me crazy. It makes me crazy." There was a noticeable dip in her usual infectious enthusiasm. And the conversation ended on a downbeat note.

A couple of weeks after I left, her office sent me her basic campaign brochure. On the front was a picture of her smiling with a constituent. Underneath was this quotation from a local reporter's appraisal: "Thurman is the kind of congresswoman every voter dreams about." I went back to the reporter's original article and found his explanation. "I'm not talking about the politics of her votes in committee or on the House floor," he wrote.

> That stuff naturally is debatable and I'm not taking sides here on those issues. But Thurman has a folksy demeanor that just sits well with people. She's friendly. She gets along well with young and old: Florida crackers and snowbirds. Thurman's people have a reputation for helping people cut through red tape for veteran's benefits, prescription drugs and medicare issues. She is in the community, and often doesn't hog the spotlight at functions. It's normal to see Thurman at an event with 200 people and she knows nearly everybody in the room. She recognizes those folks with a handshake or a few words. It's sincere. Thurman would behave the same way if she worked at Florida Power. She generally avoids the attack mode. . . . The people of this district keep electing Thurman because she is one of them.[86]

These were the sorts of personal strengths I had observed, too. She was everyone's next-door neighbor—of whom it could be said that "to know her is to like her." But that rendition served to frame, once again, the key question: Could 250,000 people whom she had never represented get to know her and come to like her enough to vote for her in a few weeks?

An Accounting

When the results of Karen Thurman's reelection campaign came, it was over. And the answer to my last question was: They couldn't. She had lost 51 percent to 49 percent, by a margin of 4,241 votes. She carried every county or "chunk" that remained intact from her previous district. And she lost every county or "chunk" that was new to her. Most of the latter had been represented in the state senate by her opponent.[87] Voters from brand-new Republican Lake County, with their 5,734 vote margin for Brown-Waite, took credit for making the difference.[88]

Interpretations were uniform in attributing the result to the pro-Republican redistricting. President George W. Bush had lost Thurman's old district in 2000 with 46 percent of that vote. In 2004, the Republican at the top of the ticket, Governor Jeb Bush, carried the new district with 61 percent of the vote and led Brown-Waite by 11,000 votes. The governor carried every county that Thurman carried, and he led Brown-Waite in every county that she carried. Analysts credited Bush family coattails as critical. "In the end," one said, "I think having Jeb Bush at the head of the ticket helped Ginny Brown-Waite across the finish line."[89] And another said, "The President's endorsement probably put Ginny Brown-Waite over the top."[90] A Washington analysis concluded that "a large GOP political tailwind provided by Gov. Jeb Bush's overwhelming reelection pushed Brown-Waite across the finish line in the lead."[91]

For her part, Thurman ran 8,000 votes ahead of the Democratic candidate for governor. Even with "two times as much money," analysts concluded that Thurman "still would have lost because of things outside her control."[92] Her new district was born Republican and it voted Republican.

As it turned out, Representative Thurman did not lack for money. It came late; but it came sufficiently. Given her financial worries when I was there, it is worth noting that she did eventually raise the half-million dollars she worried about—and more, indeed, than she ever raised before. She outspent Brown-Waite by $1.79 million to $858,000. Both candidates ended up receiving two-thirds of their contributions from PACs, with a majority of their donors coming from out of state.[93] Local analysts concluded that at best, Thurman's financial advantage allowed her to keep it close.[94] It could not change the political reality: The Republicans now owned Florida's Fifth District. And they had secured ownership the only way they could: by removing enough of Thurman's longtime supporters.

Publicly, Representative Thurman took her loss philosophically. "I don't know that there's anything I could have done differently. . . . I had no control over the fact that I couldn't be in the district because I was in session."[95] She chalked up her loss to a success for Republican redistricting—to "political gerrymandering."[96] And she added that, "For me, it was gratifying to know that the folks I was closest to still believed in me." "Who knows," she said. "I might even enjoy retirement. I think I've been a pretty lucky person. As my grandmother always told me, 'There's a reason for everything.'" She announced no plans, but said "I'm not closing any doors to any ideas that might be available to me." The hardest part, she said, was "saying good-bye over and over to friends and staff. . . . The office always felt like family."[97]

Commentary

Jim Ross, the veteran *St. Petersburg Times* political reporter, wrote, "She dedicated herself to constituent service and gained many admirers in the process."[98] A Florida political science professor, Susan McManus, summed up, "She was superb at constituent services. Within her district, she will always be remembered as being very, very accessible."[99] A senior citizen activist agreed. "I guess my feeling is there never was anybody who sought her assistance that didn't get it. She was really incredible as far as her constituents go."[100]

In the circumstances of 2002, however, her proven person-to-person strengths were not enough. Moreover, the more she depended on her personal abilities for her political support, the harder it became for her to impress those abilities one on one, on the large number of new, Republican-leaning voters. They did not know her, and they resided across an extended territory that she did not know. There were no policy or partisan shortcuts available to her—except television, a medium not known for major conversion effects. In 2002, time was what she needed to sell herself to new constituents in unfamiliar territory. And she had too little of it.

In the divisive context of contemporary American public life—the increasing dominance of partisanship in the drawing of congressional districts and in congressional decision making—it was the way of the political world that Karen Thurman would lose. In time-honored fashion, her electoral playing field at home had been deliberately and legally changed from one that was tipped in her favor to one that was tipped against her. Looking back to her own complicity in drawing the district's original lines favorably—and looking at her opponent's complicity in redrawing the district lines favorably—a biblical conclusion may be apt: that "(S)he who lives by the sword shall die by the sword."

Of special interest to this observer was the reaction of the *Washington Post's* congressional correspondent, who used the national results to write about three especially close Florida congressional elections. The reporter's announced topic was "Florida Republicans (who) managed to win House seats by running in districts they helped to shape." Yet she did so without any mention whatever of Ginny Brown-Waite's victory in Florida's Fifth District.[101]

By any measure, Representative Thurman's defeat was the most noteworthy Florida redistricting story. And certainly it was a prime case where the eventual winner had "helped to shape" the new district.

The reporter's postelection blind eye to Florida's Fifth District brought this observer back to the earliest string of contextual puzzles. And back, too, to Thurman's own frustrating description of "nowhere." Like the proverbial tree in the forest, she had fallen, and (almost) nobody had heard. At the beginning of her congressional career in 1994 and at the end of her career in 2002, Washington commentators—who had purported to help us understand a cluster of "first-term women" in 1994 and "losing incumbents" in 2002—failed to do so. From the beginning to the end of this account, it seems Washington's journalists had been out of touch.

For someone who has written to urge Washington journalists to spend more time "soaking and poking" in congressional constituencies, this failure supports the argument for doing so. Assuming that political scientists want to understand the politics of representation, there is added evidence and reason here indicating why we should go do some of it ourselves.

Postscript

In 2005, former Representative Karen Thurman was elected as Chair of the Florida State Democratic Party. She retired from that position in November 2010.

Addendum I

Two Representatives: Two Connection Patterns

Representatives Karen Thurman and Glenn Poshard were chosen for study independently. But they had enough in common and in contrast to encourage comparison. Both were open, down-to-earth, unpretentious individuals. They took their work seriously and worked hard at the tasks they valued most. Neither one made a noteworthy splash inside the House. They came; they set their goals; they fought their fights in and out of Washington; and they left. They were easy to travel with and to learn from.

Both members were Democrats in their fifties; and both were schoolteachers by profession. Both came to Congress directly from service in their state legislatures. Both represented large, multicounty districts, heavily populated with economically struggling individuals and communities. Both lived with the perils of redistricting. Their roll call vote patterns placed them close to one another in the more conservative one-third of House Democrats.[1]

Not surprisingly—since they had accepted the presence of an academic stranger—both of them had open, "what you see is what you get" personalities. Neither one had any sense of entitlement. They had worked hard to get where they were. And they had modest aspirations. They were acquainted with one another. The "colleague" who approached Karen Thurman in the House chamber to ask: "What have you two got going? He has such a good time"—was Glenn Poshard.

Except for the impact of sheer constituency size—which had to be experienced to be appreciated—the constituency similarities listed above could have been known without visiting the two districts.

Learning what matters to each person and what guides each person's representational relationships, however, requires more. It requires observation and conversation with each individual in the context of a legally defined geographical constituency and a recognizable reelection constituency. One member-constituency relationship had strong personal roots. The other was a recent transplant. In one place, a producing economy dominated. In the other place, consumption economics prevailed.

Place was the beginning of understanding in each case. Representative Poshard had been steeped from birth in the textured problems of his dominantly rural, small-town, working-class Illinois district. It was culturally conservative and politically Democratic. Its economy was heavily dependent on natural resources—coal, oil, timber, waterways, and agricultural land. He called it a "blue-collar" district.

His strength came from his total immersion in that place and from the diligence with which he tended to it. His constant concern was jobs. He operated with a strong—even stern—sense of duty; and he connected to his constituents with compassion and empathy. He represented settled communities. His travel talk was a running commentary on his relationships with, and his worries about, the many small places and the varied economic interests that appeared outside his car (or pick up truck) window.

Representative Thurman was a latecomer to Florida and to her congressional playing field—which she, as a state legislator, had helped construct for herself. It was a fast-growing, nondescript constituency—filled with a fairly random collection of lower-to-middle income newcomers. Whereas her colleague's Southern Illinois communities were old and settled, Thurman's Northern Florida communities were new and ever changing. And she did not—nor could she—express any of his lifelong attachments to a place. Her district was heavily populated by recently arrived retirees—many of them military veterans. They lived close to the margins of income and of health; and they worried a lot about the availability and adequacy of Social Security and Medicare.

A signal difference in the Thurman and Poshard representational relationships came from her especially strong interest in the legislative elements of the job and his especially strong interest in the representational parts of the job. From that difference in perspectives and preferences came two different ambitions, two different presentations of self to constituents, two different bases of constituent trust, and two different patterns of authenticity.

Whenever Karen Thurman had the opportunity to direct our travel talk, or to answer my favorite all-purpose, open-ended question "How's it going?" she usually answered with a reference to her legislative activity and to the craft of legislation. In that activity, she came across as a busy and gregarious participant.

She often discussed her activities and her relationships inside the House by comparing them with her previous experiences inside the Florida State Senate. She wanted to talk about her workaday relationships with her fellow House members—about policy interests shared, coalitions created, amendments worked on, collegial norms observed, and the facilitation of personal relationships and prospects for success. When she was at home, she wanted to tell her constituents (and me) about her legislative involvements—what she was working on and fighting for and what she had accomplished inside the legislature for the benefit of her district's needy areas, groups, and individuals. She was, first of all, a legislator.

By contrast, whenever Glenn Poshard shaped our "How's it going?" travel talk, he focused heavily on his homegrown representational prescriptions and on the factors—personal and cultural—that kept him close to his constituents. Because he was so deeply embedded in a recognizable place—Southern Illinois—his various constituency connections had a laser-like focus on the needs and the activities of the many small, recognizable, and struggling places in his territory. His supersaturation of the district with staff allocations provided convincing evidence of his perceptions and his priorities.

His textbook representational canons and his lifelong constituency immersion drew, at the margins, unreserved praise at home. He was unfailingly on the job. His flawless attendance record, his unbroken pattern of weekend trips home, his busy round of widely scattered local meetings, his determined resistance to PAC influences, and his philosophical devotion to term limits underpinned his constituency strength.

By noteworthy contrast, there were few, if any, mentions of his participatory activity on Capitol Hill. In contrast to Karen Thurman, Glenn Poshard never, to my notes and recollections, mentioned his apprenticeship in the Illinois state legislature. Similarly, while she talked constantly about her various friendships and alliances with specific individuals inside the Congress, he did not. Except for a couple of passing references to Democratic House Leader Dick Gephardt, Representative Poshard did not discuss any of his House colleagues by name.

He felt strongly, and he talked constantly, about his obligations to his constituents. And he readily claimed credit for numerous constituency projects—talking broadly and almost philosophically—about them. Yet he never discussed or explained "how I did it" or who "I worked with to get it." He pointed out large committee projects that benefited his district. But he never tracked any personal or collegial accomplishments inside his committee.

My main impression was, therefore, that Representative Poshard probably got in line inside his large distributive-style committee, took his turn, and fought hard for his fair share of whatever money for projects there was to get. For lack of any Illinois travel talk about inside committee bargaining or about any maneuvering on the House floor, it remains a best guess. Whatever the inside story might be, the representative centric/legislative centric contrast with Karen Thurman was stark.

A question that arises out of these comparisons is whether Glenn Poshard's self-imposed term limits restriction might explain his legislative behavior as well as his representational behavior. Why, if it was his intention to leave on a certain date, would he invest in—and why would any colleague pay attention to—the cultivation of person-to-person influence inside the House? Which, we might wonder, is chicken and which is egg? The view adopted here is that both behavior patterns stem from the same set of ideas and preferences that emphasized citizen participation and public service.

In our time together, Glenn Poshard never expressed any desire to be an active legislative player in Washington or to pursue a career there in order to increase his influence on any public policy. When he spoke to his constituents, he was articulate, passionate, and convincing to a degree unmatched by his Florida colleague. He was a persuasive public speaker. And perhaps his floor speeches were persuasive, too. Yet he never expressed any interest in their effect on his colleagues. And he seemed never to have thought in terms of making a career for himself in the House.

His political ambition, as I saw it, was to set the highest quality representational standard while in office, to work tirelessly to fulfill his representational tasks, and, after serving a preset limit of five terms, to return to devote his considerable heart-and-mind talents to other kinds of work in his beloved and benighted section of Illinois.

The two total strangers I had met by chance, one in Florida and one in Illinois, showed me two very different perspectives on their world and their work. The midwesterner presented himself to me primarily as an active representative. And he worried most about his representational choices. The Floridian presented herself to me primarily as an active legislator. And she worried most about her legislative choices.

How one might explain their differences in outlook, calculation, and behavior is a larger question. In the two cases at hand, sheer length of residency and depth of attachment to a constituency suggests itself as a relevant factor. Representative Poshard was more deeply embedded and attached to his constituents by lifelong experience, personal and family, in his district. And he was closely attuned to the needy economy of his home territory. He emphasized—and epitomized—representation by personal attachment to the people of that place.

Karen Thurman's home place defied easy definition. Understandably, therefore, her attachments to place were much less defining. For her, helping to make good public policy was the dominating concern and one that distinguished her among her colleagues. So too, and relatedly, was her very natural cultivation of effective interpersonal working relationships—even across party lines—inside the House. Unlike her Illinois colleague, she talked a great deal about her legislative activities, and she placed a high value on her facilitating networks inside the institution.

Despite their substantial surface commonalities, and despite their similar voting patterns, therefore, Glenn Poshard and Karen Thurman were—as I saw them—quite different working representatives. They were different with respect to their personalities, preferences, experiences, perspectives, priorities, and practices. They were different in their perceptions of, their presentations to, and their connections with their constituents. For political scientists, they display two sets of career ambitions, two workplace patterns, two trust-building relationships, and two authenticities.

— 5 —

Jim Greenwood

Moderate Republican

Suburban Playing Field

In 1994, the research year that had begun in Karen Thurman's sprawling, multicounty Florida constituency ended in a compact, single-county constituency in Pennsylvania. The trip had taken the researcher from an artifactual and unorganized 4,200-square-mile territory to a 600-square-mile cluster of identifiable and interrelated parts. The new playing field was Pennsylvania's Eighth Congressional District, located in the suburbs of Philadelphia. Ninety-eight percent of it was contained within a single well-bounded, historically rich, and politically organized place, Bucks County.[1] The county, in turn, divided itself into three well-recognized sections—Upper Bucks, Middle Bucks (a.k.a. Central Bucks), and Lower Bucks.[2] Each of the three was further divided into townships, which doubled as election districts.

This compact constituency was represented by freshman Republican James Greenwood. We became acquainted in his home place in the fall of 1994. The relationship grew from wariness to acceptance to openness. It ended, after three election-time visits, in the fall of 1998.

Congressman Greenwood was a purposeful choice. In contrast to the Thurman and Poshard selections, he was handpicked by the author from *The Almanac of American Politics: 1994*.[3] Having spent time, fairly recently, in two rural, small-town districts with two conservative Republicans—one in South Carolina, one in Indiana[4]—my objective was to find a representative who fit a very different Republican mixture—northeastern, suburban, and moderate. The first-term

Pennsylvanian seemed made to order. In the manner of Karen Thurman, and with the same successful outcome, he had influenced the boundary-drawing deliberations as a member of the state legislature.

His entry in the 1994 *Almanac* told us that Representative Greenwood had unseated a six-term incumbent Democrat in 1992 with 52 percent of the vote. Two biographical notes drew special attention. First, there was his early employment as a "case worker" in the Bucks County Child and Youth Services Agency. Second was his "legislative experience" of twelve years in the Pennsylvania state legislature—six in the House and six in the Senate. He was described as "a shrewd campaigner" with "an unusual background for a Republican . . . as a social worker." "His real world experience working with troubled families," it suggested, "should make him distinctive in Republican ranks." His own description of a legislator's job was especially appealing. "You do it by paying attention to detail. You do it by amendments in committee. And you do it by offering good ideas that are hard to resist."[5] From a distance, he came across as an active legislative player, a nonlawyer with unusual GOP interests.

The campaign in suburban Philadelphia was marked by the total absence of competitive political activity. No messages awaited me at the designated motel in the Bucks County seat, Doylestown. No phone calls came; and there was no answer at the Greenwood campaign headquarters. The next morning, there were three people at headquarters. The congressman, they said, was out campaigning "somewhere" and would return "sometime." Helpfully, however, they pointed me to their campaign news files. And my time was usefully spent reading clips, listening to conversation, and joining the group in folding and stamping invitations to an end-of-the-campaign fund-raiser. "The two big (!) problems here," I noted, "are setting Jim's schedule for half a day on Sunday and making name tags for an upcoming fund-raising event! That's what all their campaign conversation is about!"

Representative Greenwood's reelection "campaign" was, at best, leisurely. Which is not to say it was unorganized. The next day, his campaign manager and a fellow staffer provided an unusually helpful lunchtime "heads-up"—combining a lesson in local political geography with a campaign update. They confirmed the impression—from the news clips—that he had no serious opposition. There was a liberal

Democrat labor leader on his left and an Independent Party conservative candidate on his right, neither of whom had generated any heat—not even in a couple of debates. As one measure of the incumbent's confidence, his team had used no television. By comparison, in his initial 1992 campaign he had spent 40 percent ($280,000) of his budget on "electronic media."[6]

Representative Greenwood, his staffers emphasized, had "built the district from the ground up" through his six (three House, three Senate) successful state legislative campaigns. His Eighth Congressional District was—except for a small piece of adjacent Montgomery County—coterminous with Bucks County, which, historically, had been divided into three separate areas—roughly distinguished from one another by economics and politics.

In shorthand, Lower Bucks is adjacent to Philadelphia, tends to be working class, unionized, and leans Democratic. Middle Bucks tends to be middle- to upper-middle class, commuter-oriented, and politically independent. Upper Bucks, furthest from the city, is notably small-town, rural, agricultural, and traditionally Republican. Campaign planners used these three constituency segments as precampaign targets and postcampaign benchmarks.

Jim Greenwood was born and raised in an area straddling Middle and Upper Bucks. From that perspective, he observed, "Bucks County is a textbook case of an agricultural county becoming a suburban county."[7] These various county-level descriptions provided a more useful picture of geopolitical patterning than anything available to me earlier in Karen Thurman's meandering Florida district. As a political place, the Pennsylvania Eighth was, by that contrast, easy to locate and easy to describe.

The Greenwood staffers explained that their major district-wide campaign advertising featured a series of direct mailings to the three parts of the district. And the variety of his mailings served thereafter as an introductory guide to his constituency.

There were five colorful, glossy, large, four-page brochures, each with numerous pictures, a distinctive text, and distinctive covers. They were altogether larger and more attractive and more expensive-looking than anything I had ever seen. Three of the five had been sent exclusively to residents of Lower Bucks—which had voted for his opponent (48 percent to 52 percent) in 1992, and was now his special campaign target. One of the three mailings highlighted five specific job-producing legislative "projects" of his that had been custom tailored to benefit the Lower Bucks area. Of the two other brochures, one went to all voters in Middle and Upper Bucks—and one went only to registered Republican and Independent voters in those same two areas.

His campaign's total reliance on mailed material was a modest indicator of the greater residential stability and the higher education/income levels in this suburban place. And his tripartite mailing program underscored the accepted tripartite subdivision of his constituency. Because specific "mailings" went to specified places, they helped to locate and define subconstituencies.

His five mailings were issue oriented—in a carefully protective way. They portrayed incumbent Greenwood as a frugal, antitax, budget-cutting reformer who refused to accept PAC contributions and who was also a welfare critic, a consumer advocate, and an environmental protector. Conspicuously absent, however, from all five brochures was any hint of his two most controversial policy positions—pro-choice on abortion and pro-gun-control. Those two high-profile policy stands—and his related votes—were at once a noteworthy source of his intra-Republican opposition and a noteworthy source of his Democratic and Independent support.

Overall, district registration was 52 percent Republican, 38 percent Democrat, and 10 percent other. In 1988, Bucks County had voted solidly for Republican George H.W. Bush. But in 1992, it had voted narrowly for Democrat Bill Clinton. Electorally, "the Pennsylvania Eighth" was a marginal congressional district.

"The sense I got from our lunch talk," I noted, "is that Jim fits the district, because he is (in their words) moderate. All previous Republican challengers to Democrat Peter Kostmayer, his manager said, "were too conservative." To which he added, "The mail Jim gets is of two kinds. 'Jim, you're too conservative,' or 'Jim, you're too liberal.' So he must be doing something right." Their informative luncheon talk reinforced my earliest impressions: Representative Greenwood's reelection had never been in doubt, and his campaign had effectively ended. In time, I would learn more from his campaign aides than from their counterparts in any of the other constituencies in this study.

Inspection of their news clips revealed a consistency of media focus and of judgment that had not been prominent in either the Karen Thurman or the Glenn Poshard districts. The difference suggests that constituency characteristics do affect media coverage, impact, and judgment. In this case, territorial compactness served to focus local media attention on one recognizable congressional player. The Greenwood collection of "news clips" came from a cluster of three suburban newspapers and one central city newspaper. All of them, I was told, had a significant readership in the Eighth District. At first notice, they seemed to agree on the issues and the stakes of the campaign. And all of them had given similarly favorable endorsements of the congressman's first term.

The locally important *Bucks County Courier* praised "his stature, his record and his potential," plus "his social conscience, tempered with fiscal responsibility." "Although a freshman," they wrote,

> he became a player in the health care reform debate, working toward a realistic alternative that serves the public need without a big government, big brother approach. He does not just jump on the popular "tough on crime" bandwagon, but seeks to address the root causes of dysfunctional families . . . (he is) active in causes closest to his heart: advancing constructive approaches to welfare reform, health care and the crisis of pregnant teenagers.[8]

The attentive next-door *Allentown Morning Call* commented that "where Representative Greenwood comes down is never far from the moderate Republican analysis he promised the first time he entered legislative office 14 years ago. If every member of Congress applied his depth of analysis, Congress would work better."[9]

A short, supportive editorial in the more regionally oriented *Philadelphia Inquirer* observed that he "has started to develop on Capitol Hill the kind of respect that he earned in 12 years as a state legislator. Hard working, he studies the issues and stays in touch. (And his) voting record generally reflects the interests of his constituents."[10] A few days later, the *Inquirer* added "independent-minded" and "fiscally responsible" to reinforce their earlier endorsement.[11]

Local journalists had a common idea of his developing Washington career. And they were extending a solid measure of early approval. Their summaries depicted a prototypical "moderate Republican." He was an antitax, cut-spending, balance-the-budget conservative. He was a welfare and health care reformer. And he was a pro-choice, pro-gun-control, pro-environmental liberal. The local media defined him and judged him as an active, issue-oriented, and ideologically moderate representative. And his policy preferences dominated their editorial views.

The congressman later identified these three newspapers—plus the county-based *Intelligencer*—as "the big four" in his political world. "Every six months, we arrange for me to visit with each of those editorial boards," he said. "I don't want to get out of touch with their thinking. And I want to establish a personal connection. *The Inquirer* editorial board is especially intelligent and broad gauged. A meeting with them is like an oral exam."

I had not read or heard House member comments like that in Florida or Illinois. This made Bucks County newspapers a helpful place to begin an acquaintance. The local media were, recognizably, the leading describers, interpreters, and judges of politics and of players in this communication-rich suburban environment. They identified "moderate" politics; and they supported moderate politicians. Newspaper notice, commentary, and approval were central features of politics in his suburban playing field. And the commonalities of their commentary seemed to reflect the coherence of a compact territory.

To the end of my acquaintance, Representative Greenwood would be followed by favorable, policy-centered newspaper coverage and judgments. Looking back, a happenstance, first-day exposure to a pile of news clips had a lasting influence on my picture of one person I had chosen to follow. But lacking a similar experience elsewhere, this one had no comparative punch.

Early Learning

When the congressman arrived at campaign headquarters in the late afternoon, he was reminded that "This is the man who is writing the book and will be traveling with you." "I'm sorry I haven't been able to spend more time with you," he said. "Thanks for letting me come," I said. We shook hands. He went to shave. When he returned, he had cut his face and was trying to stop the bleeding.

Soon, he motioned for me to come along with him and his campaign manager. "What's your name?" he asked. As we rode along, I was given the third degree. *Congressman:* "I don't mind you studying me as a congressman. But, frankly, there is nothing in it for me. And, politically, it could be a risk. What are you doing? How did you choose your people?" *Manager:* "Is this your first book or second or what? Who publishes them? How are you funding them? What are the ground rules?" *Congressman:* "This is what I want the ground rules to be. Anything I say in public is fair game. Everything I say in the car is off the record— for your use anecdotally and for background—unless I say it is on the record." *Fenno:* "Fine, provided that if I come to you and ask you explicitly if I can put it on the record?" *Congressman:* "Yes, if I give you my permission." It served as a cautionary "heads up." He never repeated it. And I never followed up.

"He worried (about my project) more than any person I've ever been with," I noted. But, in time, I came to interpret his early quizzing as an indication of his own determination to "make it" as a moderate-to-liberal "player" inside a conservative-leaning local Republican Party. His third-degree questioning indicated an acute awareness of the vulnerabilities he would take with him into any such intraparty political effort. Put differently, his hesitations had nothing to do with me. But they had everything to do with his own ambitions. As I came to know him, Jim Greenwood would always be looking ahead and thinking "up."

Two events were on his evening schedule—a Planned Parenthood cocktail party in the Middle Bucks Township of Lower Makefield and a Republican Party dinner in Upper Bucks for the Republican candidate for US Senate.

"This group should be a good group for me," he said as we walked into the first event. "I have been strongly and totally pro-choice throughout my career in the House. I voted against the Hyde Amendment (prohibiting the use of federal funds for abortion). People here loved Kostmayer. Now, I ought to pick up (their) support." "In Lower Makefield Township," he added later, "there is a huge difference between a normal Republican vote and a good Republican vote. These people are affluent, well educated, and they pay close attention to the issues. When I was in the state senate, I made a special effort to get a better than normal vote out of Lower Makefield. It was a mark of success when we did."

On the way to the Republican dinner, the congressman explained, "I vote pro-choice and Rick Santorum (the Republican Senate candidate) votes pro-life. I voted for the (pro-gun- control) Brady Bill and the (anti-assault-weapon) crime bill. He voted against both of them. Despite our differences on those two issues, I'm supporting Rick because I believe, at this juncture in our history, it is very important for the Republicans to take control of Congress." Then he disappeared into the crowd.

His hard-line position on these two party-splitting votes contrasted notably with Karen Thurman's willingness to give ground to her conservative constituents on the same two issues. And they promised a more issue-centric picture of politics than I had encountered in either Florida or Illinois.

Catching Up

The next day, Representative Greenwood's leisurely schedule began with a breakfast pep talk to party workers in the district's most hotly contested state senate race. It was followed by some shopping center campaigning, a side trip to do a political favor, and a meeting in a private home with a group of volunteers. All four events took place in the campaign-targeted Lower Bucks section of the county, the same target as his campaign literature.

Driving down from Doylestown to his partisan pep talk in Republican Bensalem, a more relaxed congressman filled in some early steps in his political career. He began with a preliminary redistricting battle when he was a state senator angling to move up to Congress.

> Fifty percent of my battle for the US House seat took place in the fight to preserve the Bucks County Congressional District during the 1991 redistricting by the state legislature. [Incumbent US Representatives] Peter Kostmayer (D) and Don Ritter (R), who had the districts next door, cooked up a plan that would give each of them a safe district—by dividing Bucks County. . . . The Democrats told the Republicans they could do anything they wanted in redistricting if they would just give Kostmayer a safe seat. As someone who already represented much of Bucks County, I did not want it cut up. And Representative Paul McHale (D),

who eventually defeated Ritter and who served with me in the (state) legislature, did not want that either. . . . We worked together. It was a hellish, brutal war that went on around the clock till we won.[12]

Like Karen Thurman, Jim Greenwood had worked effectively inside the state legislature to obtain, for himself, a winnable playing field. In both cases, proven precongressional legislative ability was a forecast of effective legislative performance as a member of Congress.

About his initial decision to run for Congress, the Pennsylvanian said,

I had been watching (Democratic incumbent Peter) Kostmayer for some time. When I talked to people about it they would say, "If you do it, you'll only get bloodied and lose your good reputation. You don't have a single mark against you. Why get dragged through the mud. Wait and try for governor—or something." But two things happened. First, Kostmayer opposed the Gulf War, which was fine, that was his choice. But as soon as the yellow ribbons came out, there he was leading every parade, riding in the open car waving. Then later he began to say "why the hell did we go there anyway?" It bothered me that he was so duplicitous. Second, his former wife . . . said that she supported me; and she told me that the thought of my running "has given Pete nightmares for ten years!"

I believe that a decision to run is partly psychological, the feeling that you have an advantage and can win. I thought if I had been giving him nightmares for ten years, I could beat him! Before we announced, we took a poll. I was 12 points behind, 36–24, I think. With his reelection number below 50 percent and several months to go, we thought I could do it. So I jumped into the primary and won.

Then he added, "Guess what? Our postprimary poll showed we were behind by 19 points! ("How come?" "I think he turned up his franking (free mailing) privilege full blast.") When I saw that result, I was dumbfounded. I put it down and went straight to a shopping center to meet voters. I decided if I was going to win, I had to do it retail." It was a predictive choice, too. The congressman and I would do a heavy amount of retail campaigning in suburban shopping centers during our time together. It was his way.

His description of how, as a freshman, he had won an appointment to the much-prized House Committee on Energy and Commerce (E and

C), was extensive. "As usual," he began, "I'll give you the long answer," (and, again, he encouraged me to take notes):

Former Congressman Gary Lee called me the day after the election to congratulate me. He said, "You have to win three campaigns to do this job. The first is the primary and you have won that. The next is the election and you have just won that. The third is to get your committee assignment. And while the other newly elected members are yawning and lounging around, you should get on the plane to Washington and start campaigning for your committee assignment." He had been on the "E and C" Committee and we talked about it and its broad jurisdiction.

When party leader Newt Gingrich called to congratulate me, I talked to him about the E and C Committee. He said it was one of the best committees from which to get PAC money. . . . He also told me that the Republicans ranked committees red, white, and blue and that the three blue committees were the most asked for—Appropriations, Ways and Means, and E and C. So I went to Washington to make my pitch (to the party leadership) for E and C. I liked its broad jurisdiction, because I like the legislative part of the job. I like the substance of legislation. And (in the state legislature) I had been interested in environmental and health legislation.

I went to see Representative Joe McDade, the leader of our Pennsylvania delegation. I wrote a letter to every member of the Committee on Committees; and I went to see every member of that committee. My pitch was that I had defeated Kostmayer, that he was a member of that committee, and that left Pennsylvania without membership; that Kostmayer had come back from defeat once before and that he might very well try to come back again, and that I would be helped greatly in holding the seat if I could be a member of that committee. I think the Republicans considered the defeat of Kostmayer as one of the two biggest upsets of the year.

I also told them I was qualified by my years on the Environmental Committee in the state senate. I talked to people in the associations I had worked with in the senate. I knew I would have trouble with the Texas guy, Bill Archer, because the energy states don't like northeasterners on that committee. So I asked the Sun Oil people to tell him that "Greenwood is okay." And I asked for help from people in the health industry—people with whom I had worked closely in the state senate.

And Joe McDade (senior Pennsylvanian and spokesman for the state's newcomers) was a good horse trader.

His success was testimony to the value of his state legislative experience. As he had explained his choice to a reporter, "It's a legislating committee; and I'm a legislator."[13] "The irony was," he added later, "that after I got on the committee, I pledged not to take a dime of PAC money. Newt Gingrich said to me, 'We gave you the best committee for PACs and you gave it away.'"

His detailed story displayed two personal qualities that became central to his career in the House—preparation and savvy.

Of equal importance, he believed, to his future was a second early decision: his postelection pledge to refuse contributions from political action committees. That pledge would become central to his presentation of self during all of my visits in suburbia. He did not discuss his decision calculus. But newspaper reports of his winning campaign highlighted his TV attacks on his Democratic incumbent opponent for his fifty overdrafts–that is, "bounced political checks"—at the House bank.[14]

During my second trip to the district, the congressman touted the benefits of his refusal to accept PAC money—to a room full of supportive Middle Bucks constituents.

As I guess most of you know, I made a decision soon after I was elected for the first time that I would not accept political action committee funds. It is a very difficult thing to do. There are 435 members of the House, and 24 of us have made the decision to try to go without the PAC money, and half of them are millionaires, and I am not. So we have to rely upon the willingness of individuals, almost all of whom live in the district, to write their own personal checks. It is a liberating thing that you do for me . . . because . . . no matter how hostile the audience may be here in the district, and no matter how controversial and involved with the issues, when I finish my discussion with people, I am able to say, "Listen, one thing you need to know is I don't take any PAC money. So this is a decision that is based on my judgment of what people in our district want, and not based on what a particular interest group is going to offer my campaign." And that usually has a tendency to change the mood in the room because it leads to trust. And all of sudden the suspicion that a congressman is bought and sold dissipates—and now we get down to business, to the substance of the issue. It also enables me to go to Washington and tell the other 411 members of the House who haven't decided to do this that it works, that you can do it, that people will respond if you ask them to. So, I thank you for that.

Afterward, the young state representative who had succeeded to Greenwood's seat in that body came up and introduced himself to me. "I have patterned myself after Jim," he said. "He's my mentor. I figure if I can persuade people in the quiet, soft, gentle way Jim does when he talks to you, I'll be just fine."

The setting for this get-together—a comfortable, suburban home—was a more familiar and a more distinctive campaign venue for Jim Greenwood than it had been for any of the other House members in this study.

A Constituency Day

Private homes and suburban shopping plazas characterized the congressman's playing field. During each of my three visits, we campaigned in shopping centers—as he phrased it—"to meet voters and change minds."

After his breakfast pep talk to his fellow Republicans, we went to a large shopping center where he greeted shoppers and handed out brochures for over an hour in front of K-mart and Acme Market. His comfort level in these two face-to-face places far exceeded his comfort level at either the previous evening's party dinner or his partisan pep talk at breakfast.

As he handed out each piece of literature, he would say, "Hi, I'm Congressman Jim Greenwood. I'd appreciate it if you'd read this when you get home. And if you agree with me, I hope (or I'd appreciate it if) you'll vote for me." "At a shopping center with open shirt and baggy pants," I noted, "Jim looks like 'Joe-grab-a-sandwich'—blue collar, approachable, 'one of the boys.' He is short and anything but a prepossessing person physically. But he has a warm smile, a soft voice, and plenty of patience." "I campaign every day and spend time in shopping centers just about every day," he said. He was the most natural "shopping center politician" in all my travels.

A noteworthy encounter began with a man outside of K-Mart who said, when offered a pamphlet, "Greenwood? I would never vote for that bastard." Whereupon, Jim, having overheard the comment, went over, grabbed the guy's hand just as he was going into the store, and said, "Here I am; I'm the bastard." The guy said that he had seen Greenwood's name on a billboard with the slogan, "Turn in your guns." And he was furious with Jim for taking away his right to own and use guns. They went at it for about ten minutes—Jim calmly trying to explain his pro-gun-control votes and the gun owner firing off volleys of argument.

Later, the congressman reported,

> He's a member of the Falls Gun Club, one of the more radical groups around. I told him that my job was to represent the citizens of the district, and that opinion in my district was 7–1 for banning assault weapons. He said he didn't believe it, that no one had called him. I said that with a 400-person sample, the chances of reaching him were one in 2,000. I also told him that I was going to win on Tuesday by the largest margin in the history of Bucks County, and that he was going to have to deal with me in the next session, too. I also said that even if the crime bill was the camel's nose under the tent, he shouldn't punish me for putting the head under, too. That there just might be a gun-control bill sometime that I can't vote for. He apologized for his language. And I said I'd come to his gun club some time.

His calm manner during the exchange—in an unexpected, unorganized encounter—was noteworthy at the time. And it proved to be characteristic.

From the shopping center, we took a one-hour detour to visit a tiny gun shop in a nearby town. There, he was doing a favor for his long-time Bucks County Republican Party chairman. ("Next to Kim Il Sung, Harry Fawkes is the longest surviving leader in the world!") He chatted for a while with the conservative husband and wife owners. "One of Jim's characteristics," I noted, "is that he will talk at length with individuals. No matter how opposed they might be, he wants to talk it out, explain, and educate." For this campaign, at least, he seemed never to be in too much of a hurry to talk with people—whatever the place, the impact, or the outcome.

Our day in Lower Bucks ended with a visit to a private home where a group of a dozen or so women had gathered before launching a leafletting campaign in several tightly packed lower-middle-income neighborhoods. It was a time-honored, suburban style, house-to-house literature drop. The congressman was there to give them an energizing send-off talk, which, I observed, they did not seem to need. I took a doughnut and sat down with one group in the living room and listened to their comments. "I'm so excited, I can't wait till Tuesday." "I know. I wake up at night and I can't get back to sleep thinking about it." "I went out and raked leaves all day, and I still couldn't sleep." Their enthusiasm was a tonic.

The candidate's assessment was pure cost-benefit. "It's a close call whether you go to cheer on your supporters or go out to the shopping center 'to meet voters and change minds.' Two years ago, I sometimes felt like the party meetings were sucking the blood out of me. I'd keep asking myself, 'Where are the voters? Why aren't I out there?' With these party supporters, the problem is not the positive effect you get from going. It's the negative effect from not going."

On the way home, he assessed campaign atmospherics.

I think there was more anger two years ago (1992) than there is this year. . . . There was the congressional bank scandal and the [Independent Ross] Perot [presidential] candidacy; and Kostmayer and I were whipping things up. . . . Thursday, I spent eight hours in shopping centers and didn't get any hostility directed at me. . . . People are fed up with negative campaigning. . . . The general reaction I get is: "you did what you said you were going to do and we like what you are doing."

I think they like the idea that right off the bat (after the first election) I said I would not take PAC money. . . . I don't think people expected me to make a big change in the Congress. I do think they expected me to be a different kind of congressman. And I have done that. Pete Kostmayer was a classic liberal. He voted regularly for the biggest spending budget. He took loads of PAC money. The National Taxpayers Union says I have a better record on spending than 90 percent of my colleagues.

Pete Kostmayer had a great reputation for constituency service. He realized from the beginning that he had a Republican district, that it was a bad marriage, and that the only way he could hold it was through constituency service. The first thing I told my staff after the election was that the worst thing that could happen to us in the next two years would be to have people say we did not come up to the standard of constituency service set by Pete Kostmayer.

But the sitting congressman added that, in time, he would hope to engender more of a "do what you can for yourself" expectation among his constituents.

Three days later, Representative Greenwood carried Lower Bucks with 56 percent, Middle Bucks with 72 percent, and Upper Bucks with 69 percent. His vote totals were 61,000, 74,000, and 23,000 respectively. He carried his "bellwether" Lower Makefield township with 73 percent of the vote. His overall winning total was 66 percent.

Nationwide, the 1994 congressional election was historic. For the first time in forty years a Republican Party majority took control of the US House of Representatives.[15] After a single term, therefore, Jim Greenwood would be able to pursue opportunities on Capitol Hill that a multitalented Republican, Barber Conable—for all of his twenty years—could only wish for and dream about. The "Jim Greenwood research project" was about to proceed in a radically transformed majority party setting.

When we parted at trip's end, he had asked, "When will I see you again?" And I had said, "I'll be in touch." "Considering how our relationship began," I noted, "that was a good sign." I wasted no time taking him up on it.

A Player in the House

DECEMBER 1994: Jim Greenwood's "morning after" reaction to the national election combined a partisan's exhilaration with a moderate's caution. "There's a spectacular feeling of accomplishment and promise," he told a local reporter. "On the other hand, there's the very sobering task of governing . . . of promises we need to keep. And we need to make sure we do not become splintered and divisive among ourselves." Calling himself "a fiscal conservative and a social moderate," he cautioned that "if the Republicans try to run . . . far to the right

. . . the pendulum will swing back . . . and our majority status will be short lived."[16]

Speaking of his party's campaign document "Contract With America," he said later, "I remember walking over to the Capitol to sign it and being suspicious of what was in it—wondering whether it had antiabortion language in it. . . . The contract was not [included] in my [campaign] literature; but I did talk about it. I knew a lot of it was very popular. Nationally, I think [the] 1994 [election] was 25 percent the contract, 50 percent [anti-] Clinton, and 25 percent that people were shopping for something that would work."

When I visited him in Washington in December, he immediately offered, "Do you want to 'shadow me' while I talk to a [*Philadelphia Inquirer*] reporter?" And as we walked to his private office, he said to an assistant, "Get me an appointment with [Republican leader Newt] Gingrich within the next 24 hours. I need to speak with him for 15 minutes." He was already involved—putting his social service profession to good use in the new context.

The interview subject was welfare reform. It had already been reported back home that he was pushing a "proposal for group homes for unwed teenage mothers" and a proposal "to give them education and job training to wean them from a life of welfare."[17]

Reporter: Are there any other members of Congress with as much experience in the (welfare) area as you? *Greenwood:* "Not in the Republican Party. I'm a minority of one. I've found that to be true throughout my career. . . . Not only have I had hands-on experience (as a social worker), but I chaired the Select Committee on Welfare Reform in the Pennsylvania Senate." About Gingrich, he said, "I want to inject a little reason into his talk about orphanages. I want to tell Newt that it's not Boys Town—that the system does not work that way. . . . We left the idea of orphanages half a century ago. I want to explain the alternatives to him." And he added, "The question is whether my advice will be treated as knowledge or just 'more of Greenwood's moderate mush.'"

He added that if there was to be a Republican Task Force on welfare, he would want to be a member of it. The reporter suggested that if that happened, Greenwood would be the only person with hands-on social welfare experience and, as such, a major player. To which the congressman added, "People will read your story in the *Inquirer* and say, "There goes that liberal Greenwood again. All he wants to do is give welfare mothers more money." Two weeks later, Representative Greenwood was appointed to the task force on welfare reform by Speaker-to-be Newt Gingrich.[18] He had begun to multiply his prior experience.

Discussing the election results, he found everything to like. He had not expected the Republicans to take over the House. He had predicted his own election margin at 62 percent, but received 66 percent. "We checked back to 1938 and found that 66 percent was the highest margin ever." In literature-targeted Lower Bucks, "(we did) extremely well, better than anyone expected. That's where we built up our lead. . . .We ran a good campaign. Both the (state) senator who took over my old seat and the (state) representative who took over the local seat ran behind me."

As he read the election:

Almost all the criticism of me came from the extremes. The extreme liberals—the Kostmayer people—say, "Don't vote for Greenwood, he's a right-wing Gingrich clone." The extreme conservatives say "Don't vote for Greenwood, he's pro-choice, for the [gun-control] Brady Bill, and against assault weapons. He's not a real conservative, he's a liberal." Most politicians get their support from the extreme to the middle. My support came from the middle; and my opponents' came from the extremes. My 66 percent came from the middle. I think that is where the district is. So the message of the election returns is "steady as you go."

On the other hand, I tell my conservative friends here [in Washington] that my district elected Kostmayer seven times, and that he taught them a way of thinking that can't be changed overnight. . . . I tell them that it will take time for me to bring my votes to where I think I can explain to my constituents why I voted conservatively. And in that way, I can bring the district along. But I tell them I can't get out ahead of my district. . . . I'm as fiscally conservative as anyone around. But I'm pro-choice and I know something about the environment—so I guess "moderate" is appropriate.

"Moderate" had become, and would remain, his dominant political persona—inside the House and out.

MARCH 1995: When we talked for the second time in Washington, in March, the moderate, centrist Republican campaigner from Bucks

County had become a moderate, centrist Republican "player" in the House of Representatives.[19] He had found a legislative niche. "This past week has been the most historic time for me in terms of 'getting my oar in' on legislative politics," he began. And he seemed happy to talk about it.

He had been a leader—if not "the" leader—in "the revolt of the (House) moderates" against an antiabortion amendment that was about to be attached to an important piece of economic legislation. "I don't think I've mentioned this before," he began,

> but I'm a member of the "lunch bunch," a group of forty or fifty Republican moderates who get together once a week for lunch to discuss issues. Sometimes, in the last Congress, we took a position on an issue. But we never drew a line in the sand. When you are in the minority, after all, it doesn't much matter. But this week [now that we are in the majority party], for the first time, we drew a line in the sand. We said to our leadership, "If you don't remove this antiabortion amendment, we are going to kill the bill."

He explained,

> The Istook [Republican Ernest Istook] Amendment came from the far right wing of the party. As soon as it appeared, I argued inside the "lunch bunch" that if we were ever going to have any influence in the party, we had to take a stand against it. I got twenty signatures on a letter to the leadership stating flatly that we could not support the recision [i.e., appropriations revision] bill, if the Istook Amendment was in it . . . I called [Speaker Newt] Gingrich over the weekend to tell him about the letter. And I told him there were at least a dozen more members who would vote to kill the bill, but did not want to sign the letter. He said that was interesting and thanked me for calling.

Because the amendment was considered "legislation on an appropriations bill," it needed a special waiver from the Rules Committee before it went to the floor of the House for consideration. Jim and three others went to the Rules Committee to argue against it. "It was the first time I had ever set foot in that room." The Rules Committee decided to delay their vote on the special rule while negotiations went forward.

During the Rules Committee delay, Greenwood explained, he worked to win the support of the economically conservative Democrats—and their "Conservative Coalition" members—who, for their own reasons, were unhappy with the economic legislation. The coalition, he said, had asked to come to a "lunch bunch" meeting to talk about mutual interests.[20] And the two groups had met. "They had said that we could take over the Congress if the two groups could cooperate with one another. I went to their leaders [actually to Louisiana Democrat Billy Tauzin], and I said, 'the Republican leadership is counting on you guys to fill their tent. If you meant what you said about cooperating with us, you should not help them.'"

The Republican leadership made a bid to persuade these deficit-hawk Democrats to support the amendment by offering a "lock box" provision that all the realized savings would be devoted to deficit reductions. But it did not work. And when the Rules Committee found they didn't have the votes, they came back into session and rewrote the rule without the Istook Amendment.

The intraparty battle—and the Pennsylvanian's involvement—drew media attention in and out of Washington. *Newsweek* wrote that in a party meeting afterward, Majority Leader Dick Armey insisted that Representatives Istook and Greenwood publicly shake hands and make up.[21] *Roll Call*'s story highlighted "Greenwood's letter to the leadership."[22] *Newsweek*'s account called him "the leader of the moderates."[23] The *Boston Globe* story also featured "Greenwood's commentary." And they added that Greenwood "said he had signed the Contract With America after assurance that it would not contain the language about abortion sought by Istook."[24]

Back home, Greenwood concluded,

> If we had lost this fight, we would have been out of business for the rest of this Congress. We would not have been consulted. We would have been on the sidelines, without influence. Now that we have won, we have served notice that we must be consulted. We are 20 percent of the Republican membership and we want 20 percent of the legislative business.

The sophomore Pennsylvania representative was beginning to achieve some legislative traction inside his congressional party. And he was "thinking up."

A major follow-up, career-building decision came at the beginning of his third term. "After the 1996 election," he explained later, the Tuesday lunch group had a retreat at the Library of Congress. We decided that we would demand of the Speaker that he give us a seat in the leadership group—that the party needed us, that they couldn't do anything without our support. He agreed to give us a seat and also the [very conservative] CATS a seat. And he wanted those two members to be on a rotating basis—three months at a time.

At that point, I made what turned out to be a very strategic decision. I decided I wanted to be the first representative from our group to join the leadership. I wrote a letter to every member stating my wish. When no one objected or contested it, I became the Tuesday group representative. And I got to know the Speaker and [Majority Leader] Dick Armey that way.

A local newspaper reported that Greenwood had been "awarded a quasi-leadership position by moderate colleagues looking to cement relations with conservative Speaker Newt Gingrich."[25] In contrast to Democrats Glenn Poshard and Karen Thurman, who had joined a long-established and securely settled party hierarchy, Republican Greenwood found himself in a newly empowered party in flux. And he had taken full advantage of that favorable circumstance.

His intraparty abilities were becoming evident, too, on the policy-making side of House activities. As a first-term member of the Committee on Energy and Commerce, he had sought and gained membership on its Health Subcommittee. And in that position, too, his performance had led to advancement. "The best thing that happened to me [in 1996]," he explained, "was being chosen [as one of four members from E and C] for an eight-person task force committee to reform Medicare." Why, then, had he been promoted to such higher level duty? Because of his behind-the-scenes performance as an apprentice on the Health Subcommittee.

"In my first term," he explained,

when we held hearings on the president's health bill, I sat all the way through every one. Many times, the only people there at the end were [Henry] Waxman [Subcommittee chair] and myself. The staff had piles of questions they had to have asked in order to do their job. I studied House documents hard, and I learned a huge amount about the health care system. When it came to naming a member of the revision committee, the staff recommended me. They said I was a nerdy guy that would actually read the material. I was the most junior member of that committee. We sat for days, in Newt's office, slogging through that bill. And we changed Medicare. It was my most historic accomplishment.

He was both a policy-making and a policy-implementing contributor. In only his second term, a home-town newspaper was calling him "a player in the health care reform debate."[26]

In that capacity, he was appointed, subsequently, to the conference committee charged with the task of reconciling House/Senate budgetary differences in Medicare reform legislation.[27] That promotion landed him on national television's *MacNeil-Lehrer Newshour,* where he was introduced as "one of Speaker Gingrich's chief lieutenants in this [Medicare reform] fight."[28] A newspaper review at home reported that "Greenwood's dogged pursuit of health care matters helped him land a leadership role in efforts to reform Medicare, the federal health program for the elderly."[29]

In the same post-1994 period, between my first two constituency visits, Representative Greenwood was asked by his committee chairman to lead a full committee task force in "pulling together" legislation to reform the Food and Drug Administration. Its charge was to "restructure the FDA to provide the American public with access to life-saving and health-promoting drugs and medical decisions in a timely manner."[30]

In announcing his choice, the chairman of the Energy and Commerce Committee described his junior colleague as

> a thoughtful man, a compassionate one—one who developed his own innovative program for health care reform, one who spent the first years of his life as a professional social worker, helping emotionally troubled young people. Most of all, he is fiercely independent, a leader in the effort last year to develop a bipartisan alternative to the Clinton and the Republican proposals.[31]

As chairman, Greenwood was given two weeks to propose legislation, after which the full committee would begin hearings. The process, which began in March 1996, finally ended in legislation reforming the FDA in November 1997.

The early work he was "most proud of," however, was his own successful bipartisan Greenwood Amendment to the proposed 1996

HEW-Labor Appropriations Bill. As written in committee, the bill would have eliminated a long-standing abortion-sensitive program by abolishing its independent line in the federal budget. By a vote of 224–204, with the support of fifty-five pro-choice Republicans, the Greenwood Amendment restored the freestanding budget line. "I saved the Family Planning Program," he said. "And by doing so, I prevented more abortions than the pro-life people ever saved."

A women's group lobbyist, with whom he worked, described his involvement. "He worked very hard behind the scenes. He nailed people in the stairwells . . . there was no person he was not willing to approach to have a conversation with on this issue . . . when it comes to who was doing the arm twisting, who was making the phone calls, that was Greenwood."[32] The congressman said privately that he had successfully solicited a procedural assist from the Speaker—who said to him, "Because you came over here and talked me into it, I'm going to do it. And don't you forget that for the rest of your life."[33]

The Pennsylvanian's second-term, health-related activity took place within the larger context of a long-running budgetary war between President Clinton and House Republicans—a war marked by a partial government shutdown and an ultimate capitulation by the Republicans. Throughout that high-profile confrontation, and despite a spate of anti-Gingrich plotting by House colleagues, Representative Greenwood stood publicly with the Speaker.

In private, however, he urged compromise. "Newt thought he could ram the budget down the president's throat," he recalled.

> I pleaded and pleaded with Newt. I wrote memo after memo telling him that we were getting killed in the public relations war. I came home every weekend. And people were saying to me, "What do you guys think you are doing?" I kept telling Newt that we should do a poll and focus groups every week. But he was convinced that we didn't need to do any of that. . . . He bought into the crazy idea that "public support would go down and then go up again and we would triumph." I was terribly frustrated. It was a disaster.

The important point, however, was not his substantive action, but his intraparty nonaction. When other disgruntled colleagues openly questioned and defied the Speaker, Representative Greenwood remained solidly loyal.[34]

Lest he be accused of having lost his constituency bearings in all this activity, the congressman took pains, in his own news releases, to remind his constituents that he was "the most independent member of the Pennsylvania delegation," that he voted "only" 84 percent of the time with his party, because "I came to Washington to represent the views of my constituents, not my party's leadership." He acknowledged his "maverick" tendencies and emphasized his "willingness to break from" his "party when it best serves the residents of Bucks and Montgomery Counties." And he concluded by promising "to be an independent voice in this Congress" and "to continue to vote in a manner that presents the moderate views of our district."[35] The local media, weighing both sides of that comment—and emphasizing both his intraparty advancement and his "maverick muscle"[36]—seemed to agree.

In two terms, the suburban former social worker had established constructive working relationships with both his moderate Republican colleagues and with his conservative Republican Speaker. The companion political imperative was, of course, that he keep his policy activity in Washington in harmony with his electoral activity in Bucks County. That question served as the underpinning of my second visit to his home territory in the fall of 1996.

Constituency Relationships: October 1996

A "drop-in, drop-out" constituency research regimen—one that must be tailored to the rhythms of academic life—has its hazards. One of them is that important events on the home playing field will be missed. With Jim Greenwood, the 1996 case in point was a surprisingly energetic summertime primary election attack mounted by a conservative, antiabortion Republican. Incumbent Greenwood turned it aside by 60 percent to 40 percent of the vote. And it was a low turnout primary. But the unexpected closeness left a sufficient impression on the incumbent—and on his campaign advisors—to produce more than one idea for the incumbent's campaign strategy in the fall. These differences greeted me when I returned to Doylestown in October 1996.

One advisor had reacted to the 60 percent to 40 percent primary split by emphasizing the 40 percent number and advocating a more conservative-leaning campaign to prevent further erosion. Another advisor emphasized the 60 percent number and advocated sticking to the candidate's normal moderate stance in order to prevent the erosion of his centrist support. The latter's memorandum laid out the "two options": "[Either] emphasize right of center themes so as to calm down those in our Party upset with your liberal record (mostly abortion). [Or] go with a more traditional Greenwood campaign, [which] has a better chance of maintaining your moderate GOP base and holding Greenwood Democrats."

The author of the memo recommended the second course.

> Although it sounds good to assume that because you have the moderates locked up, so you can now move right-ward, I believe this is risky business. Social conservatives don't care for you, and nothing short of becoming "pro-life" will prevent them from messing with you in a primary. You cannot abandon the moderate Republicans who have come to rely on you . . . (even though they are) the same moderates who despise (Republican House Speaker) Newt Gingrich and will be voting for (Democrat) Bill Clinton this fall.

The more conservative advisor acknowledged "a difference of opinion within our group" and conceded that the congressman had already decided "to stay with our base." Even so, he still thought Jim ought to move in the conservative direction inside Congress in anticipation of a primary in 1998. To my question, "And how might you do that?" he answered, "Have him vote for the partial birth abortion bill. That's the big thing. He cast his vote against that bill (prohibiting the practice) just nine days before our primary!"

Later, when I asked the congressman about that June vote, he answered, "In my four years in Congress, I've cast thousands of votes. And the partial birth abortion vote was the toughest vote I've ever cast—horrible, horrible." But nothing would make him change it. And, predictably, his "steady as you go" campaign strategy prevailed.

When I arrived in early October, the complacency of the 1994 campaign was gone. A top campaigner greeted me with: "This is not a conventional campaign. A moderate gets it from both sides." As a result of the primary, and in sharp contrast to 1994, he said that they felt less of a need to campaign in the liberal-leaning parts of Lower Bucks County, but a positive need to campaign in the conservative-leaning parts of Upper Bucks County. And because of the candidate's definitive, post-1994 promise not to accept PAC money, he said they had scheduled far more fund-raisers [thirty thus far] than ever before.

The aide was drafting a letter to campaign workers entitled "This Ain't 1994." It conveyed the central premise of the campaign that—as a result of the summer primary—the political environment in the Eighth District had changed. In 1994, they had run an expansionist campaign. In 1996, they were running a protectionist campaign.

Their mailings, which had been distributed selectively across all three Bucks County locations in 1994, were targeted in 1996 exclusively to registered Republican voters. A "supportive letter" from Jim's mother went to "the over-60" Republicans who voted in three of the previous four primaries; a letter criticizing his primary opponent was sent to all 1996 primary voters. A brochure featuring Jim and Rick Santorum, the Republican candidate for US Senate, went to the same group; the brochure "Our Dad," featuring Jim's family, went to all 1994 and 1996 Republican primary voters; and the brochure "Republican Values" went to selected Republican-voting areas. Mailings still carried the burden of his "media" campaign.

The August primary had put the spotlight, too, on the representative's career-long difficulty with the conservative leadership of the local Republican Party. As he rehearsed it for me, "My relations are good [now]. [But] they were not good in the beginning. I spent years fighting my way into the party."

Looking back, his first intraparty conflict had come with his very first bid for public office—an open seat for state representative. His own Republican state representative—whose campaign he had run and for whom he worked part-time—decided to retire. "I was 29 and I was a Republican committee man and they'd had a hard time finding a candidate to run for office," he recalled. "I was scared to death. I spoke to the Newtown Political Club and my eye twitched for two weeks after."[37]

He was not the choice of the local Republican Party leadership.

I went and talked personally to every committee member in the district, asking for their support. The candidate of the party leadership was a guidance counselor who had no political experience and no political talent. I had already managed a state representative's campaign and I knew what it was all about. When the committee met to vote and make its endorsement, I won. The leaders shook hands with me and grudgingly congratulated me. I went home, opened a bottle of champagne, celebrated, and went to bed. The next morning, I opened the paper and the headline said, "GOP Challenges Endorsement." I was very angry. I went down to headquarters and I said to [County Leader] Harry Fawkes, "If you try to take this away from me, we will be at war as long as I'm around." The upshot was that they dropped the idea, but I never got any active party support.

Once in the state assembly, he demonstrated his issue-oriented independence—for example, on an environmental issue involving river basin integrity.

I got very involved in a major controversy that split the county right down the middle involving the Point Pleasant Pumping Project. The idea was to pump water from the Delaware River across a big part of the county into the Schuylkill River to cool the nuclear plant at Limerick. The developers loved the idea because they could tap into the pipeline along the way. I read and studied everything I could find about the environmental aspects of taking water from one river basin to another. I knew a lot about the subject. And I opposed it.

A lot of my supporters came from the pro-environment, former hippie types. They brought in Abby Hoffman for some great street theater. We would go down to Apple Jacks bar and sit and plot strategy. It was all very exciting. But my relations with the party were so bad that people got up in committee meetings and offered resolutions. "Tell Jim Greenwood to back down." I told them "You can pass all the resolutions you want. I will not back down."

"When the state senator retired, I decided to run for his seat. Again, the party refused to endorse me. That was the nature of my relations with the party. The party's candidate was a strong backer of the Point Pleasant Project. I won the election. But the upshot of the controversy was that we lost, and the Project went through.

His pro-environment leanings, as will be noted, remained steady and visible to the very last moment of our acquaintance.

When he decided to run for Congress in 1992, he again confronted a party regular—the man who had run two years before and wanted to run again. "We had a power lunch. He told me he was going to run again. I told him that whatever he did, I was going to run for Congress. He eventually backed down." "Why did the party finally endorse you?" "I think [chairman] Harry Fawkes had tried every other which way to take that seat from [five-term incumbent Democrat Peter] Kostmayer; and he reluctantly concluded that maybe I had a chance to win it. . . . After I won the primary, I had a long talk with him. He said, 'If you win the election, you will be the titular head of the Republican Party in Bucks County.' Since then, our relations have been good." In this lengthy process, Jim Greenwood had helped to move the local Republican Party toward the moderate political center.

Campaigning: 1996

In 1996, the Eighth District Republican Party was preoccupied with the presidential campaign of Bob Dole against President Bill Clinton. Despite a registration advantage of 160,000 to 115,000, the Republican was running well behind. And Representative Greenwood spoke pessimistically about the national outcome. He was tending to his own campaign and looking ahead to another four years of divided party government.

For this visit, there would be no hanging around the headquarters. Upon arrival, I was whisked off to a local school where the congressman was helping to convene a high school "Model Congress"—involving a couple of hundred students and a fair number of teacher/parent organizers.

In a short talk, he discussed his philosophy Pennsylvania-style. It was tied on the one hand to Ben Franklin's fiscal conservatism, that is, "a penny saved is a penny earned" and "neither a borrower or a lender be." On the other hand, it was linked to founder William Penn's "liberty of conscience," that is, no governmental interference with religion or abortion or sexual preference. It was a skillful coupling of "individual liberty" with "individual responsibility."

He spoke about his committee work on revamping procedures at the Food and Drug Administration. "I was given a gargantuan assignment to reform the FDA . . . how to streamline the agency to maintain the gold standard on efficiency and safety and yet recognize that it does matter if people die while the FDA does its work. We pushed it 99 yards. And we'll get it done next time!"

Questions and answers came hot and heavy. On party differences: "Republicans fear the tyranny of the masses will take away their individual freedom. Democrats want to protect people from the overbearing power of capitalists and people of great wealth." On trade with China, "Used to be against it, now I'm for it." On "the Christian Coalition," "I'm glad they participate in the political process." On same-sex marriages: "in favor." On the best Republican woman as president? "Can't think of one!" Colin Powell? "I wrote to him offering to manage his [presidential] campaign in Pennsylvania." School uniforms? "The farthest thing from the government's responsibility. I was the guy who broke the no-blue-jeans rule at Council Rock—I wore them every day for a week until they changed the rule!" Cheers. A student says, "I was always a Democrat—until today." Greenwood quips, "Hallelujah, come to Jesus." Everyone laughs. Then the student says, "I'm undecided now." More laughter. And so it went.

"Jim is very good in a dialogue," I noted. "He seems to enjoy it." "I'd a lot rather talk to these kids than I would to their parents," he said afterward, "there's a lot less tension." He came across as intellectually independent. And later, he offered confirmation.

> I lost fifty days of school in my junior and senior years in high school. The teacher had no incentive to teach me what I needed to know. I was bored to death. I read a lot at home and made honor roll every time. My parents took the view that if I made the honor roll, it [missing school] was all right with them.

It was an early preview of his self-described "maverick tendencies."

The next morning, he commented, "In our September poll, we were ahead 55 percent to 20 percent. Our polls tell us that our message has gotten through to our seniors. Last week, I went to four senior centers. I took my charts showing the Medicare increases over the several years on our budget. The most interesting thing from our last survey was the 10 percent drop in our Republican support." It was a reminder of his unexpected and unwanted contest in the summer primary.

Most of the day was spent meeting Republican voters at shopping plazas in "the most conservative part of my district"—the Upper Bucks towns of Perkasie and Quakertown. A conversation in front of the Clemens Market in Perkasie—a township that would produce a pro-life primary opponent in 1998—provided a whiff of his abortion problem.

Greenwood (handing woman a brochure): "I'm Congressman Jim Greenwood." *Woman shopper* (rejecting the brochure): "I know. You lost my vote." "I'll bet I know why—partial birth abortion." "Yes. I believe life begins at conception. You lost my vote." "Will you take this brochure and read what I have to say about abortion?" "No (walking away). They did things like that in the Holocaust." "I'll survive" (calling out). "I hope not" (calling back).

The local Republican leader, who was helping us hand out brochures, broke in. "That vote is hurting you real bad in this district. It's made my job much more difficult. It would have been much better if you hadn't voted at all. I wish you'd stayed home that day." "But that's not what I'm elected for," replied Greenwood. "The day I walk away from a vote is the last day I'll be in Congress." His pro-choice strategy was firmly set.

There was no repetition at our next shopping plaza. After ninety minutes of shaking hands and distributing brochures in front of the Acme Market in Quakertown, he noted that most comments had been favorable. "The nice thing about getting out and actually meeting voters," he said, "is that—unlike what you see in the media—on TV and on the radio and in letters to the editor—every voter in Bucks County is not consumed with abortion." Only one person had mentioned it to him, he said. And "she was undecided about her vote." Speaking of his general election polls, he reported, "we have a reverse gender gap. I do better among women than I do with men." "Pro-choice Democratic women are strong for Jim," explained a staffer.

The next event, a League of Women Voters debate—at 4 on a Saturday afternoon, on local cable TV—had few prospects for influence. It served, however, to display the season's cast of characters. There were six fist-waving, sign-carrying ("Greenwood Stinks," "Save OSHA") union members outside. And inside there was the incumbent Republican, a union leader Democrat, and a pro-life Independent, plus a moderator. It was definitely not the congressman's preferred outing. He complained that the moderator "shut me up and wouldn't let me speak." As someone who was most comfortable in face-to-face conversation, he was notably sober and soft spoken. The next morning he asked, "Did you see the story of our debate in the paper? How many people do you think read that article? Not many."[38]

In a major change from 1994, the campaign was spending money this time on television—$104,000 for three regular channels and $17,000 for cable.

> I thought that with the attack ads the unions are putting on and the negative ads in the New Jersey Senate race, that people are tuning out most TV campaigns and that a low-key ad might get some attention. I guess I'm finally convinced that we are in a television society. . . . My TV ad has been running on cable for two days. At our debate, one woman said, "I liked your ad."

Recalling how much of our earliest conversations had focused on his predecessor, I asked if he had yet been able to put his stamp on the district. "That's a good question," he answered.

> Not enough. The people who read the papers know me and know that I'm a fiscally conservative moderate Republican. But those who do not pay much attention may know my name, but they do not know who I am and what I stand for. I've worried a lot about that. And I can't decide whether the problem is that it just takes more than four years or whether we aren't doing something we should be doing. If people read the papers, I'm in them two or three times every week. But if people don't read papers, there's not much you can do.

"Does Pete Kostmayer still come up?" I asked. "In 1994, he still cast a shadow over the election. But now he's pretty much history." Later, he added, "As bitter as my campaign against Kostmayer was—and it was bitter—he was the only opponent of mine out of twenty-two who called my headquarters on election night to congratulate me. 'Jim, you had a helluva come-from-behind campaign.'" That comment had effectively put 1992 to rest.

To another question, "Who are your strongest supporters?," he answered,

> That's the greatest single difficulty of being a rational, sensible, moderate centrist. There are no groups like the pro-lifers or the NRA who will take the bullet for you. The pro-choice people, for whom I fight so hard,

just aren't as passionate or as committed as the other side. They aren't as likely to get involved in politics. For them, it's not the only issue. The people who call themselves Rockefeller Republicans are fiscally conservative and socially against government intrusion—they love me. But I have to get support by appealing to particular groups on their particular issues. For instance, the Sierra Club is coming to endorse me and that will help. Environmentalism is strong in this area.

To a third reelection inquiry: "Do you spend more time fund-raising [now] than you did when you took PAC money?" He answered, "Yes, very much more. We've had about thirty fund-raisers and you have to spend the summertime lining them all up. I wouldn't have little meetings like the one we had last night [net $700] if I took PAC money." He added,

> I have what I call a Freedom Group—a play on words since they free me from PAC money—of $1,000 givers. I get on the phone and ask them for a check. I raise a lot of money this way and I'm very good at it. Some candidates just ask for the money. I don't. I say to them: My campaign manager has chained me to my desk here until I raise $10,000. But my children are home and they need me to be there for their activities. I need to get home for them. So I'm not asking for myself, it's for my children!' And I get the money.

He did not enjoy—and he resisted—stylized campaign events: town meetings or Republican clubs. "He hates town meetings," said a political advisor. "He used to do them, but all he heard there was 'guns.' We sent out 15,000 invitations; about 20 came. And they were all opponents of gun control. We aren't doing them any more—not now anyway." As for Republican clubs, "He keeps asking me, 'Why do I have to keep going back to the Republican clubs?' And I keep telling him, 'It's important to maintain your base. The quickest way to lose is not to maintain your base.'" For the record, he appeared to be maintaining it. In the 1996 election, with an expenditure of $614,000, he carried the district with 59 percent of the vote.

With respect to the time-honored methods of publicizing constituency problems and pursuing outside assistance to cope with them, he did his part. Enough, certainly, to attract favorable press attention. In

1996, he was widely praised for his efforts to bring a Lockheed-Martin Center for Excellence—with its 1,200 new jobs—into the district and for helping to bring a new Penn State Research Center to the district to compensate for the loss of a Naval Air Station. He was always ready, too, to go to bat for the building of new highway exchanges and the paving of roads.[39] It was part of his duty. But constituency service was in no way his representational stock in trade as, for example, it was for Glenn Poshard with the egregious problems of poverty in his rural countryside.

When we dipped into Montgomery County for a Republican luncheon, it opened up a new Greenwood subject—higher office ambition. On the way in, he said, "I have only one ward in this whole area, but I'll go to show the flag." On the way out, he explained, "There was only one person in that restaurant who can vote for me. But it's the kind of thing that will help if I run for the Senate."

He was, again, "thinking up"—this time about the incumbent Republican senator currently blocking his path.

> In Pennsylvania, a Republican can put together a winning campaign either from right of center or left of center. If [Senator] Arlen Specter runs, he will have a primary opponent from the right. I will not challenge him because we would split the moderate vote and the right-to-life candidate would win. If he doesn't run, someone will take that seat and hold it for a long time. I do not want to run for the Senate in 1998. My girls will be going through adolescence and they need me at home. In 2004, my girls will be grown, I'll be 53 years old and I will have served the 12 years I set for myself. Then I'll have to sit down and decide whether or not to roll the dice for the Senate.

Only this once did he talk about the political long run.

And only once did I hear a staff member do so. Referring to the congressman's 1996 "gender gap" as "very unusual for a Republican," the staffer commented, "and that's what it takes for a Republican to be elected to the Senate. . . . I told Jim that whatever (activity) he thinks might work in a Senate race should be tried in 1998." He, too, was "thinking up" in the long run. In the short run, however, "Jim" was increasingly preoccupied with his activity and his standing among his fellow House Republicans.

Advancement in the House

In the months following his 1996 reelection, he began receiving notice and credit for his activity inside the House. In March, a Capitol Hill reporter wrote that Representative Greenwood "has emerged as one of the Republican Conference's most important moderates at a time when the bloc of 45 moderates is crucial to maintaining the GOP's 227 seat majority." She noted further that his leadership of the "lunch bunch" had given him "increased stature by placing him—along with GOP Representative Mark Souder—on the Republican expanded leadership team." And she quoted others to the effect that he was "fair," "open," "analytical," "well informed," and "can break down barriers."[40]

One month later, Speaker Gingrich came to Bucks County for a Greenwood fund-raising "roast," which raised $85,000 for the Pennsylvanian's campaign.[41] And he returned four months later to raise another $15,000 and to tell his Bucks County audience that their congressman "played a big role in the successes of the Republican-led Congress."[42]

A few months later, he received a major promotion inside the party organization in the House. As he told the story afterward,

> When they [Gingrich and Armey] set up a leadership task force on planning, they put Bill Paxon in charge of it. He selected me, [Mark] Souder and three others for his group. The leadership just piled work on Paxon on all sorts of issues. He was overloaded. One day he said to me in desperation, "Jim, you take over long-term planning." Which I did; and I prepared reports on various party problems.
>
> When the revolt against the Speaker caused Paxon to be fired by the Speaker, I went to see him. I asked the Speaker if he was going to continue his task force on planning. He said yes he was. And I said to him, "Then I'm your man. I've been doing the long-term planning already." He said, "Well, I think you probably know enough to do the job." So I went to each of the other members of the task force and asked for their support. I went last to Souder, so as not to stir things up among the conservatives. He agreed. . . .
>
> In that position [chairman of the Speaker's Planning Advisory Team], I have had a great deal of advantageous exposure to others in the leadership and in the party, and I've had a lot of input in developing several issues.

His appointment as head of the House Republican planning committee drew favorable public notice on Capitol Hill and at home.

A lengthy front-page story in Capitol Hill's *Roll Call* described the Pennsylvanian as "a pro-choice activist and strong environmentalist who has emerged this year as a leader of the moderates in the Tuesday Group."[43] "You'll never see a northeastern moderate running this party," commented a party observer, "but he's done a hell of a job being a silent leader who listens and proposes constructive changes.[44] *Congressional Quarterly* explained that "the move was widely seen as a 'thank you' to the moderates for their support during the abortive July coup against Gingrich." They described him as "a member who was able to put aside personal political ideology in favor of pulling together disparate factions of the party." And they quoted a Gingrich aide to the effect that the Pennsylvanian was "a known consensus builder [who is] likely to run the group as a model of 'gathership.'" "I have come full circle with the Speaker," said Greenwood, "and I hope the country does, too."[45] Representative Souder—with whom he was cohosting party unity dinners—was reported expressing concerns that his "good friend" might exclude social issues such as abortion from the party's agenda.[46] Capitol Hill's *Roll Call* referred to the Pennsylvanian as "a key power broker."[47]

At home, too, he was receiving flattering media judgments. Calling him "one of his party's shining stars," a *Philadelphia Magazine* survey wrote that "after 1997's House Republican leadership shakeup, Greenwood was the only member to emerge better off, stepping up to join Speaker Newt Gingrich's inner circle of advisors."[48] In their ranking of six senators and six congressmen in the three-state surrounding area, the magazine ranked Greenwood as "the best" of the twelve. They buttressed their judgment with adjectives "energetic and principled," "evenhandedness," "accessibility," "frankness" with a "future (that) is probably going to shine brighter."[49]

A profile in the *Morning Call* had a similar upbeat tone. "Repeatedly over the past four years, (Speaker) Gingrich and his top deputies, firebrand conservatives all, have handpicked the Bucks County legislator for sensitive posts within the House Republican conference despite his contrary views on social issues."[50] And Speaker Gingrich was quoted: "If there's a middle management of the Congress, he's part of the middle management that makes things actually happen every day."[51] The legislator from Bucks County put it this way: "I'm pragmatic. My objective on any issue is not simply to stand up and articulate one position and then call it a day, but rather to see how much I can get done."[52] These 1998 judgments established an upbeat tone for my third and final campaign-time constituency visit.

Bucks County: October 1998

1. RECONNECTING: By the time of my 1998 visit, the wary and awkward atmospherics of 1994 had been replaced by a welcoming receptiveness. The congressman had easily dispatched (67 percent-33 percent) another antiabortion primary opponent. The staff arranged for me to stay in the cozy, small-town cottage that had recently been the secret, hideout honeymoon suite of two well-known House Republicans. And, when I had settled in, the campaign manager and three staffers took me to dinner. The next morning, two of the staffers drove me to a campaign breakfast in Upper Bucks—where the congressman jokingly referred to the designated "staff" table as "Fenno's cult." When the eating, patriotic singing, and speech-making had ended, he called me over to the table where he was schmoozing and answering the questions of a handful of Upper Bucks Republican notables.

The gathering at his table hashed over matters of the day—mostly national in scope and mostly in Q and A form—Social Security, land-based missile systems, impeachment of the president, terrorism, Russia, antitrust, drugs, taxation, education, Al Gore, etcetera. The state representative who asked the congressman a question about immigration put the relationship just right, I thought, when he said, "Jim, maybe you could give us a focus on that." He was asking his representative for some idea-based leadership. "It was all very rational—pretty intelligent and pretty informal," I noted—with the congressman displaying "impressive virtuosity."

As a wind-up topic, he said to the group, "For all the issues we've talked about today, the bottom line is campaign finance—the ability of special interests to buy access and protect big incomes. Many times when I think about it, I think if only we could eliminate money from the process." It was his trademark constituency-driven "no PAC money" conservatism. When talking to conservative groups, he explained afterward, "I try to focus on good government, fiscal conservatism—on mainstream subjects—to keep the conversation from veering off in a strongly conservative direction. . . . Upper Bucks is the most conservative part of my district. As you can tell from my talk, what I'm trying to do here is to let people see more dimensions of myself." It was a textbook "presentation of self."[53]

He had announced his reelection bid in February. And he had done so using a covering constituency idea that was not—and could not be—available to either Karen Thurman or Glenn Poshard—that is, the idea of "our community." "As long as I am at the table where the big discussions are made, able to voice the concerns and represent the interests of our community, I will continue to serve."[54] It was an inclusionary suburban-sized comment.

In what was described as "a quiet campaign,"[55] editorial commentary was favorable. "Greenwood is a popular, middle-of-the-road Republican in a district that is strong on middle-of-the-road Republican thinking, and he has steadily moved into a position of prominence among GOP lawmakers in Congress."[56] "His ascendancy as a clear-thinking moderate in the GOP camp is impressive. It's a rare congressman with just three terms under his belt, who's invited into leadership meetings and asked to head up House Republican long-term planning."[57] "He is so adept as a consensus builder . . . that he was chosen to lead the House GOP's long-range planning team."[58] Both the congressman and the newspapers referenced his *Philadelphia Magazine's* ranking as "the best of the area's elected U.S. Senators and Representatives."

During our now familiar shopping center routine—that is, from Perkasie to Quakertown, with Wendy's in between—he updated the campaign outlook. "Are you holding onto what you have, or are you expanding your support?" I asked.

> Very definitely, we are expanding. In 1994 and 1996, we mailed the hell out of the Republicans—and only the Republicans. Last time we sent five different pieces of literature, all to Republicans. We never did anything to court the Democrats. This year, the Democrats have put up their weakest candidate ever. He's raised about $7,000, he's inarticulate . . . he spent the first minute of his opening speech at our debate yesterday explaining why he was not a crook! If ever there was a year that a Democrat would consider voting for a Republican, this is the year.

"So this year we are mailing out five pieces of literature—to the Democrats and Independents," he continued, "the first was on education. We liked it so much we are going to send it to Republicans, too. The second one has an endorsement of me by a former chairman of the Bucks County Democrats, a former Democratic County Commission, and other Democrats. They said, 'this one year, I'm voting for Jim Greenwood.' We hope that if those Democrats vote for me once, it will change the pattern. This year, it is outreach, big time." In a pattern first noted in his 1994 campaign, the 1998 campaign was "primarily conducted . . . through personal appearances and mailings."[59] "Mailings"—not television—remained the centerpiece of his extra-personal, campaign-time connections in suburbia.

As a counterpoint to his upbeat appraisal, he singled out the long-time opposition of the Pennsylvania State Teachers Association (PSEA). "Pennsylvania," he said,

> was once the teachers' strike capital of the world. And the most important thing I did in the state legislature was to pass the teacher's no-strike—mandatory arbitration first—law. They supported Kostmayer. And in the last two elections, they supported my [teacher's union organizer] opponent. . . . This year, on October 15th, I met the PSEA representative from my congressional district for the first time. When he came up and introduced himself, I said, "Doesn't it strike you as strange that here it is, October 15th, and you are only now introducing yourself?" I told him, "My opponent is a right-winger. I'm going to win. I'm your congressman. I'm a moderate. I also serve on the House Education Committee. And that's the strangest part."

The group remained an immovable part of his unforgiving—and organized—opposition.

"In our polls," he concluded, "my name recognition is just about as high as you can get—99 percent or something like that. My job approval rating is 69 percent. So, with respect to my 'favorables,' they are high. And from that standpoint, I am doing fine."

2. WASHINGTON UPDATE: When travel talk turned to Washington, he updated his ever-increasing responsibilities inside his congressional party.

He talked about his work as the Gingrich-appointed "Chairman of the Speaker's Planning Advisory Team":

The first thing I did was to talk with all the committee chairman to find out what issues were coming up and what larger issues were on the horizon. I got pages and pages of notes. (My staff director) and I got together one day in December and distilled it down to eight issue areas or eight items. I'm not sure what we called them. We prepared a document and gave it to Newt. . . . He called and wanted to talk about the plan. He had looked at the eight ideas; and he had decided we would have four ideas. He was making sure I knew he was the leader. They were his hopes for the future—drugs, retirement, education, and reform. The planning group has spent long hours talking with Newt about planning and training. He is at his best in those meetings. He loves to talk about ideas; and the meetings always last longer than they should.

Asked to sum up his work since my previous visit, he said, "I've had a great deal of exposure to others in the leadership and in the party. And I've had a lot of input developing several issues. . . . There was no one thing compared to the Food and Drug Administration in the last Congress. I guess I did 1,000 different things. . . . The planning team took a lot of my time."

Without a doubt, he had reached his early goal to be an inside player among the House Republicans. And he was still "thinking up." "I have asked the Speaker for the appointment to fill a vacancy on the Intelligence Committee. And my staff says, 'Which of your 1,000 projects are you going to give up?' He'll probably say 'Greenwood, you're too busy.' But he has already asked me to lead a congressional delegation to India and Pakistan."

3. IMPEACHMENT: Very early, our travel talk came around to the dominating issue of the day—the pending impeachment of President Bill Clinton: its prospects, alignments, voting, and possible consequences.

A week before my arrival, the House Judiciary Committee had been authorized by vote of the House to begin public hearings—preliminary to the question of House impeachment proceedings. [House approval of those impeachment proceedings would come four weeks after my visit.] Off and on for two days, the Pennsylvania congressman worried about, and played out, the full range of intra- and interparty considerations and consequences of his upcoming vote decision. On this issue, he was clearly not in the Republican Party leadership loop. And, in the end, his key vote decision was marked more by constituency politics than by partisan or personal preferences.

Constituency opinion, he said, was divided into thirds—for, against, and no opinion. By party, "three-quarters of the 'yes' votes are Republican; three-fourths of the 'no' votes are Democrats; and the rest are all over the place."

But it was always difficult to be sure about such calculations. As he once generalized, "When you're inside the machine you lose sight of larger trends that are developing outside. We are so intent on holding hearings, going to committees, voting on the floor, processing things, working the process, we can lose touch if we aren't careful." In this case, he noted,

> I go to small-town fairs and ask people, what do you think we ought to do about impeachment? The most conservative people in my district want him impeached. Sometimes you can guess what sentiment is because you know what certain people are like. But when I talked to the Northington Women's Club and I asked them their opinion, three-fourths of them said "drop it." I think a lot of people want him impeached, but they are also afraid of what will happen if we do it.

He was nervous about the entire enterprise; and he wanted to tone down the conversation.

Inside the party in Washington, he argued against open hearings and against making Prosecutor Kenneth Starr's entire report public. I asked them, "Are you sure you want to put all this on the Internet? Are you sure you want all this put out without having someone inspect it? Once it's out, it will be too late for second thoughts." They had none. And he had no influence on agenda-setting. "The whole impeachment thing is being run through Republican whip Tom DeLay's office," he said. "That's where the outside conservatives get their leverage."

As for the probable outcome,

> I think he will be impeached. Too many Republicans want him impeached and too few, if any, will stand against it. I'm not sure whether any of the moderates will vote against it when the time comes. It's a runaway train and I don't know how we can stop it. My great fear is that the whole process will be driven by the right wing, and it will hurt the party terribly in the long run. It could cost us the presidency in 2000.

And later,

> I dread that vote. I don't know how it will play out. But [for me] it is a no-win situation. If I vote to impeach, half of my supporters—the moderate Republicans—will be mad at me for prosecuting the president and hurting the country. If I vote against impeachment, one-half of my supporters—the conservative Republicans—will be mad at me for letting 'that immoral man' off the hook.
>
> The political calculation is that the moderates will be mad at me, but in time, they will forgive me. They will still think I'm better than any alternative. But my conservative supporters will not forgive me. They will say, "first abortion, then guns, now impeachment. We never liked that guy and this is the last straw." And they will come at me in a primary. That's the politics of it. I'm determined not to let the politics of it dictate my vote.

Finally, "When I tell people my story—that he will be impeached, but that it will end there, and he'll finish out his term—I find that most people are satisfied."

There was political calculation on all sides. And "the politics of it," that is, the balance of constituency relationships, surely determined his eventual "yes" on the key vote in favor of impeachment.[60] Afterward, he worked to minimize the political fallout by joining a futile effort to change the punishment to censure. It failed. When the Senate later voted not to convict, his various dilemmas were over.

Back home, afterward, he encouraged a small group of friendly constituents in a Lower Makefield living room, to "look beyond the impeachment mess. As my mother used to say, 'this, too, will pass.' I urge you to look beyond this problem to the problems that lie ahead." It was advice from his personal playbook. His waffling on the subject of impeachment was not typical. And it had done him no good.

Last Day, Last Look

Our final day together took us to five meetings in four Middle Bucks townships. I asked him to rank them on their "importance" for his constituency relationships.

The day began with a Republican Party brunch in his birthplace, Newtown. "I haven't seen half of these people since yesterday," he laughed. "But these are the troops; these are the people who sell you to others. It's important to show the flag here. Now they can say, 'I was talking to the congressman about impeachment, and this is what I said to him . . .'" In the congressman's later "importance" ranking of the day's five events, he placed the Montgomery County brunch with the party-faithful in third place.

From there, we went to a sparsely attended poolside fund-raiser at a private residence. "I met six new people there," he summed up. "And they were all longtime supporters." A second fund-raiser, in a crowded private home, put him, once again in the company of old acquaintances. "I had dinner with [the hostess] two nights ago. She's very active in Planned Parenthood, and this was a heavily family-planning-oriented group." In all of those first three meetings, he was reinforcing his primary constituency, demonstrating that he had not "gone Washington," and, in general, enjoying the luxury of weak Democratic opposition. On his "importance" scale, he ranked the two small reinforcing, in-the-home events—interchangeably—in last, and next to last, place.

On the way to visit with the more familiar people in the second Lower Makefield home, I asked him if the township was still the stronghold it had seemed to be in 1994. "Yes," he said. But he also spoke of constituency change—the long-term hazard of every incumbency.

> Even here, the Christian Coalition is beginning to make inroads by taking over the [Republican] party committees. There is a lot of change taking place. I have represented Newtown–where we were at the brunch this morning—for eighteen years, going back to my days in the assembly. But it is growing so fast that there are areas in town I could walk through where nobody knows who I am. The primary in 1996, when the Republican got 40 percent against me, made me understand how many people there were who had just arrived and did not know who I was.

It was a fitting valedictory talk and a fitting assessment. The congressman was always at his most impressive, most persuasive, and most comfortable talking low-key, face-to-face with individuals in shopping centers or with small groups of constituents in private venues. As an all-purpose campaigner, he would never be confused with emotional, stem-winding, grassroots-driven Glenn Poshard.

Between the two fund-raisers, he performed at a flag presentation ceremony at the opening of a new middle school. We raced there at warp speed. We arrived just as the MC was about to designate a substitute. "Unless Congressman Greenwood is walking down the aisle," he intoned, "we'll have to . . ." He looked up and there was the out-of-breath congressman running down the aisle! His job was to present the school a flag which had flown over the US Capitol. He bounded onto the stage to much applause. And he remained there for a few minutes, till the ceremony was over. After which there was a busy period of greeting and hand-shaking.

Without hesitation, he ranked this event as number one in "political" importance. He explained,

> You meet people here—parents, teachers—who have nothing in common with you except that you have kids in school. They are not the same people whose events you attend over and over. I talked about Katie and Laura [his children] and how they go to Paradise Middle School and how proud we all are of this beautiful school. I don't do this as much as I should. Which is why I urge my staff to set me up with high school graduations. Several hundred people saw me who had never seen me before. I presented them with a flag that had flown over the White House. Pretty good stuff.

"It was, at best," I noted, "a ten-minute appearance"—plus hand-shaking. But I had long since discovered—with Barber Conable—that winning new supporters could be a lot less time-consuming than maintaining old ones.

Our travel time provided a final opportunity for him to relate his home routines to his connection preferences. And he did it by comparing himself to his predecessor.

> When Peter Kostmayer was the congressman, he would come home every weekend, and do what I'm doing today. He'd go from event to event to event. He did not have a family life, and did not see much of his children. He was a one-dimensional congressman. He went to every Eagle Scout installation—things like that. He was always organized. He

was very liberal—more liberal than the district, but people loved him. Everywhere he went, people knew him.

I don't do that. And I think a lot of people feel they don't have that personal contact with me that they would like—that they do not feel they know who I am. I don't go to Eagle Scout celebrations. I fight the schedule constantly. My staff always wants me to do more than I am willing to do. It's a battle. I won't blow a Saturday with my kids by getting up, putting a suit and tie on, and going somewhere. If I did, it would be my children who didn't know who I am. It's a trade-off.

It is noteworthy, perhaps, that Jim Greenwood would sometimes make a point by contrasting his attitudes and behavior to that of his predecessor. Neither Karen Thurman nor Glenn Poshard had the opportunity to "go to school" on the performance of an immediate predecessor. Where such comparison is available, it can help a researcher in thinking about connection patterns.

After comparing himself to his predecessor, the Pennsylvanian commented more generally on the relevance and the importance of personal relationships and assessments.

From the day I began in political life, I have believed that in order to succeed, people have to have three opinions about you. First, they have to respect you. And you gain respect by demonstrating competence, that you know what you are doing, that you know the issues, that you do your job. Second, people have to like you. And that comes from the interpersonal relations you develop. Third, people have to trust you. People trust you when they say, "I wouldn't have voted the way he did. But if he voted that way, he must know something I don't know." I think you earn that trust by acting on principle in ways that are contrary to your own self-interest.

In that last sentence, his post-1992 pledge—to take no PAC money—could be heard. That pledge, I believe, had become one—perhaps the—essential underpinning of all of his constituency relationships.

The last event of the day was the Annual Bucks County Sierra Club Banquet, at which he was to receive their "1998 Outstanding Congressman Award." It was the last of my Pennsylvania visits and my last exposure to Jim Greenwood, representative.

In anticipation of the event, he ranked it in second place (to the flag presentation) on his "importance" scale of weekend events. "It's two weeks out and we are trying to court Democrats and Independents," he explained. "It gives me a chance to fly 'the green flag.' And not because I say I'm 'green,' but because the Sierra Club says so. And there has been some publicity on it." To which he added, "The environment was Kostmayer's claim to fame. That and family planning were the ways he endeared himself to the most people."

In our final conversation, the congressman had brought us back, full circle, to the main subject of our earliest conversation. His first race had been his toughest race. And no other constituency memory equaled its staying power.

As the "wrap-up" event of my Pennsylvania travels, the Sierra Club dinner brought into focus a career-long pattern of environmental interest and activities. His high school social studies teacher once recalled that "a few years after he got out of college, he [Jim Greenwood] dropped in to see me. He was very involved in environmental concerns."[61] I remembered, too, his lively account of his early fight, along with other high-spirited environmentalists, to stop the diversion of Delaware River water for commercial purposes.

A summary treatment of his state legislative career described him as "an activist (state) legislator" who "played a large role in passing a solid waste act that mandated recycling and set up a state superfund for compensation for hazardous waste clean ups."[62] They also noted his efforts to spur the cleanup of hazardous "brownfields," that is, abandoned industrial sites left polluted and unusable by toxic waste. In pursuit of this early cause, he had cosponsored the first bipartisan "Land Recycling Act" in the US House in 1997.[63]

Three weeks before my initial visit, in 1994, his "big four" local newspapers were already following and praising his effort—as a freshman—to pass national legislation putting limits on the amount of out-of-state trash that could be shipped—as was being done in large quantities—into Pennsylvania.[64] His bill, setting such limits on state-to-state solid waste disposal, passed the House, only to be buried permanently in the Senate. With this history, newspaper endorsements in 1998 would describe him as "a pro-choice, pro-gun-control, friend-of-the-environment moderate."[65]

It was no surprise, therefore, to hear that a national environmentalist group was going to honor this particular Republican. His credentials were securely in place well before I arrived.

With about one hundred environmental enthusiasts in attendance, the National Sierra Club president handed him its annual award. "Jim Greenwood," he said, "has done it all. And I am confident that he represents the future of the pro-environment majority in the United States House of Representatives."

Representative Greenwood's talk rested on the premise that, in matters involving the environment, he was not a representative Republican. At the dinner, he spoke of his postcollege summer spent living in a Bucks County park "as resident caretaker, park ranger, and assistant naturalist." He called himself a "moderate environmentalist," and he played on the theme the club president had handed him. He argued that environmentalists should not be partisan—that Republicans and Democrats should talk more to each other in order to find bipartisan agreements in support of the broadest, common-interest environmental causes.

Of special interest to this observer was the story of his recent trip to Alaska—taken at the request of the House leadership—to check out a local conflict between a small fishing village that wanted a medical access road built through a national wildlife refuge in a wilderness area. Representative Greenwood's investigation had bypassed—for the moment—the pro-road-building chairman of his House Transportation and Infrastructure Committee, Don Young of Alaska. Committee member Greenwood met on-site with the two sides to the controversy. He concluded that compromise was impossible. And he recommended against building the road.[66]

Chairman Young's reaction to the Pennsylvanian's trip and to the decision was delivered informally on the House floor! As Greenwood told the story privately: *Young:* "Who the hell do you think you are! I heard you were up in Alaska looking at the King Cove road project. *Greenwood:* "I was hoping we could get together." *Young:* "Well, I'm not going to do that, god damn it." *Greenwood:* "Well, it's your call, Don." "Then," said Greenwood, "he walks away and yells back at me, 'You're a jackass.' It seems that I had gone to Alaska without getting Don Young's permission!" An expurgated version of this "good guy" "bad guy" story was a rousing, unifying hit at the Sierra Club dinner.

The congressman did not, however, tell his audience the price he had already paid for his decision. As he explained privately, "The one bill I got through the House this year had to go through the Senate with unanimous consent. I got ninety-nine senators; but one stopped it— Murkowski of Alaska. It was payback time! I'm going to have to try and make up with Young," he added, "because I have several things— especially my Delaware River Basin projects—I need to get through his committee." The score? A Sierra Club award at home; a defeat in Washington.

It was one more reminder that "representing," like "legislating," involves choices. And that the interaction of legislative and representational choices never ends. After dinner, we said our good-byes; and we have not connected since.

Afterword

Jim Greenwood won reelection easily a few weeks later. Two of his post-election reflections gave some closure to his constituency career as I had observed it. "This is a mainstream county and I've taken mainstream positions. Throughout my career in Congress, I've refused to cater to extremists of the right or left."[67] "I've tried to be a bridge-builder. I've tried to reflect the views of the great two-thirds of folks in the mainstream, and to avoid being shoved around by extremists either on the right or left."[68] Taken together, they articulate the aspirations, the maneuvering, and, perhaps, the accomplishments of a suburban-centered, moderate Republican member of the US House of Representatives.

The Pennsylvanian continued to serve in the House of Representatives for three terms and six years after we said good-bye at the Sierra Club event.

At home, the local newspapers remained attentive and supportive. A June 1999 summary carried a familiar headline: "Greenwood: A Major Player." And its subhead read, "(he) has acted as a bridge between the party's influential moderate wing and its conservative base."[69] He was described, too, as "still mulling" a 1998 run for the US Senate. That option, however, closed down when incumbent Republican Arlen Specter decided to run for reelection in 1998.

As for his later life, I recalled a hint from a top aide in May of 1997. He had said to me:

> Jim is . . . going to Silicon Valley to meet with the biotech group. He is all over the biotech field—from his work on the Federal Drug Administration. There may have been other names in front of his on the FDA bill; but it was his bill. He wrote it; and he pushed it through. Most people didn't notice. But the biotechs did.

Doubtless, "the biotechs noticed" him even more after they and he had worked closely (but unsuccessfully) in 2001 to protect stem cell research during the legislative battle over human cloning.[70]

In the summer of 2004, seven years after the staff member's story of the Silicon Valley visit, Representative Greenwood announced that he would not seek reelection. Capitol Hill's *Roll Call* called him "the rare moderate who has both a key committee position and the ear of the leader (and) has often been an important swing vote and a centrist emissary to the leadership table."[71] The *Philadelphia Inquirer* called him "an excellent congressman . . . one of the diminishing breed less interested in posturing and hardball than in dialogue and getting useful things done."[72]

Shortly thereafter, it was announced that as of July 2005, James Greenwood had been chosen as the new president and CEO of BIO, the Biotechnology Industry Organization. He has served in that capacity ever since.

— 6 —

Zoe Lofgren

Liberal Democrat

Urban Playing Field

In Northern California, in the fall of 1996, this political scientist's closing adventure began in the home constituency of Democratic Congresswoman Zoe Lofgren. Her birthplace and playing field was San Francisco Bay Area's Santa Clara County—primarily the city of San Jose, plus a few outlying towns.[1] She was a lawyer—a graduate of Stanford University and of Santa Clara University Law School. She had been elected to Congress two years earlier, in 1994.

We traveled her congressional district at the end of her first term in the fall of 1996, and again at the end of her third term in late summer, 2000. The first visit focused on her home connections. The second visit opened up her expanding legislative involvements in Washington. At neither time did she face a serious challenge at the polls.

She was, deliberately, a West Coast choice. She had been recommended by a friend of mine, one of her professors at Stanford. He noted her feisty—but unsuccessful—legal effort to add the description "mother" to her "occupation" ID on California's election ballot. Her handwritten reply to my initial inquiry conveyed a similar spunky quality. If, indeed, I had a serious interest in "Home Style," she wrote, she might even be willing—"subject to agreement by my husband and my two children—to cook you a meal." We did eat together, a couple of times, but only at "the best burrito place in San Jose." Her assistance came entirely from her willingness to help "the professor" to understand the confluence of electoral politics, representational activity, and policy interests in her lifelong home territory.

Throughout four years of research in her district (and in sharp contrast to Rep. Greenwood), the congresswoman labored under one dominant contextual constraint. She had entered Congress as a member of the new minority party in the House of Representatives. Unluckily, she entered Congress along with the first Republican majority in forty years. And the Democrats would not regain control of the House until 2006—two years after my constituency travels had ended.

I never, therefore, saw Zoe Lofgren perform as a member of the majority party in the House of Representatives. Her legislative opportunities in the body were vastly more circumscribed than those of Jim Greenwood during an election campaign. Furthermore, I did not travel with her at election time—as I had done three times in Pennsylvania. (She had no serious competition.) So a side-by-side campaign-centric comparison, of the Thurman-Poshard variety, was not possible. She had no electoral difficulty at home. But the differences in timing and campaign connections made comparisons between the two House members more difficult and more tentative than with the previous pair.

On a late October afternoon in 1994, I landed in San Jose, settled in a recommended motel, called her office, and took the trolley downtown. She was not there. My contact, her chief of staff, took me around to a warren of backroom offices to introduce me to the staff as "the man who will be shadowing Zoe for a couple of days." They all "shook hands dutifully," I noted, "and that was the last I ever saw any of them." No one offered assistance. I sat alone for a while, tired of it, and left. The atmospherics were notably different from the warm and helpful staff receptions in Illinois and Pennsylvania. "The office was businesslike, a little uptight, and much less hospitable than most," I noted. It left a lasting impression. But it had no calculable effects.

Her reception area had one dominant motif—children. A collage of children's drawings with the theme "it takes a village" covered one wall.[2] Beside it was a congratulatory letter from President Clinton on their "village project." The next day, a couple of dozen children in Halloween costumes trooped in during her office hours; and they were ushered immediately into the congresswoman's inner office for hugs and candy. She later declared their visit to be "the highlight of the day." Her attentiveness was a preview of her exceptionally strong child-centered policy interests.

Invariably, my earliest exposure to the workaday life of each new constituency left one lasting impression. (Riding through the poverty stricken community of Benton on my first day with Glenn Poshard had been an earlier example). In San Jose, the relevant impression had occurred during my first ride on the light rail, from my motel to the legislator's downtown office. Inside the trolley, and outside at each stop, directions were printed in three languages—English, Spanish, and Vietnamese. From that point on, the multiculturalism of this urban district would be central to my perspective and my calculations. None of my other five constituencies began to compare with it in this respect.

When we met the next day, and I mentioned the multilingual signs, Representative Lofgren noted matter of factly that she had sponsored "the sign project" when she served on the Santa Clara County Board of Supervisors. Four elections and fourteen years of service on the Board had been her precongressional apprenticeship. And it bulked large in her view of her constituency.

"There is no dominant ethnic group in the district," she added.[3] "We have Vietnamese, Latinos, Cambodians, Philippinos, African-Americans, Hindus, and Sikhs. We have more Buddhists than Baptists. What is more, they get along. There are a few rumbles, but not many. They are all very proud of that fact." She spoke with enthusiasm about constituency diversity.

> When I was on the county board of supervisors, only one of the five of us was a white male. I represented the district with the largest Latino population. An Asian represented the area with the largest Anglo population. A Latino represented the area with the largest African-American population. The other Anglo woman represented a mixed Asian, American, Anglo area. People were very proud of that—as they should be.

She wanted me to know, up front, that she and her multicultural congressional district were in touch and in tune.

She elaborated, "I was talking to one of the freshman Republicans . . . who was arguing for a constitutional amendment providing for a spoken school prayer. I asked him 'Who gets to pick the prayer?' He said, 'The local school does.' I said, 'How would your child like it if he or she had to say a Sikh prayer?' He said, 'What's that?' She laughed and said, 'There actually is a Sikh school in my district.'"

Her staff, I soon learned, was overloaded with immigration problems. One staffer did nothing but process these cases; and several others worked part-time to cover the overflow. For her part, Congresswoman Lofgren enthused, "We wallow in our diversity; we love our diversity; we cherish it." It was a trademark comment; and it quickly distinguished her from all the others in this study.

From the beginning, she was open and helpful. Immediately, she invited me to sit in on her morning appointments—with a woman from Africa on the subject of female circumcision, with a Vietnamese group opposing (as too restrictive) an anti-affirmative-action proposal on the state ballot, with an Iranian concerned about repressive trends in his country, and with a local university student doing research on public health problems. If the ethnic diversity of her appointment list were not enough of a reminder, five wall clocks kept the time of day—in Viet Nam, India, Greenwich, Washington, and San Jose.

With each visitor, she would lower expectations—"I've only been in Congress for twenty-two months," or "I'm not as knowledgeable as some," or "I'm only a freshman," or "I rely a lot on people like Tom Lantos who have been here a lot longer than I have" —but she listened quietly and patiently without making promises. It was a markedly modest, self-effacing stance.

For fourteen years, she had been one of five Santa Clara County supervisors with decision-making authority covering three-quarters of what became her congressional district. Reminders of her tenure— its length and breadth—emerged most vividly during the day's final appointment.

With the public health student, I noted, "she showed a complete command of the issues . . . (and) a broad view of public health—not just immunization, AIDS, and epidemics, but also violence, domestic and nondomestic." To the surprised student's question "Where did you get all your information?" she answered, "I got most of it informally. Because I served on the county hospital board, I know these people and I talk to them all the time." And when the student gave her a copy of the "Health Status Report of Santa Clara County," she said, matter of factly, "We started that when I was on the board."

It was an early introduction to her lengthy and constructive immersion in local affairs. And it became clear, too, that when she thought of her constituency, she pictured Santa Clara County—unless she said otherwise. In strong contrast to Karen Thurman, Zoe Lofgren could get her arms around a functioning community. And she operated with a strong sense of engagement within it.

She spoke proudly about her working-class background, starting with a grandfather who came from Sweden "with his clothes on his back and no money." "When we visited," she said, "I always ran straight to my grandfather. I would sit with him for hours and listen to his stories about how poor he was and how he found work and became a citizen." "I grew up in the Bay Area," she told a campaign brunch for nearby Democratic hopeful Ellen Tauscher. "My father was a truck driver; my mother was a cook at a school cafeteria—they still use her spaghetti sauce." During World War II, her mother worked in a factory as a riveter. She had died a number of years earlier. Her father, who volunteered the day after Pearl Harbor, had served in the US Army. He was a truck driver. She cherished their relationship. "I call him every night," she said. When they occasionally differed over a public policy, they would talk about it.

Zoe Lofgren was born to politics. "It was a political family," she told a reporter. "I walked my first precinct when I was five. . . . We would talk politics at home. I thought everyone did."[4] It was a strong Democratic family. And she was as devoted a working Democrat as I had met in thirty years.

Education had been the way up for her.

> I had the good fortune to go to California's public schools at a time when California valued and put money into education. I got a scholarship. I was the first person in my family to go to college. It made my life bright. It changed my life from one of dreariness to one where I can go ahead and dream.

Later, she elaborated, "One day, the teacher pulled me out of class and said, "You should go to college." I said, "How can I go to college? We have no money." "You can get As instead of Bs, and get a scholarship." "So I worked hard and I got As and I got a scholarship." It was a message she carried wherever she spoke. "People will try to fulfill the expectations that other people have for them." The luncheon speaker, too, emphasized, as characteristic of San Jose, "the respect for other cultures" and the absence of any "politics of resentment."

Later that day, the congresswoman ceremonially opened a job fair run by the Hispanic organization, MACSA. "I helped organize this group," she said. Afterward, I noted, "She seems to be a veteran of countless community campaigns. And the dominant thing about her career was how little she had to change her priorities or her practices at home when she moved from county supervisor to Congress. As much as anyone I've studied, she keeps finding her prior (county) work applicable to her congressional work—seamlessly in some cases."

And she was still learning. Walking from the luncheon, she recalled an early learning experience with the luncheon speaker—one that had taught her the advantage of keeping her political avenues open. "We fought when I was on the board of supervisors," she said,

> and when I got to Congress, the two of us sat down one day and talked. I reminded her of how we had fought over money. She said to me, "Is that what it was all about? I thought you just didn't like me." "No," I said. "I always liked you. It was only about the money." Since then, we have worked well together. Sometimes we still disagree. . . . But it is never personal.

And she added, "I wish now that we had had that talk much earlier."

Connections

When I asked Zoe if hers was an easy district to represent, she said that it was. "I grew up here, and I am so much a part of the district—by experience and by outlook. It's not just the community activists. When I stand on the school playground talking with other parents, I think like they do. . . . I love it here. I love the people here. I love to talk with them. I love to listen to them." And, later, "I love San Jose. I think it's the best community in the country to live in." She was unusually enthusiastic about her place, her people, and her connections. Person and political geography seemed to be a reinforcing fit.

Her comfortable sense of community was in striking contrast to the absence of same with Karen Thurman. The Floridian never thought of her constituency in a comprehensive way. Nor, in view of his three intraparty primary fights over abortion, did Jim Greenwood.

Making note that several Democratic women had been elected to the House of Representatives from surrounding districts, I asked Representative Lofgren whether she could have run and won in their districts. "I could never have gotten elected in those districts," she answered. "My family was not wealthy. All of those women came in at the top—with money. . . . I came up 'scrappily' through local government."

The story of her "scrappy" 1994 election to Congress began with the retirement announcement of Representative Don Edwards—a fifteen-term congressman and liberal icon, for whom Lofgren had interned as a student and for whom she had worked as a part-time San Jose staff member for six years. "I called him to urge him to run again; and I got the feeling that he wasn't. So we [she and lawyer husband, John] began to think about what we would do if he decided not to run. . . . Then one day the phone rang and a friend said, 'He's not running.'"

The prominent former Democratic mayor of San Jose jumped immediately into the Democratic primary; and he quickly signed up Lofgren's previous county campaign manager. After some back-and-forth—"could the family work it out, did I really want it," County supervisor Lofgren followed suit. "I remember thinking, all of a sudden, 'of course I want to go to Congress.'"

"When my opponent announced," she recalled,

> the San Jose Mercury News wrote a long, glowing editorial saying how lucky we all were that he was willing to run. Then, for almost a week, they ran a series on all the improvements he had brought to the downtown. It was the greatest piece of unpaid publicity you ever saw. I was not expected to win [the primary]. No one thought I could win. I can remember calling my campaign manager and asking "Do you think I can win? Because if I can't, there's just no sense in knocking myself out the way I am." He said, "it can be done. You can do it. . . ." That energized me and we went back to raising money [$200,000] and organizing the phone banks.

She summarized, "We did it with phone banks. We had forty going in the Valley for six weeks. I hate to walk precincts. We relied on phone banks. I went from one to the other, to keep up morale. And I allowed the phone bankers to say, 'Zoe is right here. Do you want to talk with her?' Then I would talk to the person directly. The volunteers were unbelievable—the hours they put in on the phone banks." "It was," she said, "a race between the downtown business community and the grassroots." In her one-party district, the primary was the only contest that mattered. And election, of course, followed.

A framed front page of the *San Jose Mercury* election issue hangs in her inner office. Her victory (45 percent to 42 percent)is described as a "surprise"; and her defeated opponent is described as "once the most powerful leader in the region." When I commented on the paper's apparent shock, she said,

> On election night, there was not one single reporter assigned to my headquarters. The *Mercury* sent one photographer to take a picture of the loser. When the returns started to show I was winning, he had to start writing copy for the paper.
>
> It was a low-turnout election. We won by 1,000 votes, because we were able to turn our folks out, especially in the working-class areas of East San Jose. The phone banks were the key to my election.

After a school fund-raising meeting of parents at McDonald's, where she met and talked with other mothers, she said, "You asked me about my best supporters. Those women in there would work the phone banks—three hours at a time, three nights a week." Later, she revisited that theme, listing her "strongest supporters" as "my neighbors, parents of my children's friends at school, people I worked with (as county supervisor) in health and human services, health workers—especially public health nurses. They are the best people in the world at walking precincts. . . . These are the people who, when you vote in a way they disagree with, will say, 'I must be wrong.'" "I became a cause," she added. "I became an icon of the women's movement." It was a totally different view—more place-specific and more gender-centric—from that of her Democratic House colleague from Florida.

Her election-day recollections were spiced with down-to-earth, one-on-one connection stories. There was the man with his head under the hood of his car, who looked up and said, "I know you. I just voted for you. You saved my son's life" (through the county drug rehab program). There was the man who said he had "memorized" her campaign brochure, and proved it to her by saying, "I know you; you are the truck driver's daughter." Two elderly women going into the supermarket told her, "We're going to vote for you." To which she answered, "You only have fifteen minutes before the polls close." They go in to the store, immediately turn around and come out, saying "We decided we'd better vote now. Shopping can wait." These Election Day encounters, she said, were "omens."

A longtime coworker commented that Zoe's close rapport with her constituents marked a complete change from the stance of her predecessor. "Don Edwards," she told me,

> was a marvelous, courageous spokesman on all the great issues of our time. He represented the views of his constituents well. But he did not know his district well. He did not live in the district. He did not answer his mail. When he first ran, he bought the seat with $900,000—much of it his own. He became untouchable. He had only one challenger that anybody can remember.

The congresswoman nodded in agreement. "People were surprised when I answered their letters. They weren't used to that." Nothing more was said by way of comparison with her mentor. He had helped her mightily along the way. And she knew it. Without a doubt, however, Zoe Lofgren had brought an unfamiliar and radically different—more personal, more hands-on, more in-touch, closer-to-home—representational style to the district.

Her idea of representation was unusually personal. And it remained so during both my visits.

> Sometimes I wonder whether the job is to find out what people want and do it, or do what you want and hope people want it. In the end, though, when I do what I want, I'm so much like them that they'll agree with me. For that reason, I think its better not to come home and make speeches, but rather to come home and go to barbeques, sit on the front porch with your neighbor, get in the supermarket lines and talk to people to keep up with the rhythms of what they are saying.

In the same vein,

> Sometimes we go out, unannounced, and set up an ironing board in front of a grocery store and invite people to come talk. If they have a problem,

they can talk to a staff person then. Sometimes, we announce these visits. We'll set up a card table and a couple of chairs and people line up. One very hot day, an elderly man stood in line for over an hour, got to the table and said, "I just wanted to say 'thank you.'" I said, "Don't you want to talk about anything in particular?" He said, "No, I just wanted to tell you that you're doing a good job and thank you." Wasn't that sweet!

The Vietnamese community makes up, she said, "25 to 30 percent of the district by population . . . but the voting participation is much smaller." She correlated these numbers with their immigration patterns—with the first wave consisting mostly of the conservatives associated with defeated President Ky, followed by ordinary refugees escaping the victorious communist regime. Ever since, the Vietnamese community, said Lofgren, had been split between a politically experienced, early group and a nonpolitical late-arriving one.

Presently, however, they had come together in opposition to statewide ballot Proposition 209, which forbid affirmative action in university admission. One day, we walked with several Vietnamese allies to an anti-Proposition 209 rally at which she spoke with passion. "It's shameful when people say Proposition 209 will help. Proposition 209 legalizes discrimination, and it forbids special treatment—depending on one's interpretation. People new to our community need help. They need outreach efforts to tell people what opportunities there are that will help them to succeed. I am present to stand with you once again in your efforts." An African-American, too, spoke strongly in opposition.

Walking away, she noted that the presence of both conservative and liberal Vietnamese at the rally reflected "a new maturity." "How did that come about," I asked. "I think I helped," she said. In her current, barely contested reelection campaign, she had spent $35,000—one flyer to each of the 82 percent of households with a woman in residence—plus one small, but indicative, mailing—to leaders of the Vietnamese community.

The next day, she presided over a unique and unforgettable swearing-in ceremony, granting American citizenship to a former major in the North Vietnamese Army. The empowering law had been proposed, defended, and shepherded through Congress by Representative Lofgren.

The background was this: Three American airmen were shot down over North Viet Nam during the war. A North Vietnamese officer found them, hid them, and then led them to safety. Later, that officer lost both his arms in combat. After the war, he reached the United States and settled in San Jose. He was repeatedly denied citizenship. And he appealed to his member of Congress. She had a private bill written granting Major An citizenship; and she shepherded it every step of the way through Congress. The formal awarding of citizenship by an INS official was the centerpiece of the ceremony—Representative Lofgren presiding.

A very large community room with balcony was filled to overflowing with Vietnamese. There were dignitaries and citizen groups who had come to honor their—and our—hero. There were bands, color guards, veterans' group representatives, lots of flags, and "more TV cameras," I noted, "than I have seen in one place." For sheer emotional drama, the highlight came when one of the three rescued pilots was piped in through the loudspeakers to tell his story firsthand, blow-by-blow, detailing the acts of bravery and humanity that had saved three American lives. There were few dry eyes in the house. It was the most emotional event I ever attended in my travels—"like a wedding," I scribbled. In that room, Representative Lofgren was every bit a certified hometown hero.

Accomplishment

Driving away after the Major An swearing in, she said,

> I have very good relations with the veterans. You might think that strange since I voted in favor of the assault weapons ban and against the [antidesecration] flag amendment. They oppose me on those things, but it doesn't matter to them. It's the little things that matter. For instance, the county has a twenty-year contract to keep up the graves of the Santa Clara veterans who have no family. It costs $6,000. The county proposed to cut that out of the budget as a cost-saving. I said, "Are you crazy, $6,000?" I fought for that and got it put back. . . . Those men went to war, put their lives on the line, and saved civilization . . . why shouldn't they

get their due from the rest of us? I also helped facilitate their veterans' benefits. Those things gave me a pass on the flag amendment.

Judging by her commentary as we traveled the district, she had been a resourceful Santa Clara County supervisor and had enjoyed every minute of it. Recalling a winning (57 percent-42 percent) 1984 fight to pass Measure A—a one-half-cent county sales tax dedicated to road construction—she said, "I knew it would pass because I talked to people on their porches and in the supermarket lines. I asked them if they would be willing to pay a half cent more on the county tax to improve three highways. Traffic was so bad, businesses were threatening to leave." Asked, during my visit, to name her "foremost political accomplishment," she answered, "In an odd way, it was probably the highway program, in terms of its biggest impact."

She and two other women commissioners campaigned, on another occasion, to remove the county jails from the sheriff's department. "We were just three girls, not to be taken seriously," she recalled. "The sheriff raised a million dollars. He used money set aside for a new building. He mortgaged his home. We raised $200,000 and we crushed them. They hate me for it. They have not forgotten. But the jails are less costly, and our programs on literacy, drug abuse, and teaching skills are a huge improvement. . . . People here are hard pressed," she said. "But they will sacrifice for education and for the future."

She told another story involving her head-on collision with a local judge. He had ordered the board of supervisors to complete the renovation of the county jail within thirty days or else be thrown in jail. Whereupon she and her top aide drove to the State Capitol in Sacramento and asked their friends to pass legislation essentially forbidding local judges to throw county supervisors in jail. "We got it passed through the house at 12, through the Senate at 3; and the governor signed it at 7. We got a bill passed in one day! The judge was furious. And we rebuilt the jail [as we wanted it] in a reasonable time."

During our second visit, she pointed to a large church and recounted another involvement.

This is the largest Portuguese area in the county.[5] That lovely church is the center of their community life. When I was on the board of supervisors, CALTRANS wanted to put a huge railroad bridge over the creek, right where it would block out the view of the church. It was awful; and the community was up in arms. I organized a little group from all over the area; and we came up with an alternate train route.

CALTRANS is almost impossible to deal with. But I went to the president and asked him to look at our alternative. He said, "We've committed. It would be impossible." I said, "Just look at it." He did; and they changed it. . . . The architect who designed the plan came to see me later with tears in his eyes, and thanked me for giving him the chance to be creative. He said that working out the new plan was the highlight of his life. Later, in retirement he came and offered to walk precincts for me; and he did.

She exclaimed, "We even worked on a Planned Parenthood plan with the Catholic Church! We differ totally on abortion, but we didn't let that stop us from moving ahead with a Planned Parenthood plan. Did you ever hear of that back East?"

Formally and informally, supervisor/politician Lofgren seemed totally involved and markedly successful. She seemed to have a deep-rooted and a practical hands-on appreciation of her district as a functioning sociopolitical community. Her local attachments had the same depth and durability I had encountered with Glenn Poshard. At the end of my first visit, I concluded that her dominant representational characteristic was a broad-ranging community-mindedness.

Congressional Partisanship

The one overtly partisan event of my first visit was an instructive session with the Young Democrats at San Jose State University.[6] When asked, as a Washington newcomer, to evaluate the performance of the two parties, she attacked Republican failings. "They opened up the Capitol and put a cash sign on amendments," she said. "That was the worst thing they ever did. I've heard from lobbyists that they've never seen anything like it. On the clean water bill, between the committee and the floor, one hundred pages of amendments were added by the petrochemical industry and others. And the cash flowed in for Republican House members. . . . If that's going to be the pattern, we're in trouble."

"A second thing," she said,

> was their efforts to stifle voices of dissent. There were numerous occasions where that happened. With one minute still left on the clock to cast a vote, with people on one side running down the aisle to vote, the Republican whip . . . closed the vote. He didn't allow their votes to be cast. That's a chilling thought. The desire to win was too great. In the end, decency is more important than any vote.

"The division between Republicans and Democrats on 'where we go from here,'" she told the Young Democrats, "is stark. . . . I spend a lot of time listening to the Republicans talk about where they want to take the country. They are strict market economy people. They see almost no role for the government, except through the military." And she summed up: "The difference in agenda, life experiences, and outlook between the freshmen Republicans and Democrats is marked indeed." She had made a big institutional leap; and she had been given a cold-bath welcome to a strange two-party political world.

Her comments and judgments were strikingly partisan. Notably, too, they were focused on actions taken—and outcomes registered—visibly, on the floor of the House. In large part, therefore, her answers to the students were the natural reactions and complaints of a newcomer from within the minority party. On both counts, she had been shut out of legislative action. Coming as she did—from twelve years of face-to-face, five-people, one-party personal involvement in all decision making—her strong reactions to the congressional workplace were compounded fourfold. It was a far greater leap than state legislator Jim Greenwood had made. To say that she had a lot to react to, learn from, and make judgments about—in Washington—would be an understatement.

In her early search for strategic and behavioral yardsticks, she even puzzled over her own Democratic colleagues. "We Democrats are a diverse party. And I've wondered what our core values are. When I came to Congress, I only knew three people—all liberal California Democrats. Now I see two Texas Democrats who are as conservative as you can get. What do they have in common with the others?" Perhaps her puzzlement helps explain her oversimplified "us and them" comments to the college students. In any case, her own partisan placement—her starting point—was unmistakable. Her 1995–1996 roll call vote pattern ranked her as more liberal than three-quarters of her fellow House Democrats.[7] And that was the ideological screen through which she had spoken to the San Jose students.

As an interesting case of intra-Democratic priorities and constituency preferences, compare her reaction to President Clinton's major "Welfare-to-Work" reform legislation to the reaction of fellow Democrat Karen Thurman. Representative Thurman was torn between simply voting "no" or jumping into the legislative process to modify the legislation. She decided to get involved; and she worked to modify a provision of the bill. And having worked at it, she then voted "yes." It was, she said, "the hardest vote I have ever cast in Congress."

When I asked Representative Lofgren "was it a hard vote for you," she said it was not. While she believed "that welfare should be a work program," nonetheless, she voted "no." "If people had known what I knew [i.e., that support services would be inadequate], she said, "they would have voted against it. And that made it easy for me to explain." And she added, "the county commission passed a resolution opposing it. The city council passed a resolution opposing it. The *San Jose Mercury* wrote an editorial against it. That made it easier." The "moderate" credentials of one Democrat and the "liberal" credentials of the other Democrat remained intact.

The floor of the House and the committees of the House are, of course, two very different decision-making venues. And, given her minority party status, strong partisanship would not serve Democrat Lofgren well inside her particular committee—if, that is, she wanted to initiate and promote her legislative goals. Increasingly, therefore, she was propelled—by legislative interests and by necessity—into cross-party cooperation. Inside her Judiciary Committee, especially on her two subcommittees, political necessity gradually became the mother of bipartisan invention.

Even so, the Californian's habit was to comment first on each colleague's ideological bent and only then on the likelihood of productive personal working relationships. With less liberal fellow Democrats, her comment "I'm very fond of A, although we don't always agree on everything" was common phrasing. With Republicans, her judgments either took the form, "With X and Y, you cannot do anything with them." Or, "he's a nice person, but his views are terrible."

Over time, a third version became increasingly common. "I can work with Z even though he's a hard-right Republican." That reaction flowered during my second visit, in comments such as, "We have learned together; and our subcommittee got the best result we could." All newcomers have to adjust. But her very involved and productive one-party San Jose past magnified her adjustment problems.

Socioeconomic Agenda

Throughout her first term, Representative Lofgren coped with a double invisibility—as a newcomer and as a member of the minority party. As the only first-term Democrat elected from "the West," however, she gained a little early television exposure—as one of four House newcomers chosen to appear on the *The Newshour with Jim Lehrer*. In that forum, the Californian made several appearances during her first term. And she had a rare opportunity to state her views. Throughout, she stuck closely to her policy priorities by emphasizing that her constituents "sent me here to stand up for the working people and their children."[8]

She talked about her constituency as it suffered from unfavorable Republican legislative activity. "If you earn five bucks an hour, like a lot of people who live in the district, it [the tax bill] doesn't do anything for you. You get a very low amount, and it's being paid for by cuts in the things that really matter to working people, things that really helped me as a young person to get ahead, to be able to get a student loan, to be able to go to college. Just the fact that you're in a blue-collar family shouldn't cut off your ability to achieve."[9]

On her next visit to PBS, she echoed "we need to invest in our children . . . and the cuts in education and research and in science are not going to bode well for the prospects of our country."[10]

In a third interview, she again highlighted her child-centered policy priorities. "I think I've made a difference with Internet access for schools—which is probably one thing I can point to where I know I made a difference for kids—that will help this country. But the frustration I have is (that) I came here to change things . . . what I want to do is talk about kids and families of this country . . . it's why I ran . . . to focus our attention on education, on our children, their well-being . . . and there's been nothing of that—nothing."[11]

A *Congressional Quarterly* profile at the end of her first year emphasized her desire to "fight child abuse, juvenile delinquency, and inadequate public school education" and her "frustrating life in the minority." "My frustration is I don't get the chance to suggest things that will work better, especially the issues I know something about."[12] Throughout these interviews, she remained totally focused on the needs of her home community. She was a determined representative. There was no pretense that she was a Washington player.

A week before I arrived in California, she answered Jim Lehrer's "How is your reelection race going?"

> The feedback I'm getting from my constituents is pretty positive. They appreciate that I stood up to fight the cuts in education, that I stood up for pro-choice, that I stood up to keep the Medicaid program from being repealed and also for science and technology, which is the base of our prosperity . . . our (district's) low unemployment is really based on investments in education, in science and technology research, [in] the Department of Energy.[13]

When I arrived, she was helping reenergize what she saw as her district's faltering application to the congressionally sponsored "Gear Up" program to challenge and reward pre-high-school student performance and promotion with special incentives.[14]

"Sometimes, people pull me back" (into district matters), she said when we talked.

> And sometimes, when things don't seem to function, I get people together to make things work. With the Gear Up [national education] program, the San Jose Central School District was totally dysfunctional and couldn't act. So we got the East Side schools together, with San Jose State in the lead. It's a university–public school nonprofit partnership. We didn't have a nonprofit. So I created and organized a nonprofit. We have worked very hard on that application.

"It's a very compact district," she added. "I know everything that's going on and I've been involved in most of it. It's fun—and I care."

During my first constituency visit, Silicon Valley was not a major part of our conversation. She had commented briefly on its importance.

> The only part of my district I did not have when I was a county commissioner was Silicon Valley. So, when I became a congresswoman, I knew almost nothing about the businesses in Silicon Valley. Oh, I had met a few people when we got into transportation. Of course, they are very interested in that. Since my election, I have made it my major campaign to get to know business people there. They are worried about encryption, security, intellectual property—a whole set of issues I knew nothing about.

In 1996, direct references to Silicon Valley, such as this, were rare.

Her running comments on her district's problems did reflect, however, an early personal interest in the promise of technology as it affected her young constituents. Guaranteeing public school access to the Internet, she said, was one of her major accomplishments in her first term. When a student at San Jose State had asked a question about the future, she elaborated: "I love the Internet. It is bound to improve the country when people can get their own information and use it." And she praised "Net Day," a Saturday school learning program for students. Interest and aptitude seemed to be there, waiting for opportunities.

Relatedly, she talked about the value of quantitative analysis in policy making. On juvenile delinquency, for example, "We know a lot about what works. And I have a great bill. We have 'a set of key indicators' (i.e., troubled home life, early arrest), and 'a grid,' and a set of predictors that 'pinpoint' people most likely to get into trouble." On the basis of which, remedies could be fashioned to cope with "troublemakers" and to steer others away from crime. She also referenced a successful program in East Orange, New Jersey, where they provided a computer for every two students and found improvement in student dropout rates, discipline, attention span, and test scores.

She seemed to have constructive instincts for harnessing quantitative techniques for the purpose of treating social problems. They were predictive of concerns that surfaced later in our travels.

Because of her Silicon Valley constituents, she had set her second-term membership sights on her Judiciary Committee's "Subcommittee on Courts and Intellectual Property Rights." That relevant subcommittee, she said, had been in especially inept hands. "When the CEOs came to testify before the subcommittee—Bill Gates and the others—the [subcommittee] chairman opened the meeting reading from a sheet of paper. They were appalled. He had no understanding at all of the issues they were interested in." None of the other Californians on the committee had picked up on the subject, she said. And, a few months later, she successfully transferred to that subcommittee.[15] When I returned to the district four years later, Silicon Valley had become a central preoccupation.

Congresswoman Lofgren's lengthy immersion on the county board of supervisors had left her—more than most new members—well acquainted with the preferences, the tolerances, the needs and the decision-making practices of her constituents. On PBS, six months after my visit, she spoke again of these interests and needs, and of the tasks that, in her view, lay ahead. "For whatever reason," she said, "we're not producing results on the subjects that people really care about. What I hear when I go home is education and juvenile delinquency and prevention and how do we get our country back on the right track on a bipartisan basis."[16]

Near the end of the 1996 visit, my notes summarized:

> She's a friendly, partisan, liberal, soft-spoken, businesslike person who let me accompany her on all her activities. She's a 1960s liberal who lives and works at the connections between government and people in need. She is as aware of—and attentive to—the cultural . . . and neighborhood connections of a constituency as a member of Congress can be.

Interim Interview: 1998[17]

In March 1998, between my first and second visits to San Jose, Representative Lofgren was interviewed by the Center for American Women and Politics at Rutgers University. Their exchange confirmed opinions and practices that had appeared in San Jose two years before. And it suggested a posture that would appear two years later during my visit in 2000.

When asked to talk about her "most important personal legislative accomplishments," she returned to familiar ground: Getting the House to agree to legislation promoting portable Internet access for public schools, she said. And she added, "I think it wouldn't have happened except for what I did. . . . I just jammed it and didn't give up. . . . I (even) berated the Speaker on the floor and threw a hissy fit and finally just bullied my way into a commitment." When asked about her behavior on "issues that get classified as not women's issues"—on crime in particular—she described herself in familiar language as a player.

On a criminal incarceration measure, she said, "I think I hold the record on amendments in the Judiciary Committee." Relating her law enforcement experience, she said, "As sort of a practical person . . . I'm not a rigid ideologue. Having run a large county jail facility and having been involved in criminal justice issues in local government for fourteen years, I thought that I had practical experience that was useful."

On the matter of deciding when to get involved: "I tend to make . . . a judgment at the beginning when it looks like a piece of legislation is actually going to become law, then it's worth spending some time to make it better." And, as something of a self-revelation, "I can talk to practically anybody. I don't have to agree with them on everything."

To the Rutgers interview question "in addition to the responsibilities you feel to represent your district, do you feel an additional responsibility to represent women?" Lofgren answered, "My job is to represent the Sixteenth Congressional District. But the women of that district are not dissimilar from women across the country." When asked for "any parting thoughts," she reiterated, "I guess the only thing I'd add is that I think it's a mistake for women in public life to allow themselves to be ghettoized into only women's issues. But that doesn't mean that you shouldn't advocate on women's issues. That is the posture I've tried to take." The low-key balance she struck was similar to that of Karen Thurman.

Constituency Update: 2000

In 1996, Representative Zoe Lofgren's representational commentary had been dominated by her previous twelve years of busy service on the Santa Clara County Board of Supervisors. And her constituency emergence had dominated this researcher's attention. Inside the US House of Representatives, she was simply one more rookie—and in the minority party to boot. She had come across as talented, hardworking, opinionated, and liberal. In her Santa Clara County home place (as she described it), she was about as solidly grounded as a representative can be.

In August of 2000, I returned for a second (and final) visit to California's Sixteenth Congressional District. And four years had made a large difference. Representative Lofgren remained as solidly embedded as before in her overwhelmingly Democratic constituency. But her political talk reflected a new set of adjustments—some at home, some in Washington.

At home, there was the steadily increasing impact of a fast-growing and innovative Silicon Valley economy. In Washington, there was her work on the Judiciary Committee during the impeachment of President Bill Clinton. In both contexts, she worked, learned, and solidified constituency support. She also had begun to express a policy activist's growing impatience with six years in Washington's minority party.

Almost immediately after we said hello—"I'm fine; but I'm tired"—she unloaded on the state of congressional politics. "The right-wing Republicans have blocked everything," she said. "The NRA [National Rifle Association] owns the Republican Party in Congress—that's all there is to it. [Majority Leader] Tom Delay calls the shots, and he won't do anything. I'm sure [Speaker Dennis] Hastert gets his orders from DeLay every morning. They have blocked everything." Her comment set a tone for the visit. It was an old tone. But, I soon learned that her four years of actual practice had made the tone less strident and more nuanced.

Chronologically, our first day began, as it had in 1994, with a series of constituent appointments. While on the surface all were nonpolitical, all did have political ramifications. For one reason or another, each supplicant had been moved up from the staff to the boss. "It's a recess-type schedule," she repeated, "because when I get home, I'm beat." Thinking back to my first experience with her "office hours," her newer, less self-effacing, more confident stance was noteworthy.

First came a young Boy Scout in uniform, accompanied by his mother, to fulfill a requirement that he ask questions of an elected official. They (mostly Lofgren) discussed the Bill of Rights. To the mother, the congresswoman explained her own child-related, experimentally grounded "Z's to A's" legislative proposal that the school day begin earlier for the youngest students because they wake up earlier, and later for older kids who have trouble waking up. The *San Jose Mercury,* she said, had given it a friendly write-up. It was a rare mention of the local newspaper. As they were leaving, Zoe acknowledged the mother's support. "Thank you for all you have done for us." And later, an explanation, "She is a great person. She has been with us from the very beginning."

Next came a woman in trouble, asking for help in getting a public housing "certificate of necessity." She began, "I'm glad to meet you. I've voted for you many times." Then, "I'm just hanging on. I'm that close (two fingers) to being homeless. I've worked all my life; but I've lost my job. My Social Security won't kick in for six months. I'm taking care of my mother. I've been on the public housing list for eight years. I'm near the top of the list. But the director won't listen to me. I'm not complaining, but I need a little help. We need to look after our seniors." Should she get the certificate, she hinted, "There are 149 units in the building. I'd like to start a voter registration drive, to get people together."

Next and in order, a small business administrator asked Zoe to help persuade President G.W. Bush to inaugurate their new Entrepreneurship Center; a staff director of the county's largest business association explored her position on the group's public transportation bond issue; and a group from the County Water Authority solicited her support for a new water distribution project.

Afterward, her reactions varied. About the businessman: "He just wanted to find out whether I was going to go public with my [privately expressed] opposition [to the proposal]. I told him that I would not. I have other fish to fry. All the rest of our conversation was window dressing. Sometimes in politics, you have to understand the message behind the message." And she dismissed him with "He's a staff guy. He doesn't know anything about business trends." The water department people, on the other hand, received a proactive hearing. "I like the water people. They have a tough job." Parts of her district, she explained, has severe flooding problems. "I applaud what they are doing. They might not have thought about the two questions I raised. But that was not crucial in getting my support."

Later, I asked, "If you could only help one of those people, which one would you choose to help?" Predictably, she said,

> The older woman who needed housing: she had all sorts of problems—
> her operation, her mother, her six-year wait. And it looks like we have

been able to help her—with her certificate. It was the most rewarding to me, to help a needy person. It was the right thing to do. She loves to talk, as you could see. And she will tell one hundred people her story and how I helped her. So it was good policy and good politics.

In the late afternoon, we visited three federally subsidized "home health units" scattered in residential areas throughout the city. (She went in to take a firsthand look. I remained outside.) We drove in her car followed by a pair of staffers. "She wheels her Mazda van around the town like a truck driver (her father's profession) and drives pretty fast," I noted. She seemed to know every street and every corner; and she pointed out landmarks as we went. "This intersection was the most crime-ridden, drug-infested part of the city. It's a little better now, but it's still pretty bad. . . . That large building belongs to a company, Mentor. They make high-tech instruments. And they have started an elementary school." "She likes to be in motion," I noted. Mercifully, "she did slow down once, when the staffer's car following us fell too far behind."

Her business day ended that evening with a meeting and an elaborate dinner with the council of the regional Muwekma Ohlone Indians. Their problem was the pursuit of formal "recognition" as an American Indian tribe by the US Bureau of Indian Affairs. Without it, they have no legal standing and cannot own or conduct a business. Representative Lofgren had been working since her election to push their case with the Bureau.

The basic research, tracing lineages and legitimizing the origins of the tribe, had been conducted by an anthropologist at San Jose State University. He spoke eloquently, ending with, "Zoe, you are the rock on which our future will be built." She assured the group that "I will stand by you and push your case in every way I can, because it is a matter of justice. The reason I took up the tribe's case in the beginning and have argued it ever since, and will continue to argue it, is because it is a basic matter of justice—a matter of civil rights."

Her private concern is that when the Muwekmas do gain official recognition, they will purchase land and go into the gambling business. So her talk centered, too, on the importance of going into some other business. The group was elaborately deferential to her; but the lure of big money hung in the air. And they were keeping their own counsel. Altogether, the evening's adventure illustrated the sheer range of her involvements in a culturally diverse constituency.

Silicon Valley

In the four years between visits, Representative Lofgren had deepened her working relationships with her district's high-tech business community. "This valley exists," she said, because of science and innovation." "The growth of Silicon Valley," she agreed, had turned her district into "two worlds." But, she added, "That's not inconsistent with the rest of the district, because they have done so much to help the poor by providing jobs and supporting education . . . Silicon Valley has been a terrific resource for my constituency—providing money for schools."

"My kids went to school in multicultural schools, with kids who were very poor," she said,

> with kids whose parents had no education and had no interest in technical fields. Now, Cisco Systems is hiring these poor kids. One of my daughter's friends spent fifty hours a week at a fast-food place. Cisco found her, hired her, and sent her to USC. Cisco has established a Networking Academy at the high schools—an after-school program. Kids can learn (some high-tech skills) even if they don't go to college. And they make good money. These companies are hungry for personnel—going all over the country looking for people.

As for herself, she was undaunted and enthused.

> I'm not a high-tech person. But I'm very interested in technology. In high school, I took computer classes—they called it "business machines" then. After I got elected, I started learning the high-tech business. And I found it came easy to me. I enjoy it. And it's not just a high-tech matter. It's a civil rights issue. It's a privacy issue. And these issues interest me deeply. You have to catch on fast, because the industry is so volatile—up, down, up, down. If you miss one product revolution, you're out of business. Time is money for these companies. You have to be able to talk with them in their language, at their speed. I've learned to do that.

In answer to my question about her working relationship with leaders in the high-tech industry, she told a couple of icebreaker stories.

One relationship began with a call from the Clinton White House telling her that the Secretary of Commerce, Mickey Kantor, could be made available for an event in her constituency. "They wanted a meeting of some kind," she said, "to help him get acquainted with Silicon Valley people." She called an involved individual—whose wife had been a fellow county supervisor. He suggested, "Don't have a straight fundraiser; have a fundraising luncheon"—And the Lofgren staff proceeded to organize a fundraising luncheon in the "comfortable library room" of giant Cisco Systems.

She finessed the problem of enticing people to come to the event by translating one person's "maybe" into a "yes." "Then they all fell into line," Lofgren recalled. "We had a rousing discussion of encryption.[18] Kantor saw how deeply these people felt about it and how absolutely crucial it was to their business. When I pitched in on their side, they realized that I knew the subject. And we bonded." Encryption, of course, was central to her work on the Judiciary Committee's Subcommittee on Courts, the Internet and Intellectual Property.

In 1998, she worked with her Republican subcommittee chairman, Robert Goodlatte, to pass legislation that eased the effects of encryption on trade by bringing restrictions more in line with those of competing countries. "We still have a long way to go, but this is a good start," she said.[19] It was her most noteworthy bipartisan effort. And the careful delineations in her story were familiar.

> It was his bill, and he asked me to join him. I did. I disagree with him on a lot of things; but we worked well together on encryption. He had some ideas that I agreed to; I had some ideas he agreed to. I gave him credit and he gave me credit. I don't agree with him much. But we worked well together, and got the bill passed.

Her meeting and her legislative effort were especially central, she observed, to her career inside the House. "Women do have a better understanding of some issues than men. There are 'women's issues.' And it is very important that women work on those issues. But if that's all you do, you are not taken seriously in this institution. You aren't respected; and you don't count. Encryption is not a 'women's issue.'"

A second "getting acquainted" story centered on her personal activity in combating a statewide ballot proposition that had the effect of encouraging frivolous legal attacks on high-tech companies. Venture capitalist and Valley billionaire John Doerr had begun to raise money to back his "No on 11" campaign. And Representative Lofgren joined in.

I got the local Democratic Party to join the fund drive, by calling all my friends from the board of supervisors. Then I went to my friend, the head of the building trades, with whom I had worked when I was on the board. And he rounded up trade union support. In that legal fight, I got to know John Doerr. And he has been friendly to me ever since. I can't raise forty million in two weeks like he does, but I can be of help to him from my position.

"High-tech is easy to learn," she said, "I learned it in the Judiciary Committee. And I've gotten to know many of the high-tech CEOs. . . . I love Cisco. They are the most socially sensitive and socially helpful company in the world. They are wonderful citizens, better than any of the others—and the others are very good. They are now the biggest company in the world—bigger than Microsoft or GE."

She had enlisted in another of their causes—the relaxation of immigration requirements for highly skilled workers. And she was taking the lead, along with centrist Democrats, in legislation to increase their numbers.[20] Much harder, and more costly, was her vote in favor of increased international trade. "I knew what the right vote was. And I did it. It made a lot of my union supporters unhappy. It was the right vote for my constituency."

Summing up, I noted, "Her (constituency) connections are now full of Silicon Valley. They were not in 1994. That's the big change." It was not, however, her only new activity. Another, more temporary, "big change" in her public policy activity lay ahead.

Impeachment

By design, a research project focused on House member representational activities at home leaves little space for House member activities inside the legislature. Jim Greenwood's intraparty impact had been unusual. In Zoe Lofgren's case, her involvement in a one-time national event—the 1998 impeachment proceedings against President Bill Clinton—also forced an institutional detour.

By law, the impeachment process begins in the House and in its Judiciary Committee. The process requires that a majority vote in that committee is needed to send a recommendation to the full House for a yes or no impeachment decision. A majority "yes" vote to impeach will trigger an expulsion trial in the Senate.

In 1974, the House Judiciary Committee voted to impeach President Richard Nixon. But before the full House could act on that vote, the president resigned. During that confrontation, San Jose's representative, Democrat Don Edwards, was a member of the House Judiciary Committee. And he had brought Zoe Lofgren—a young, part-time lawyer on his district staff—to Washington to help him in his preparations. Now, in 2000, she was a member of the decision-making House Judiciary Committee in her own right. And when the Clinton impeachment controversy surfaced in 1994, press accounts noted her earlier involvement. "I knew something from Watergate," she said. "I wrote the Cambodian bombing resolution"—that is, one of the Articles of Impeachment.

In 1996, therefore, she had a head start. "It became clear to me that [the Republicans] intended to take him [the president] out." In her view, the effort to impeach President Clinton was nothing less than "an effort to overthrow an election." And she knew she would need help in making that argument.

"First off," she recalled, "we needed a top-notch lawyer who could bring order to the thing." With the help of her lawyer husband, she found a person who fit their prescriptions. He was experienced as counsel to several congressional committees; and he had the intelligence and stature, she believed, to do the job. And so, "when impeachment struck, John Flannery came on board."

That step was especially necessary, she believed, because she intended to stick to legal arguments. "Before we begin chasing facts . . . we need a common understanding of what is an impeachable offense."[21] And she began with the ideas of the founders: "I dug out my *Federalist Papers*."[22] There, she found a limited and imprecise discussion of what constituted an impeachable offense. As a working proposition, she adopted Benjamin Franklin's conclusion: that impeachment was so extreme an act that it should be considered "the alternative to assassination. [And] it is that standard that needs to be applied in this case."[23]

She worked with her chosen lawyer to build "our 30-page document" arguing for the strictest constitutional and legal definition of impeachable offenses. Her central argument would be that whatever political or personal offenses the president may have committed, he had not committed an impeachable offense. "Impeachment," she argued early on, "requires a destruction of the constitutional form of government, and all we've got [here] is [that] the president had a girlfriend and lied about it."[24]

To take any other position, she argued, would reveal a purely partisan effort to unseat a duly elected president. Her strategy—to make impeachment a "constitutional," (i.e., a less political) matter, failed. Later, during the committee debate on whether to recommend a formal inquiry, she argued that "before we begin chasing facts, we ought to know the relevance of the facts we are chasing . . . we need a common understanding of what is an impeachable offense.[25] That effort, too, failed.

Inside the committee, she recollected, "I tried to work out something bipartisan. My idea was, first, to get the most conservative Democrat on the committee to cosponsor it. I asked Rick Boucher (D-VA) to read my 30-page document. He said it made total sense to him. He believed in the rule of law; and these, he agreed, were the facts to compare with the law." But it went nowhere. She did open the smallest bipartisan crack. "I told the committee Republicans that I wasn't going to be the Chuck Wiggins (a bitter-end pro-Nixon California holdout in 1974) of the Judiciary Committee. If you can put together an argument I can support, I will. If you don't, I won't." Given her terms, they did not try. She was, of course, only one low-ranking committee member of the minority party. Because of her experience with the Nixon inquiry, however, she received far more attention than her formal position called for.

"I was on *Meet the Press* prematurely—at Easter time," she said. "We had worked on our 30-page document on the subject of finding a standard for impeachment. And I referred to it on that program. It said, 'There is a legal matter here.' But the Republicans were not interested in our document; and Judiciary Committee Chairman Henry Hyde was not interested in it. I knew then that they were plotting to take him [Clinton] out."

Asked to compare the context to Watergate, her view was that "with Watergate, there was a very heavy sense of foreboding and gravity, which isn't present here. Then, it was widely perceived as a committee coming together in the face of a national, cataclysmic threat. This time, it's just one party going after the president of another."[26]

The Judiciary Committee's recently hired Special Counsel prepared a lengthy set of his taped interviews with all persons involved, together with a set of anti-Clinton pro-impeachment "findings." At a small meeting of House Democrats in Minority Leader Dick Gephardt's office, Representative Lofgren spoke against the public release of these findings. And she lost. "I said we should not release the tapes—that we didn't know what was in them, who might be hurt, or what security secrets were in them. They didn't listen to me." Recalling the ultimate floor vote, she said, "I think sixty-seven of us voted against releasing the tapes—and a lot more later wished they had. I was right."

At one point, she said that she and a colleague had tried to reach the chairman of the Judiciary Committee, Henry Hyde, to ask, as she put it, that he "bring the Constitution into play." But they could not reach him. "The party leadership controlled him; so no negotiation."

When she spoke of Henry Hyde, I mentioned that during the public hearings, when she had been questioning the committee's Special Counsel on his findings, Chairman Hyde had repeatedly referred to her as "the little lady from California." "I got dozens of emails and letters from all over the country expressing outrage at that comment," she said. "I could have taken him up on it, but I was winning the argument, and I didn't want to create a distraction." She added, "I was the only person who got [the Special Counsel] flustered . . . I knew some things he didn't think anyone knew and he started looking around and shifting his papers." At least one attending journalist noticed that her questions had been especially well targeted.[27]

Throughout the impeachment process, the Santa Clara County congresswoman received more than her share of public notice. Prospectively, in March, the Capitol Hill newspaper, *Roll Call*, profiled her as one of seven Democratic "players" in a "possible impeachment inquiry." And they noted, "Both Democrats and Republicans respect Lofgren who has consistently emphasized that concern for the institution of Congress should take precedence when it comes to questions of political misconduct."[28] "The President," she said, "gave a very straightforward and emphatic denial (of political misconduct). Therefore, I would conclude that is correct. I am 50 years old and I have been disappointed in life. I hope that doesn't happen this time."[29]

In September, *CQ Weekly* profiled her as one of five Democrats "Worth Watching on the Judiciary Committee."[30] A week later, *Time Magazine's* impeachment story pictured her as one of three "Democrats to Watch" on the committee—as someone who "could emerge as an important moderate, female defender of the President."[31] Midway through the inquiry, a California journalist commented that "Zoe Lofgren has made her mark as one of the more measured lawmakers who consistently asks deeper questions about what the Founding Fathers had in mind."[32]

"The vote was upsetting and wrong," she commented, "it frightened people to think we were undoing an election." And, "When the issue is overturning the government that the American people elected," she added, "you end up with the kind of comments I've been getting in San Jose, in grocery stores and on the street, where people tell me they think this is a Republican coup d'etat."[33] "I came here to Washington," she told colleagues, "and I find people on a different reality plane. And then I fly home, and normal people say, 'What are those nuts doing?'"[34] In a closing comment, she noted that considering the work she did, "for the first time when I worked for Don Edwards, a member of the Judiciary Committee [in 1974], it does come out to about two years of research on this issue."[35]

When we talked at home in 2000, she reflected on the impeachment experience and its effects. Her level of self-satisfaction was far more definitive and positive than it was with the conflicted and fence-sitting Jim Greenwood.

> Personally, I learned the mechanics and learned how to do it, and it raised my profile. I also found out something about myself—how important the basic principles of the Constitution and our values are to me. I learned that they are more important than who has the job. I didn't know I felt that way until I was tested. I did not know at the time whether my decision would be the end of my political career. But I decided that it didn't matter.

Institutionally, the impeachment episode accelerated her adjustment to the institution. She said, "I learned how to put things together. And I raised my profile because I had been guided by the law. At first, I didn't speak to the press. Then I realized that the Republicans were going to try their case in the press. So I did." As a result, she said,

> I became a well-known figure relative to what I had been. It changed the way the local media handled me, because I had become a local celebrity. It took a while for the media to catch on, however. The people understood at a gut level what was involved—the upsetting of an election—but the media didn't. It was interesting to see the media learn.

"It was fun to be on TV. At first, I shunned it. Then I realized I could do it. And I think I became effective at it. I had to learn not to be anxious and just do it."[36]

In addition, "the experience helped me in the House because they knew I had no leadership ambitions, that I was only interested in accomplishing something—that I was not a goofball." And with one peek into the future, she added, "I won't think about leadership as long as my son is in high school. Leaders can't get home every weekend."

The Home Front

When she was at home during impeachment, she recalled, constituency relationships often centered on that subject.

> People at home would mob me. They would hug me in the supermarkets. Strangers would come up to me crying. A mother with two kids came up to me crying; and the kids were crying. "What will become of our country?" Once I was standing in line at the supermarket checkout, and the women said to me, "You go to the head of the line. We know you don't have time!" I went to the Dress Fair and the clerk said, "Can I talk to you?" And two of them took me outside and they started to cry. "Save the country," they said. They called impeachment "a coup d'etat." And it was.

Beyond impeachment and thinking more generally about "staying in touch," it was very much business as usual, with an ever-changing constituency.

> Since 1997, I have gone to the Fourth of July parade and barbeque in my neighborhood. I never go to big citywide festivities. I only go to my own

neighborhood. This year I went; and I said "Who are these people?" They have moved in during the last ten months. And they all have PhDs—all in high tech. They are all Anglo. And they are Democrats.

Apropos of "staying in touch," I asked whether she still used the "ironing board" approach.

> It's a struggle to connect with constituents in a way that's comfortable for them. When I set up the ironing board, it makes them nervous. They have to wait in line. They don't know what it's for. If you do a mailing, mostly it's constituent service. I tried telephoning, but then they all come at once. And if you make them wait, it seems disrespectful.

Short answer: no. Still, she stated a preference.

> Staying connected is done better by shopping in the supermarket than by formal outreach. I like to shop in different parts of the district. I can talk while I shop. And people will talk. I like that. It fits my comfort level. It drives my daughter crazy.

The same openness was demonstrated soon after. She took me to walk through her newly purchased home—still under some renovation—but with her son asleep upstairs. It was a large, Spanish style, older home on a wide and winding city street, with a spacious backyard and pool under a landscape architect's management. It all seemed inviting but not pretentious. "Our mayor does a lot of entertaining," she said. "I hope to do some entertaining here, too."

Updating her constituency relationships, she singled out changes in ethnicity and income. "The ethnic mix has changed, with Asians increasing. Ballparking it, I'd say the Asian population is now about equal to the Hispanic population in the county. North San Jose has seen an influx of Chinese—mostly working in Silicon Valley. A large number of Indians, Sikhs, and Hindi also work in Silicon Valley."

Hand in hand with ethnic change had come economic change. And it was being registered in an exploding housing market.

> We are in a time of dislocation here in the Valley. New people are coming in and displacing old people. Housing costs are going through the roof. The new people are buying up the homes of old people at outrageous prices. It's a very high-cost area. . . . The General Counsel of

Cisco, my friend, says "It's the modern gold rush. And we sell machines to all the miners."

A 2006 census study of housing reported that San Jose had "the highest median income" among "larger American cities."[37]

Constituency changes had brought new constituent policy preferences. Among the most visible was growing support for reducing and/or eliminating the federal estate tax. "I voted for the Republican bill lowering, then ending, the estate tax," she said. "It may have gone too far; but I voted for it to make a point. A group of us (three nearby Democrats) did. And that's not a Republican group! We were voting our districts." It was a learning experience.

She continued,

> The story that brought the whole thing home to me was the story of [Representative] Sam Farr's gardener—a man who worked hard all his life, bought a small house, and then watched the value of his house skyrocket. Working in the garden one day, he asked Sam to vote to repeal the estate tax. That says it all!

And,

> With housing values going up the way they are, working people in my district who have worked all their lives now have something to pass on to their children. And they want to be able to do that. The legislation was not about Bill Gates. He is not worried about his estate tax! It is about working people in my district.
>
> My father does not understand this at all. He hung up on me three times when I tried to explain! He's a union man. To him, there are the rich managers and the poor working people—nothing in between. He cannot understand that working people might have something to pass to their children. He could not understand that I had voted my district.

The next day during her town meeting in a middle-to-lower-income neighborhood, a young woman, holding her baby, got up and said to her representative, "I never thought I would ever say this, that I'm in favor of repealing the estate tax. I never imagined I would have an estate. But I have a house, something to give my daughter here; and I thank you for your vote." "Did you hear what that young woman said?" Zoe asked afterward. "She's a yuppie. What a change! The best solution would be to raise the exemption."

Congress later passed, with Lofgren's support, a compromise, gradual multiyear elimination of the tax. In her calculation, it was a Silicon Valley induced compromise.

Inside the House, she said, her own postimpeachment adjustment was not easy. "It took me a long time before I could work with the Republicans again. Their behavior fell so far short of what was called for that I lost all respect for them." But as a minority member, she had to form policy alliances or be left out entirely.

Despite the disruptions of impeachment, cross party talk had begun inside her two Judiciary Subcommittees. She now distinguished between "the good Republicans" and "those way out on the right wing . . . . I do get awfully tired of the right-wingers. You can't work with them on anything. Other members that I disagree with, we can work together."

Inside her encryption-related subcommittee, for example, she was developing a good talking-working relationship with the Republican chairman.

> He's a good guy. I don't agree with him on a lot of things, but we talk. I tell him that I hope that I will chair our subcommittee and he will be the ranking member. But if we don't, I hope he will be the chairman and I will be the ranking minority member. We laugh a lot. We could work with each other.

She was building on her earlier encryption success. And she was working her way from partisan impeachment activity to bipartisan governing activity.

Constituency Snapshots: Town Meetings

On my last day, Representative Lofgren's schedule took us to three town meetings—two in solidly middle-class communities, and one in a less prosperous area. "This is the first time I've tried three meetings in one day," she said. "And it's been quite a while since I've done any." It was the only time that she was not in charge behind the wheel of her car. Her top staffer/confidante drove—and supplied an appropriate Edwards-to-Lofgren comparison. As we approached the second community, she said, "We drove [Representative Don] Edwards out to this place once. He looked at the thousands of new homes and asked, 'What is this place? Where are we?' We had to tell him, it's your district!" No such necessity this time. For a visitor, it was a useful introduction to the makeup of the district.

Opening each meeting, the congresswoman said "how great it is to leave the idiocy of Washington for the normalcy of San Jose," or, "to leave the crazy people of Washington for the normal people of San Jose." Then she apologized for not always being available. "I travel 5,000 miles every weekend and sometimes when I get home, I'm shot." Then, "I'm only human and I know I make mistakes. I hope you will tell me when I do. And I'll keep trying to do the best I can."

"It's a nice, low-key, pleasant introduction," I noted, "but serious. She comes across as knowledgeable (and) dedicated—nothing frivolous or flashy or lighthearted. She is empathetic and seems especially quick to see, identify, and abhor injustice. She was on the same wavelength with each audience. During or after every meeting, several people thanked her for coming."

She displayed a broad issue reach. And there was a considerable issue overlap—on health care, defense, transportation, noise pollution. Even so, each of the three meetings had its own distinctive flavor—the first one more technical, the second one more personal, and the third one more medical.

In view of the anti-NRA blast that had greeted me the day before, it was noteworthy that in all these meetings, she went out of her way to emphasize her devotion to gun control as a "priority." "I'm working," she repeated, "with Carolyn McCarthy [a crusading Long Island congresswoman whose husband was shot to death on a commuter train] on a sensible gun-control bill." To which she would add, "I am not against people having guns for hunting or sport. In the northern hills of my district—in the Hamilton Range—you'd better have a shotgun because there are wild boar and rattlesnakes." And she told each group that she had come to such strong opposition because she worried about her children.

Afterward, in the car, she elaborated,

> I took them to school one day and found yellow police tape all around
> the front door. We had to go through a side entrance. Someone had been
> shot and killed right in front of the school. It was the second killing near
> the school, and I was frightened for the safety of the kids. That's when
> I fully realized what was really at stake in gun violence—the children.

She concluded, "I learned far more about this issue as a mother than
I ever learned as a woman. And I expect that's true of a lot of other
issues, too." From my first day in 1996 to my last day in 2000, her gut-
level preoccupation with improving and protecting children's lives and
opportunities remained second to none.

In the first meeting, the first question concerned the US Patent Office.
"Welcome to Silicon Valley!" I scribbled. And I said to her afterwards,
"I've sat in dozens of town meetings and that's the first time I have ever
heard a question about the Patent Office." "You couldn't see this," she
added, "but when I mentioned encryption, I got some big 'thumbs up'
from the people in the back row." It set a tone. The group of about thirty-
five seemed to be scientifically oriented and, I noted, "very articulate."

Patents and encryption were familiar subjects. She described patents as "the economic engines driving the high-tech industry." And she
noted that "more patents have been issued in Santa Clara County than
in any other place in the world." Describing her Subcommittee on Intellectual Property as "an island of bipartisan sanity in an ocean of partisan idiocy," she discussed their work on encryption.

> There are no Democrats or Republicans on the subcommittee. It's like the
> board of supervisors—there were no Republican or Democratic potholes
> or parks. We just work together to produce a bill. . . . I spent countless
> hours talking about encryption, finally getting members of the House to
> agree in the end to do what they ought to do. That was pretty neat.

But it was an exception. "Partisan gridlock," she added, "has [legisla-
tion] bottled up in Washington." She ruminated afterward, "I'm doing
my best . . . 5,000 miles a week is not worth it unless I can accomplish
something for my constituents. . . . If I wanted to be rich, I'd stay here
in dot-com land."

The group seemed particularly concerned, too, about preserving
their suburban neighborhoods from ever-increasing noise pollution

and traffic congestion. On the subject of cutting down air traffic noise pollution, an engineer thought NASA had developed some relevant technology—about which Zoe noted afterward, "I've got to look into that NASA suggestion." On the question of "a terrific shortfall of housing in the community," she said she had just been appointed to chair a House Democratic Study Group on affordable housing.

On the closely related subject of ever-increasing immigration, she lambasted the Immigration Service. She began with a pet story I had heard her tell more than once. A young Vietnamese woman came to the United States as a baby; she lived here all her life; she was valedictorian of her high school class; she was admitted to UCLA. But the Immigration Service denied her scholarship to UCLA because she had never become a US citizen. "Now," said Lofgren, "she's a waitress. . . . What a dumb law. . . . I taught immigration law at Santa Clara Law School. I know something about immigration. The Immigration Service is a mess."

The second, less prosperous, constituency group centered their questions on a private airport, Medicare, gun control, prescription drugs, and immigration. It was the meeting with the sharpest tone of discontent.

It was held in one of the least affluent parts of her district. And it was (with more than forty people) the best attended. "This is the [East Side] area where Cesar Chavez came and organized the farm workers—most of whom are now dead," she said. "I remember when these low-income houses here were built—almost overnight—to house the poor farm workers. . . . San Jose used to be a sleepy little town. Its motto was: 'The Valley of Heart's Content.' The last canneries here closed a couple of years ago."

There was not a lot of "heart's content" expressed in the town meeting. One person wants "money to fix up my house." Another opposes a transportation levy because "What's in it for us?" An engineer complains that students from other countries are "crowding out American engineers." Afterward, Zoe singled out "the man who complained about immigration" for a critique. "There is always someone who—having come to America and succeeding here—wants to keep everyone else out."

An older woman opposes a proposed city golf course: "What are we getting over here . . . we want crosswalks and stop signs . . . why doesn't the mayor help the poor people?" Another person pipes up to correct her, "We got a stop sign." Another worries that Social Security is not safe, "You hear that every day." A man thanks the representative for her work with troubled children. And she tells him about her visits to the county jail. Along the way, it develops that there is one thing on which several of them strongly agree: opposition to the day and night unrestricted noise coming from the private plane, general aviation airport next door. After listening to several complaints she suggested, "Why don't you all get together."

At lunch, she unloaded on the neighborhood airport. "It's all for recreation. It serves no useful purpose. These rich guys don't live anywhere near here; and they have nothing but contempt for the people they fly over, making so much noise." "When I was on the board of supervisors," she continued at lunch, "I worked as hard as anything to get rid of that airport and put that land to better use. I had the three votes to do it; but one of them went south on me and I lost . . . the Pilot's Association got to him." And, she added, "There are three groups from whom I never got anything but trouble, no matter what I did for them . . . the Humane Society, the gun nuts, and the private pilots."

An uneventful third town meeting marked the end of my research in California's Eighth Congressional District. The solidly middle-class group was more senior and less technology-oriented than the first one and more satisfied than the second. Their questions emphasized health care, HMOs, hospitals, and prescription drugs. Interestingly, there had not been a whiff of "impeachment" in any of three meetings. It was long gone.

Altogether, the day exemplified the variety of political places in which our representatives go about their work—and the very broad reach of this one. When I commented on the easy relationship she seemed to have with each group, she said simply, "I have been very deeply involved in the community. And they know it." With some weariness, she added, "There is no politics-free zone. Sooner or later, every issue becomes a wedge issue. And it's not the rules. It's the culture."

We walked toward her car. I said, "Thanks for letting me come." She said, "Good-bye Professor." We shook hands. She turned away to go to her car. I walked with a staff member to his car to hop a ride to my hotel. It was an unusually businesslike good-bye. Nothing of a personal nature had passed between us. With a seven-word exchange and a handshake, it was over.

Afterward, I wondered about it. From the beginning, she had been welcoming, accommodating, candid, expansive, and thoroughly helpful. But all the while she had kept it markedly impersonal. To my recollection, she had never called me by name. When we were alone, I was always "Professor." When we were with others, I was always "the professor." There was none of the personal exchange that warmed the Thurman relationship. She had not inquired about who I was—work, family, or personal. It was her way.

I closed the study with a simple, covering generalization: that from the beginning of this research adventure I had expected to find behavioral differences across the five House members and to find behavioral consistency within each individual member. Zoe Lofgren, like the others, had fit nicely into that expectation. She was every bit a welcoming professional. Happily, in the business relationships that mattered, she had made the research a successful, clean sweep "five for five." The book could be closed.

Postscript

As of 2011, Representative Zoe Lofgren had served nine terms in the House. Until that Republican year, she chaired the House Committee on Administration—to which she was appointed by her California colleague, House Speaker Nancy Pelosi. Zoe was described, at various times, as a "top lieutenant," as a "long term friend" of the Speaker, and as part of the Speaker Pelosi's "personal circle" or "inner circle."[38] In 2002, Zoe ran for election to the position of vice chairman of the House Democratic Caucus.[39] The result was James Clyburn (SC) 95 votes; Gregory Meek (NY) 56 votes; Zoe Lofgren (CA) 53 votes. Later, she was appointed by the Speaker as Chair of the bipartisan House Subcommittee on Ethics. In that position she presided very professionally over a complexity of difficult ethics investigations of fellow House members—most notably, the one involving Representative Charles Rangel—until the Republican Party took back control of the House in 2011.

Addendum II

Two Partisans, Two Playing Fields

In contrast to the sprawling, multicounty constituencies of Karen Thurman and Glenn Poshard, both Jim Greenwood of Pennsylvania and Zoe Lofgren of California represented compact, accessible, and, essentially single-county districts. Their constituency connection patterns present a contrast between those of a successful suburban Republican moderate and those of an equally successful urban liberal Democrat. Both of them had enjoyed precongressional electoral success—he in a state legislature, she on a county-wide governing board. Their willingness to take on a stranger promised marked variations in geographical location, constituency makeup, partisan affiliation, issue preference patterns, congressional priorities, and personal opportunities.

The connection with Representative Greenwood in Pennsylvania began during his first reelection campaign in 1994. Visits with Representative Lofgren in California began soon after her first reelection campaign in 1996. Expected comparisons centered on familiar philosophical, partisan, and socioeconomic differences between two political prototypes—a suburban Republican moderate and an urban Democratic liberal. Of particular importance, their constituencies differed widely with respect to cultural makeup. In Santa Clara County, we traveled among a population that was notably 38 percent Hispanic and 23 percent Asian. In Bucks County, with its 2 percent of the same two groups, ethnicity never surfaced.

Comparisons developed under unusual circumstances. The congressional elections of 1994 had ended forty years of Democratic Party dominance in the House of Representatives, and had brought to power an untested Republican majority. Republican Jim Greenwood came to Congress, therefore, as a charter member of a newly energized and upbeat take-over majority. By contrast, Democrat Zoe Lofgren came to Congress two years later as a first-term member of a recently defeated and still unsettled minority party. They entered the same institution, but with very different strategic postures, problems, and possibilities.

When side-by-side comparison came into view, the two new political figures were embarked on markedly different career trajectories. Republican Jim Greenwood was a second-term congressman looking forward to ever-brightening prospects inside an aggressive and energetic new majority. But he had to contend with the troublesome opposition of his own party's strong conservative wing. Democrat Zoe Lofgren was a Washington newcomer looking to constituency nourishments, while seeking a viable footing among a recently defeated, demoralized, and disorganized minority party.

He was "climbing" inside his party. She was "finding a place"–and would soon "settle down" in hers. She enjoyed solid support in her district. In contrast to the Pennsylvanian, she often could—and did— speak inclusively of the community she represented. Her worrisome problems derived from her party's minority status in Washington. His noteworthy problems, by contrast, remained with persisting divisions within his party electorate at home.

This post-1994, majority/minority, Republican/Democrat congressional alignment survived throughout the period under investigation here. As observational opportunities played out, the setting for all three visits in Pennsylvania was an ongoing fall election campaign. On the other hand, both California visits took place in nonelection periods. Research patterns and opportunities for comparison varied accordingly.

Representative Greenwood spent most of our time together campaigning for reelection among issue-oriented and partisan groups. Representative Lofgren, by contrast, spent our time together in nonpartisan constituency service activities—constituent appointments, community-regarding events, and small minority group activities. The representative from Santa Clara County and the Rochester observer never did travel together in a campaign context. In contrast to the embattled Pennsylvania Republican, however, the California Democrat worked across a broad spectrum to cultivate outsized majorities in her multicultural, "one-party" constituency.

Their differences present (or reinforce) a standing analytic challenge. Returning to the basic proposition, a political scientist could not have known or pondered any of their similarities or differences without visiting their two constituencies and becoming immersed in two playing fields, and in two sets of representational/legislative activities. For this inquiring student, it was deemed a necessity. For other political scientists who accept the challenge to do more and do better, the two-person example can serve as a continuing stimulant.

— 7 —

Constituency-Centered Scholarship

Exploration: In the Constituency

There are numerous reasons why students of American politics might want to study the US House of Representatives. And there are numerous angles from which to do so. The small set of studies presented here—of a few politicians, their home places, their policy preferences, and their connection patterns—tells us that much. The studies have been presented in hopes of nudging our scholarly attention toward the comparative study of House member activity in their home constituencies. From ambition to accountability, via immersion and inquiry, we have watched and talked with a few of them as they worked in their separate and distinctive home constituencies. And we have endeavored, in both contexts, to supplement and to balance our lopsided legislation-centered scholarship with research focused on the activity of representation.

In the last half century, political scientists have accumulated a treasure trove by tracking and explaining the legislative activities of our elected members inside the House of Representatives. Our accumulated working knowledge of committee decision making, of partisan coalition building, and of vote patterning inside the House is the result of concentrated and cooperative scholarly effort. In the absence, however, of any comparable effort, we know a good deal less about the activity of the very same House members when they are engaged in representational activity outside of the institution—when, in particular, they are working for understanding and for support at points of contact with citizens/voters in their own, distinctive home constituencies.

Political scientists know, of course, that the two main House member activities—legislating and representing—are linked to one another as the two central activities of a democratic government. To date, however, House member legislative activity in Washington has commanded the lion's share of our scholarly scrutiny. And House member representational activity in the political world outside of Washington has generated a lot less. Our studies of the US Congress are rich and robust in collective action, vote-centered analyses. But in the examination of individual House member activity in their home places outside of the House, political science studies are relatively thin and notably scarce. With respect to congressional constituencies, our scholarly inattentiveness is odd. As political scientists, we "own the franchise." Constituencies are "ours," yet we do not study them.

If, as, and when our research interest moves toward the subject of representation, our scholarly focus will be pulled increasingly toward the study of House member connection patterns in their home constituencies. In the present study, it is precisely that interest in legislator constituency connections that drives and focuses inquiry.

As a day-to-day research matter, the study of representation presents something of a chicken or the egg stalemate. Unless and until we undertake additional research inside House member constituencies, we are unlikely to pose or to pursue questions concerning representation. But unless and until we first highlight questions concerning representation, we are unlikely to investigate House member constituencies and/or to engage in connection-centered research. For now, this arrested state of play contributes heavily to our lopsidedly legislation-centered research agenda.

In the study at hand, we have treated the constituency focus as providing encouragement and leverage in moving beyond any such intellectual/research stalemate. We have done so by keeping our research focused directly on representational activity as conducted by a few House members in their own constituencies. And by remaining mindful throughout of the core belief—and stimulus—expressed at the outset: that "representation is the underlying strength of the United States Congress." Given the polyglot makeup of our nation, "the politics of representation" is every bit as basic a study as is "the politics of legislation."

With these ideas in mind, we have studied the political activities and connections of several members of the House of Representatives. And we have done so by joining them when they were at work in their home constituencies. In different time spans and in different district-wide settings, we developed a working knowledge of a few House members and their constituency activities. The dominant research method was participant observation. And the results, as presented here, have been an observational/conversational learning exercise along five separate and distinctive investigative paths.

Each one of the five representatives appeared to "fit" his or her own constituency reasonably well. Enough, at least, to make it clear that none of the five individuals, as we watched them, would have been a comfortable fit in—or could have been elected from—any of the other four congressional districts. Each representative talked about a distinctive territory. And each adopted a pattern of political activity responsive to that particular place. Building upon some broad similarities and differences, we have undertaken a close-up study of these House members in their constituencies. First, the representational activities of the five members were observed and described one at a time. And second, in order to gain analytic leverage, four of the constituency activity patterns were paired and compared two at a time.

Variation in the timing and the context of observation, and in the type of activity being observed, quickly ruled out sweeping generalizations. So, too, did the differences among the individual House members—in their backgrounds, work habits, adjustment problems, group affiliations, policy preferences, and office ambitions. Thinking about some of them as pairs, however, did serve to highlight similarities and differences and, in that way, encouraged comparison. One pair shared partisan loyalties; but they were separated by personal ambition and by constituency connection patterns. The other pair displayed talented political craftsmanship. But they differed in their partisan arrangements and in their legislative opportunities.

Overall, the most visible and the most broad-based of constituency connection patterns was partisanship. Party support certainly underpinned all five representational linkages—building, solidifying, and repairing—most visibly at campaign time. But party dominance does not tell us all, or even most, of what we need to know in order to study

House member activity in their constituencies. The separate pairings, however imperfect, are helpful precisely because they do provide some extra-partisan scholarly leverage.

Observation-centered research invites questions, too, about the attitudes and activities of the political scientist as an observer. It is a credibility problem. And it, also, affects the research product. The researcher inevitably spends considerable time and energy worrying about his/her ongoing relationship with each politician—contact by contact and cumulatively. And relationships vary considerably. The author's unique accessibility to the first individual studied (Barber Conable), for example, was very different from the author's more routine accessibility to the last individual studied (Zoe Lofgren). Taking stock of our five profiles as a group, how might we generalize across five very different research opportunities and experiences? And, how might we generalize across the different constituency activities of five individuals?

Difficulties are substantial. Neither the research experiences nor the individual players can be treated as any kind of sample. They have been studied one at a time, trip by separate trip, rarely in the same time frame, often at very different points in the two-year election cycle, and in their individual careers. The two pairs have been presented in very loose two-by-two comparisons. Neither the portraits nor the narratives fall (at least not yet) into easily recognizable representational categories or themes.

Looking backward, now, at the difficulties and shortcomings of single-scholar research across a range of playing fields, one obvious question is: Can we do better? And, if so, how? One obvious answer is that we might encourage a more systematic multischolar study of House member connection patterns.

Paired comparisons have long been this author's preferred road to discovery and generalization. Previous state-centered research efforts have included pairs of US House members: in Georgia, in New York, in Ohio, and in the Midwest.[1] All of them are more suggestive than definitive. And future follow-up comparative studies will surely require more careful questions, better controls, and, above all, engaged political scientists. Joint efforts might be directed at designing and administering a common questionnaire. Which brings us to matters of coordination, cooperation, and comparison.

Collaboration: Consider the Classroom

Political science studies of the US House of Representatives have been rich in analyses of its partisan and policy decision-making institutions (i.e., parties and committees) and in analyses of roll call vote patterns inside those institutions. Our inside vote studies are broadly conceived, comparatively cast, and statistically sophisticated. They are models of cumulative social science research. And because of them, we now know a great deal about how, why, in what patterns, and to what effect our elected representatives think, plan, organize, and decide inside the House.

We are not, therefore, without guidelines. That being said, however, the research being described here comes with a less common focus and a less familiar agenda. In place of the House of Representatives and its Capitol Hill settings, our outside research begins in the election constituencies from which House decision makers have been chosen. In place of member vote patterns registered inside the House, we have examined member connection patterns developed and displayed while they are at work in their home constituencies.

This work examines a one-on-one, face-to-face component to outside constituency research that is absent from—or at least very different from—research inside the House. The difference becomes especially prominent and challenging when moving from the study of collective behavior (on Capitol Hill) to the study of individual behavior (in constituencies at home). While we may recognize and talk about constituency activity, we have not yet subjected its full range and its variety to scholarly inquiry.

Plainly speaking, and compared to our flourishing studies of inside legislative activity, studies of outside representational activity are uncommon. And the full set of connection patterns that shape constituency relationships remain complex and unexamined. For now, they can best be examined in a variety of constituency contexts—one researcher, one constituency, one House member at a time. Unless and until, that is, a coordinated study—one combining several member-constituency explorations—could be devised and implemented. At which point, a more aggressive, more wide-ranging, more open and deliberately comparative "nudge" might be possible. And suggestions for cooperative activity would be welcomed.

The difficulties facing any constituency-based, connection-centered research are not hard to identify. Data collection and observation inside a constituency are likely to be piecemeal and intermittent. Arrangements are difficult to replicate, too—over time and in different contexts. Until measurement methods are devised, agreed upon, and implemented, results will continue to rely heavily, as in this study, on one-to-one listening and talking. Conversation is inevitably disjointed and imprecise. Its value depends, ultimately, upon personal interaction—and upon informal agreement—with contextual conditions being difficult to "hold constant." In-and-out, on-the-run research yields a good deal of uncertainty—in establishing constituency connection patterns, in developing personal relationships, and in weighing a variety of observations and influences.

Short-run counsels of caution ought not, however, to be treated as long-run expressions of despair. Not while classrooms are available. If, as, and when an experienced and inventive political scientist could be persuaded to undertake a constituency-centric classroom research project within the boundaries of a single state, we might begin to uncover and specify the ongoing variety and patterning across US House members and their districts. By devising a common interview schedule and by assigning student-interviewers to specific constituencies we might begin to recognize, and explain, research commonalities and contrasts across congressional districts. Indeed, students of politics, well accustomed these days to traveling abroad, might welcome and benefit from time spent "traveling abroad in America."

Pedagogy might be optimized if all constituencies being studied could come from a single state, and hence be governed by similar rulings. In which case, smaller states—that is, those with totals of, say, four to seven congressional districts—might make the most rewarding early choices. Number of districts might well be tailored to match the number of students—who would learn and contribute via their "travels"—one student to each constituency within the chosen state. Each student might be expected to travel in the same district at least twice with the House incumbent. One trip could be used to pursue answers to a common, group-devised questionnaire; and one trip could be used to pursue a range of place-and-person inquiries. This subject seems made to order for a seminar. Presentations by individual students—of their inquiries and experiences—might spur collective efforts to challenge old generalizations and to propose new ones.

Looking forward, some of the House member-constituency connections and activities opened up in this study might qualify as preparatory groundwork for a wider disciplinary push toward more politician-centered studies of representation in Congress. Until that happens, more constituency-centric research, of the sort displayed in these pages, will remind us of important "unfinished business" in the study of American political life.

Notes

Introduction

1. Richard Fenno, *Home Style: House Members in Their Districts*, 2nd ed. (New York: Longman's Classics in Political Science, 1978).
2. John R. Hibbing, foreward to *Home Style*, by Fenno, v–vii.
3. David Glenn, "The Power of Everyday Life," *The Chronicle Review*, September 25, 2009.

   The author's earliest (1981) single member (constituency-centered) study (of Rep. James Johnson of Colorado), "What's He Like? What's She Like? What Are They Like," can be found in Richard Fenno, *Watching Politicians: Essays on Participant Observation* (Berkeley: Institute of Governmental Studies Press, University of California, 1990), 95–111.

1. Constituencies, Connections, and Representation

1. Richard F. Fenno, *Senators on the Campaign Trail* (Norman: University of Oklahoma Press, 1996), 338.
2. Richard Cohen and Michael Barone, *Almanac of American Politics* (Washington, DC: National Journal Group, Biennial editions, 1964–present).
3. *Politics in America, 2008: The 110th Congress*, ed. Jackie Koszczuk and Martha Angle, (Washington, DC: Congressional Quarterly Press, 2008).

2. Barber Conable

1. The *New York Times Magazine* was financing a January trip to Washington so that I could "shadow" two newly elected New York representatives and write an article on their earliest adjustment experiences. The proposed article was rejected—and later published by Nelson Polsby in his compendium,

New Perspectives on the House of Representatives (Chicago: Rand McNally, 1974).

2. As quoted, by James Fleming in conversation with the author. See note #3, supra.

3. James Fleming, *Window on Congress: A Congressional Biography of Barber B. Conable, Jr.* (Rochester, NY: University of Rochester Press, 2004). Fleming's study draws heavily upon his access to Barber Conable's contingency newsletters and personal journal.

4. Richard Fenno, *Home Style: House Members in Their Districts* (Boston: Little Brown, 1974), 24–27.

5. I did not mention, and probably did not see then, his world-class collection of Native American artifacts—especially masks—which would lead him to the presidency of the Museum of the American Indian and to the executive board of the Smithsonian Institution. Once, when I told him that another congressman with whom I had traveled took a similar interest in local antiquities, he said, "You mean he's a nineteenth-century man like I am."

6. Jim Fleming first opened up Conable's newsletters for scholarly scrutiny in James Fleming, "The House Member As Teacher: An Analysis of the Newsletters of Barber B. Conable, Jr.," *Congress and the Presidency* (Spring 1993), 53–74.

7. For contrast, he parodied his neighbor's pattern. "He sends out two newsletters a year, filled with pictures of himself shaking hands with every person in the world. And it says, 'I have sponsored this bill and that bill to give money to the wealthy, money to the middle class, money to the poor.'"

8. He also retained, in the rural area, a campaign advisor and friend as a part-time staffer—who kept an office in his own country home and kept abreast of the local scene.

9. Courtney Shelden, "Movers and Shakers in Congress," *US News and World Report,* April 23, 1984.

3. Glenn Poshard

1. First as assistant director of the Southern Illinois Regional Education Service Center, and then as director of the Area Service Center for Educators of the Gifted. His PhD was in administration of higher education.

2. In the 103rd Democrat-dominated Congress, 203 (75 percent) House members were more liberal than Poshard; and 55 (25 percent) were more conservative. In the 10th Congress, the yearly numbers were 83 percent and 86 percent more liberal. (Keith T. Poole and Howard Rosenthal, *Congress: A Political-Economic History of Roll Call Voting* (New York: Oxford).

3. "Gray Announces Retirement," press release, *Congress of the United States,* no date.

4. A similar newspaperman's view from inside that district is Pat Gauen's "Costello Sitting Pretty; Others Are on Ant Hill," *St. Louis Post Dispatch,* January 16, 1992.

5. Michael Barone and Grant Ujifusa, The *Almanac of American Politics,* 1990, National Journal, Washington D.C. pp. 393—394.

6. One author described him as "deeply religious," noting that in Congress, early on, he started a Bible study group (Bill Lamprecht, "Southern Populist," Illinois Periodicals-on-Line, November 1997).

7. *Politics in America, Congressional Quarterly* (Washington, DC: CQ Press), 482.

8. When he joined the committee, it was "The Committee on Public Works and Transportation." In 1996, it became "The Committee on Transportation and Infrastructure."

9. Kathleen Best, "Glenn Poshard," *SLPD,* October 16, 1994.

10. Lynn Sweet, "Compromise's Balancing Act Sways Some Illinoisans," *Chicago Sun Times,* August 23, 1994.

11. Jennifer Davis, *Glenn Poshard,* Illinois Periodicals on-Line, Northern Illinois Libraries, 7. Also, Glenn Poshard, "My central and southeastern Illinois congressional district is comprised of [sic] 27 rural and economically distressed counties," testimony, Ways and Means, Health Subcommittee, Ways and Means Committee, July 20, 1995.

12. Gayle Worland, "Poshard: Illinois' Quiet Leader," *Illinois Times,* January 5, 1995. Another estimate was that Illinois was the fourteenth largest producer of oil and led the nation in recoverable coal reserves (Lamprecht, "Southern Populist").

13. For Poshard, see Tom Woolf, "Poshard Laments Nation's Growing Intolerance," *Southern Illinoisan,* April 30, 1995. A keen and timely academic analysis is Sarah A. Binder's "The Disappearing Political Center: Congress and the Incredible Shrinking Middle," *The Brookings Review,* Fall 1996. A more recent, commanding analysis is Morris Fiorina's *Disconnect: The Breakdown of Representation in American Politics* (Norman: University of Oklahoma Press, 2009).

14. Joe Holleman, "Poshard Tried in Vain to Kill the Clean Air Act," *SLPD,* March 18, 1992.

15. Kathleen Best and Tim Poor, "War Page," *SLPD,* January 23, 1994. See also Patrick Gauen, "Lawmaker to Ask Clinton to Help Domestic Oil Industry," *SLPD,* February 24, 1994.

16. "Poshard Announces Bid for Final Office Term," *Effingham Daily News,* no date.

17. News release, "Poshard Ranked Second Among IL Delegates for Budget Cut Votes," May 11, 1996. See also, Concord Coalition Citizens Council, *Tough Choices: Deficit Reduction Scorecard,* [pamphlet], April 1996.

18. Editorial, "For Congress in Southern Illinois," *SLPD*, March 11, 1992. See also, Joe Holleman, "Poshard Leading Bruce in Battle of Incumbents," *SLPD*, March 18, 1992; "No member of the Illinois delegation eschews the trappings of power as vigorously as . . . Glenn Poshard, who just works hard and gets the job done;" "Final Choices for U.S. House," *Chicago Tribune*, February 28, 1992.

19. Poshard: "I'm a workaholic. I work 16 hours a day." Near the end of his tenure, he gave up his DC apartment, moved into his DC office, and lived there for the remaining months (Basil Talbott, "Poshard's DC Home is a Study in Frugality," *Chicago Sun Times*, August 25, 1997).

20. Key endorsements were the *SLPD* editorial, "For Congress in Southern Illinois," *SLPD*, March 11, 1992, and "Final Choices for the U.S. House," *CT*, February 28, 1994.

21. Dwight Morris, ed., *Handbook of Campaign Spending: Money in the 1992 Congressional Races, Congressional Quarterly*, (Washington, DC: CQ Press: 1994), 284. Others were more lopsided. One account said it was $690,000 to $85,000 (Patrick Gauen, "Battle Lines Drawn in New District: Campaign Financing Highlights Poshard-Bruce Race," *SLPD*, March 9, 1992). A third accounting estimated the difference at $700,000 to $120,000 (*Inside Politics*, CNN Transcript #19, March 23, 1992).

22. Ibid.

23. Robert Koenig and Daniel Browning, "Poshard Credits Budget: Winner," *SLPD*, March 19, 1992.

24. When Terry Bruce announced, later, that he would not attempt a rematch, he acknowledged that "Poshard is doing a good job. . . . It's a great match of man and district" (Michael Kilian, "Glenn the Obscure: Rep. Poshard Confines His Recognition to His District," *CT*, October 17, 1994).

25. Lamprecht, "Southern Populist."

26. Ibid.

27. Harry Caudill, *Night Comes to the Cumberlands* (Boston: Little Brown, 1962).

28. Speech, "In Defense of Freedom," *CR*, June 26, 1995, H6307–H6310. See also, "Supporting the American Flag by Supporting the Bill of Rights," *CR*, Wednesday July 20, 1990.

29. Robert Kelly, "Moderate vs. Conservative Stances Evident in 19th District," *SLPD*, October 24, 1994.

30. Ibid.

31. Robert Koenig, "Washington: For a Coal Miner, It's Black Lung," *SLPD*, March 19, 1992.

32. *CT*, March 24, 1992.

33. Killian, "Glenn the Obscure."

34. Worland, "Illinois' Quiet Leader."

35. Lamprecht, "Southern Populist."

36. Dave Moore, "Poshard Rolls Into Reelection Bid," *Herald and Review,* December 17, 1995.

37. Mike Dorning, "Term Limit Proponent Poshard Plans to Keep Vow Not to Run Again," *CT,* February 13, 1997. See also, Best, "Glenn Poshard."

38. Hugh Dellios, "Downstate Faces Tough Choice," *CT,* February 13, 1992.

39. Speech, "Support the American Flag by Supporting the Bill of Rights," US House of Representatives, 101st Cong., second session, vol. 136, June 20, 1990. See also the speech, "In Defense of Freedom," US House of Representatives, *CR,* June 26, 1995, H6307–H6310.

40. Sweet, "Compromise's Balancing Act."

41. Woolf, "Poshard Laments Nation's Growing Intolerance."

42. Ibid.

43. Press release, August 21, 1994. For earlier vote, see press release, August 12, 1994.

44. Press release, July 27, 1994.

45. Tim Poor, "US Troops Are Needed in Bosnia, Lawmaker Back from Region," *SLPD,* December 6, 1995.

46. See Richard Fenno, *Home Style* (New York: Longmans, 1978), chapter 5.

47. *CT,* December 24, 1995.

48. Worland, "Illinois' Quiet Leader."

49. Dwight, 284. Robert Koenig and Daniel Morris, *Handbook of Campaign Spending* Browning, "Poshard Credits Budget Winner; Says Support for Pact Led to Win," *SLPD,* March 19, 1992.

50. "Opinions," *SI,* October 1995; "Opinions," Peace and Prosperity: The Case for Bill Clinton," *SI,* November 3, 1996.

51. When he spoke outside his district, journalists who were unfamiliar with his style emphasized his "fiery rhetoric and populist style" of "fists waving, muscles in his neck and face tightening" as he gave a populist appeal for "simple justice" (John Kass, "Democratic Day at the Fair," *CT,* August 15, 1997, and Bernard Schoenberg, "Candidates Use State Fair," *State Journal Register,* August 17, 1997).

52. Lamprecht, "Southern Populist."

53. In a 1995 interview, he explained, "What troubles me (about the Christian Coalition) is when I see a particular position . . . being portrayed as 'the Christian position' and yet in my heart, I feel, as someone who has shared this basic Christian culture all my life, that the position doesn't match up to my understanding of the Bible. . . . Almost always the group judges a good vote to be one that agrees with the Republican position." Ronald Brownstein, "Christian Coalition in a Good Spot to Show It's More Than Just a GOP Arm," *Los Angeles Times,* April 10, 1995. See his floor speech on faith and abortion in the US House of Representatives, November 1, 1995, H11683–H11685.

54. From my notes: "As part of the after-dinner program, we had watched a video on keeping kids out of trouble—put out by a Lutheran group—in which the only two troubled kids they showed were one named (Michel) Ramirez and a black youth. All the real troublemakers in their world seem to be minorities!"

55. Bernard Schoenberg, "Poshard Popular in South, But What About Elsewhere?," *State Journal Register,* March 9, 1997.

56. An updated profile during that later period is Scott Carlson's "A President, Fighting for Every Nickel," *The Chronicle of Higher Education,* April 4, 2010.

4. Karen Thurman

1. Michael Barone, ed., et al., *Almanac of American Politics* (Washington, DC: National Journal Group, 1996) , 288; Collins Connor, "Hogan-Thurman Rematch Likely," *SPT,* September 2, 1992; Jim Ross, "Thurman Focuses on Current Issues," *SPT,* December 9, 1993; Collins Connor, "US House District Five," *SPT,* November 5, 1992.

2. Collins Connor, "A Widely Varied District," *SPT,* October 18, 1992.

3. From 1992 to 2004, candidates with Perot connections ran in every congressional election except 1994.

4. Mark Hollis, "Redistricting Plan Complicates Races," *Gainesville Sun,* April 12, 1996; Mark Hollis, "Redistricting Proposals Would Divide Alachua, Marion," *GS,* April 30, 1996; Mark Hollis, "New Districts Shift 300,000," *GS,* May 10, 1996.

5. Dan Balz, "Are the Democrats Losing It?," *Washington Post Weekly,* September 19–25, 1994.

6. Grace Browning, "Endangered Species," *National Journal,* September 3, 1994; Kevin Merida, "On the Inside Now, and Struggling to Stay There," *WPW,* August 15–21, 1994; Dan Balz, "On the Inside Looking Out: Incumbents At All Levels, In All Regions Are Running Scared," *WPW,* April 4–10, 1994.

7. Kevin Merida, "An Unhappy New Year for the Year of the Woman," *WPW,* September 19–25, 1994.

8. Alissa Rubin, "1994 Elections Are Looking Like the 'Off Year' of the Woman," *Congressional Quarterly,* October 15, 1994.

9. Michael Frisby, "Florida Race Shows How Democrats Were Hurt by Efforts to Create Black Dominated Districts," *WPW,* October 25, 1994.

10. Thomas B. Edsall, "The Democrats' Gender and Class Gap," *WPW,* June 6–12, 1994.

11. See notes 9 and 10.

12. A study that teases Washington reporters to do more constituency-based work is Richard Fenno, *Congressional Travels: Places, Connections and Authenticity* (New York: Pearson-Longman, 2006).

13. Barbara Palmer and Dennis Simon, *Breaking the Political Glass Ceiling* (New York: Routledge, 2006), chapter 6.

14. Ibid., 152.

15. Report of Dr. David Bositis, Joint Center for Political and Economic Studies, Washington, DC, January 2, 1996.

16. Rick Gershman, "Health Care is Talk's Focus," *Pasco Times,* September 2, 1994. See also the editorial, "Thurman for Congress," *SPT,* October 30, 2000.

17. *Tech Politics,* House of Representatives, 104th Congress, "Social Security Recipients by Congressional Districts," 2; Chris Cillizza, "A Senior Moment for GOP?," *Roll Call,* February 28, 2005.

18. Neil Johnson, "Thurman Reelected in House District," *Tampa Bay Tribune,* November 6, 1996; Jim Ross, "Thurman Goes from Battle to War," *SPT,* October 28, 1996; Jorge Sanches, "Women Told to Watch Social Security Changes," *SPT,* April 29, 2000; on the importance of veterans during redistricting in 1992, see Chuck Murphy, "GOP Cries Foul on New Lines," *SPT,* May 21, 1992. In the Tampa area, her southernmost territory, her opposition came from a Republican Congressman whose attentiveness to veterans was his trademark.

19. Editorial, "Return Thurman to Congress," *TBT,* November 4, 1994.

20. David Dahl, "Thurman Vote Catches Ire of Abortion Rights Backers," *SPT,* July 2, 1993, and "Her Choice Unclear on Abortion Rights," *SPT,* July 11, 1993; David Broder, "Feminist Dilemma," *WP,* July 18, 1993.

21. Associated Press, "Karen Thurman: Election 2002," *Orlando Sentinal* (no date). See also James K. Glassman, "The Voters Know How to Clean House," *New York Times,* November 3, 1994.

22. Mary Shedden, "Is Thurman Battling a Celebrity Factor?" *GS,* October 19, 1994.

23. William Booth, "High on Fuel, Low on Bull," *WPW,* October 10, 1994. A good account is *CQ,* January 16, 1993.

24. John D. McKinnon, "Republicans Now Claim Redistricting Win," *SPT,* May 15, 1992; Ken Moritsugu, "Old Hands Seek New Political Roles," *SPT,* July 14, 1992.

25. Eileen Shanahan, "Democrat Finds Squabbles, Chaos, Accomplishment," *SPT,* November 28, 1993.

26. Collins Connor, "The New and the DeJaVu in the 5th Congressional District," *SPT,* November 2, 1992; also, editorial, "Times Recommends," October 12, 1992.

27. *GS,* as reported in *Hotline,* October 27, 1994.

28. Jim Ross, "Know Your Candidates," *SPT,* November 2, 1994.

29. On her budget vote, David Dahl, "What Swayed Karen Thurman?," *SPT,* May 28, 1993; Adam C. Smith, "Rep. Thurman Defends Her Vote for Clinton's Budget," *SPT,* August 19, 1993.

30. Interview with Debra Dodson from the Center for American Women and Politics, Eagleton Institute of Politics, Rutgers University, April 21, 1995, 3–4. Note: I shall make use of three Dodson interviews with Rep. Thurman and will specify when I quote from them. I wish to acknowledge that all three interviews were conducted by the Center for American Women and Politics, Eagleton Institute of Politics, Rutgers University, and were made possible through the support of the Ford Foundation and the Charles H. Revson Foundation.

31. J. Craig Crawford, "Mica Slings A Rock, With Help from Thurman, Into EPA Bill," *OS*, February 6, 1994; editorial, "Risky Business," *Wall Street Journal*, September 15, 1994; Shanahan, "Democrat Finds Squabbles."

32. See note 1.

33. Shanahan, "Democrat Finds Squabbles."

34. *AAP*, 1994, 287; *AAP*, 1998, 356, 404. Jim Ross, "Big Daddy Garlits is Left in Dust by Freshman Lawmaker," *SPT*, November 9, 1994; Ceci Connolly, "The Power Chase," *SPT*, January 15, 1994.

35. Jean Heller, "Thurman's Water Aim: Alternative Sources," *SPT*, March 12, 1999; Sara Fritz, "House Passes Thurman's Bill for Funding Water Projects," *SPT*, May 5, 2000. Note: "Support Alternative Water Source Development Act," *TBT*, March 19, 1999.

36. Jennifer Thomas, "Thurman Refunds Contributions from Tobacco Industry," *Citrus Times*, April 17, 1996; Carl Hulse, "Thurman Swears Off Tobacco PACs," *GS*, April 17, 1996; Erika Niedowski, "Candidates Attack Tobacco PAC Money," *The Hill*, April 24, 1996.

37. Jim Ross, "Prospects for Thurman's Next Term are Favorable," *SPT*, November 13, 1994.

38. On Thurman, the best article is Jeffrey Brainard and Brian Chichester's "Trade Vote Stirs Some Unease," *SPT*, November 19, 1993. The longest Florida story was David Dahl's "Clinton Wins Showdown over NAFTA in a House Divided: In Florida, A NAFTA Odyssey," *SPT*, November 18, 1993; Jim DeSimone, "Florida Farmers Fear Free Trade," *OS*, August 1, 1993. See also, "Helene Cooper and Bruce Ingersoll, "With Little Evidence, Florida Growers Blame Tomato Woes on NAFTA," *WSJ*, April 4, 1996. A year later, she repeated her opposition to the President when she "again turned a deaf ear to President Clinton" on his GATT (General Agreement on Tariff and Trade) proposal (Dean Solov, "Thurman Votes Nay on GATT Pact," *TT*, November 30, 1994).

39. Ross, "Prospects for Thurman's Next Term."

40. Gabriel Kahn, "Democrats Give 14 Members Displaced From Exclusive Panels Hobson's Choice," *RC*, December 15, 1994.

41. Gabriel Kahn and Mary Jacoby, "Democrats Start 104th Without Final Lineup," *RC*, December 22, 1994.

42. Peter J. Boyer, "Whip Cracker," *New Yorker,* September 5, 1994; Jim Ross, "Thurman Opposes Clinton Crime Bill," *SPT,* August 13, 1994, and "Thurman Didn't Like Crime Bill," *SPT,* August 23, 1994. It is important to note that in her first election, she took campaign money from the NRA. But after that, she refused to take money from them and could, therefore, emphasize her independence during the 1994 gun-control legislation fight. "I do not want it (the vote) to be confused with campaign money" (Jim Ross, "Thurman Opposes Ban on Weapons," *SPT,* May 4, 1994). They did, of course, continue to support her. See "Your 1994 Election Guide," *American Hunter,* October 20, 1994.

43. Gabriel Kahn, "Bill Clinton's 100-Day Adventure," *RC,* April 3, 1995.

44. My own view of the context and of the contract is found in Richard Fenno, *Learning to Legislate* (Washington, DC: The Brookings Institution, 1997).

45. Jim Ross, "Thurman Pitches in on Welfare," *SPT,* March 22, 1995, and "Thurman: Vote on Welfare Was Biggest," *SPT,* August 5, 1996; Dean Solov, "Thurman Blasts Welfare Reform," *TBT,* March 25, 1995. Her floor speeches can be found in *Congressional Record,* March 21, 22, H3393–H3394, H3540–H3541.

46. Eliza Newlin Carney, "Pesky Critters," *NJ,* October 29, 1994.

47. Jim Ross and Kelly Ryan, "Thurman Hits Trail for Husband," *SPT,* August 20, 1996.

48. "Interview with Congresswoman Karen Thurman" (see note 30 Supra).

49. Ibid., 7.

50. Ibid., 3.

51. Jim Ross, "Know Your Candidate," *SPT,* October 30, 1996. See also Robert Nolte, "Welfare Vote Welcome, But Thurman is Still Good Democrat," *Hernando Today,* August 6, 1996; editorial, "Return Thurman to Congress," *SPT,* October 29, 1996; editorial, "Reelect Thurman, Miller to Congress," *TBT,* October 28, 1996.

52. Marjorie Margolies-Mezvinsky, *A Woman's Place: The Freshmen Women Who Changed the Face of Congress* (New York: Crown Publishers, 1994), 55.

53. Interview with Congresswoman Karen Thurman, Center for American Women and Politics, Eagleton Institute, Rutgers University, April 21, 1993, (see also, note 30, Supra).

54. Ibid., June 20, 1995, 11.

55. Ibid., November 4, 1997, 9.

56. Ibid., June 20, 1995, 2.

57. Margolies-Mezvinsky, *A Woman's Place,* 124.

58. Interview with Congresswoman Karen Thurman, Center for American Women and Politics, Eagleton Institute, Rutgers University, June 20, 1995, 2.

59. Margolies-Mezvinsky, *A Woman's Place,* 104.

60. Interview with Congresswoman Karen Thurman, Center for American Women and Politics, Eagleton Institute, Rutgers University, June 20, 1995, 2.

61. Ibid., June 20, 1995, 4.

62. Ibid., June 20, 1995, 13.

63. Ibid., November 4, 1997, 10–11.

64. Lindsay Peterson, "Study Suggests Elderly Get Gouged on Drugs," *TT,* June 2, 1999; Jim Ross, "Thurman's Drug Plan Takes New Path," *SPT,* June 3, 1999; Jorge Sanches, "Shalala Visits; Talks of Medicare," *SPT,* October 11, 1999; Jim Ross, "Bill Offers Seniors Coverage for Drugs," *SPT,* October 17, 1999, and "Drug Amendment Fails," *SPT,* October 23, 1999.

65. Mary Jacoby, "Long Term Care Plan Has a Chance This Year," *SPT,* March 9, 2000. "Deadline Nears for Military Retirees," *SPT,* March 28, 2001; Jim Ross, "Bill Would Help to Offset Insurance, Care Costs," *SPT,* April 2, 2001; Jim Ross, "Thurman's Efforts Result in Help for Military Retirees," *CT,* November 3, 2000.

66. Jim Ross, "Florida Delegate Addresses Medicare," *SPT,* August 16, 2000.

67. Jean Heller, "Thurman's Water Aim: Alternative Sources," *SPT,* March 12, 1999; Josh Zimmer, "Water Studies Received Funds from Congress," *SPT,* September 30, 1999; Sara Fritz, "House Passes Thurman Bill for Funding Water Projects," *SPT,* May 5, 2000.

68. Editorial, "Reelect Thurman, Miller to Congress," *TBT,* October 28, 1996.

69. Editorial, "Return Thurman to Congress," *SPT,* October 29, 1996.

70. Jim Ross, "For Thurman, Winning Becomes Old Hat," *SPT,* November 7, 1996.

71. Editorial, *TBT,* October 29, 1996.

72. Favorable editorials in 1998 and 2000 echoed the same sentiments as those of 1996. See, for example, the editorials, "Thurman for U.S. House District 5," *SPT,* October 23, 1998; "Rep. Thurman Deserves Another Term at the Wheel," *TBT,* October 29, 1998; "Times Recommends Thurman for Congress," *SPT,* October 30, 2000. On her dedication to "Constituent Service," see "Campaign 98," *SPT,* October 26, 1998.

73. "Round Table Discussion: Women and Reflections on Congressional Life," in *Extensions,* the Journal of the Carl Albert Congressional Studies Center, University of Oklahoma, Norman, Oklahoma, Spring 2000, 8.

74. Jim Ross, "Thurman Gets Ways, Means Seat," *SPT,* November 22, 1996; Phil Willon, "Thurman To Sit on Powerful Ways and Means Panel," *TBT,* November 22, 1996. Both articles noted that she had replaced retiring Rep. Sam Gibbons, a Tampa/St. Petersburg congressman, which certainly did not hurt her chances.

75. A profile of Rep. Rangel at the time is Alissa Rubin's "Many-Faceted Rangel Positioned to Become House Deal-Maker," *CQ,* December 7, 1996.

76. Bernie Sanders of Vermont was the only Socialist member of Congress.

77. John Mercurio, "Between the Lines," *RC,* March 25, 2002; Steve Bosquet, "Tailored Congress Districts Approved," *SPT,* March 23, 2002.

78. Lara Bradburn, "Showdown Brews for Washington," *TBT,* March 26, 2002.

79. Jim Ross, "Thurman PAC Aims to Redraw District Line," *SPT,* March 2002.

80. Jim Ross, "US House Map is Route to Battle Royal," *SPT,* March 23, 2002.

81. Bradburn, "Showdown Brews."

82. Jim Hoy, "Interview with Representative Karen Thurman," *Cedar Key News,* September 12, 2002.

83. The author made this assessment based on conversations he engaged in during the campaign.

84. Lara Bradburn, "Face Off: Brown-Waite and Thurman," *Hernando Today,* March 26, 2002.

85. Ibid.

86. Mike Wright, "Common Politician a Rare Find," *Citrus County Chronicle,* September 9, 2001.

87. Campaign and Election Coverage, *SPT,* November 6, 2002.

88. Jose Garcia, "South Lake Made Difference: They Cast Ballots as Expected in Fifth District," *OS,* November 7, 2002.

89. Jeffrey Solocheck, "How Brown-Waite Ousted Thurman," *SPT,* November 7, 2002.

90. Ibid.

91. "New Member's Guide," *RC,* November 11, 2002.

92. Jeffrey Solocheck, "Cash Can't Always Buy a Win in Politics," *SPT,* December 8, 2002.

93. Ibid.

94. Ibid.

95. Carrie Johnson, "Political Farewell is Bittersweet," *SPT,* December 29, 2002.

96. Ibid.

97. Lauren Whittington, "The Future is Now," *RC,* November 21, 2002; Lizette Alvarez, "Goodbyes Are Long for Congress's Lame Ducks," *NYT,* November 11, 2002. See also, Johnson, "Political Farewell."

98. Ross, "US House Map."

99. Johnson, "Political Farewell."

100. Ibid.

101. Juliet Elperin, *"Experience Counts," Washington Post National Weekly* edition, January 6–12, 2003.

Addendum I

1. On average in the Ninety-Second, Ninety-Third, and Ninety-fourth Congress, 82 percent of the House Democrats had higher Poole-Rosenthal liberalism scores than Glenn Poshard. And 69 percent of the House Democrats had higher Poole-Rosenthal liberalism scores than Karen Thurman. The

difference may also reflect the relative importance she attached to working with Democratic colleagues in shaping legislation. Both of them resisted liberal dogma on gun control and, to different degrees, on abortion and budgets (Keith Poole and Howard Rosenthal, *Congress: A Political-Economic History of Roll Call Voting*, New Yale: Oxford University Press, 1997).

5. Jim Greenwood

1. The district also included a very small section of Montgomery County.
2. For administrative purposes, Bucks County was further divided into fifty-four municipalities—forty "townships" and fourteen "boroughs." They rarely appeared in political commentary. It proved too difficult to allocate election districts among townships.
3. *Almanac of American Politics, 1994,* ed. Michael Barone and Grant Ujifusa, *National Journal* (Washington, DC: pp. 1097–1098).
4. Lindsey Graham in South Carolina and David McIntosh in Indiana. See Richard Fenno, *Congressional Travels: Places, Connections and Authenticity* (New York: Pearson-Longman, 2006), chapters 4–6.
5. *Almanac,* 1097–1098.
6. In 1992, he spent $717,000; in 1994, he spent $360,000.
7. Winslow Mason Jr., "Greenwood Plans County-Wide Flood Meeting," *Bucks County Courier Times,* June 19, 2001.
8. Editorial, "Send Greenwood Back to Congress," *BCCT,* October 1994.
9. Editorial, "Reelect Holden, Greenwood," *Allentown Morning Call,* November 2, 1994.
10. Editorial, "Greenwood for House," *Philadelphia Inquirer,* November 1, 1994.
11. Endorsements, *PI,* November 6, 1994.
12. Another analysis linking the views and activities of neighbors Greenwood and McHale is John Harwood's "How Clinton's Plan for Health Reform Lost Two Moderate Voices," *Wall Street Journal,* August 23, 1994.
13. *Congressional Quarterly,* January 16, 1993.
14. A contemporary story of the Greenwood and Kostmayer race is Jackie Calmes and David Rogers's "The Perot Sweater Makes Incumbents Sweat; So Do Too Many Checks, Not Enough Balances," *WSJ,* July 16, 1992.
15. An expanded account of the Republican takeover and its early effects is Richard Fenno's *Learning to Govern: An Institutional View of the 104th Congress* (Washington DC: The Brookings Institution, 1997).
16. Leslie Klein Funk, "Greenwood is Elated, But Also Cautious About GOP Take-over," *Morning Call,* November 10, 1994.
17. Ibid.
18. *PI,* Section B, December 21, 1994.

19. For an early Washington press focus on the new influence of Republican moderates, see Eric Pianin, "Look Who's Holding the Marbles Now: GOP Moderates Rise to a Pivotal Role in the House," *Washington Post Weekly Edition,* January 23–29, 1995.

20. On Blue Dog activity, see Jackie Calmes, "Conservative 'Blue Dog' Democrats in the House Believe Their Bark is 'Useful' and 'Influential'," *Washington Post,* March 28, 1995.

21. Thomas Rosenstiel, "Politics, Oprah Style," *Newsweek,* May 27, 1995.

22. Gabriel Kahn, "In Intramural Skirmish, the GOP Moderates 'Tuesday Lunch Bunch' Wins First Big Victory," *Roll Call,* March 16, 1995. See also, *National Journal's Congress Daily A.M.,* March 15, 1995.

23. Rosenstiel, "Politics, Oprah Style."

24. Peter Gosselin and Jill Zuckman, "Congressional Panel Passes GOP Tax Cuts," *Boston Globe,* March 15, 1995. Editorial, "Send Greenwood Back to Congress."

25. Peter Leffler, "Greenwood Will Lead Group From New Office," *MC,* November 27, 1996.

26. Editorial, "Send Greenwood Back to Congress."

27. James Greenwood, congressional press release, October 31, 1995.

28. *MacNeil-Lehrer News Hour,* September 1995, 1.

29. Peter Leffler, untitled article, *MC,* February 20, 1996.

30. James Greenwood, congressional press release, March 18, 1996; "Greenwood Contends FDA Reform Plan Not 'Radical,'" *National Journal's Congress Daily,* March 26, 1996.

31. Ibid.

32. Mary Hawkesworth, et al., *Legislating By and For Women,* Center for Women and Politics, Eagleton Institute, Rutgers University, New Brunswick, NJ, 2001, 41–42. Another account, in a broader context, is Linda Killian's *The Freshmen* (Boulder: Westview Press, 1998), 137.

33. My best recollection is that the Speaker supported a rule that prevented an antiabortion proposal from being offered as a separate bill during the debate. Floor action occurred on August 2, 1995. See *Congressional Record: House,* H8249–H8265. See also Juliet Eilperin, "The Truth About Bipartisanship," *RC,* February 20, 1997.

34. An account of the unsuccessful "coup" against the Speaker will be found in Richard Fenno, *Congressional Travels* (New York: Pearson Longman, 2006), chapter 10.

35. Pete Leffler, *MC,* February 20, 1996.

36. Ibid.

37. John L. Nicek, "Greenwood's GOP Roots Run Deep," *Intelligencer,* October 18, 1998.

38. Laurie Mason, "8th District Hopefuls Debate on TV Forum," *Intelligencer,* October 17, 1996.

39. Editorial, "Greenwood and Hoeffel for Congress," *MC,* October 28, 1996. See also campaign publication, "Greenwood for Congress," March 20, 1996.

40. Juliet Eilperin, "Pennsylvania Rep. Finds His Place in the Middle," *RC,* March 6, 1997.

41. Joseph Ferry, "Gingrich Jovial at Fund-Raiser," *MC,* April 19, 1996. See also, Juliet Eilperin, "Despite Washington Troubles, Gingrich Remains Huge Fund-Raiser on the Road," *RC,* July 10, 1997.

42. Rena Singer, "Gingrich Offers Goals and Backs Greenwood," *PI,* October 1997.

43. Jim VandeHei, "Greenwood Follows Paxon as Head of GOP 'Strategy Team,'" *RC,* August 11, 1997.

44. Ibid.

45. "Legislative Affairs, Gingrich Taps Greenwood to Head Strategy Team," *CQ,* August 16, 1997.

46. "Morning Business," *RC,* September 1, 1997.

47. Eilperin, "Pennsylvania Rep. Finds His Place."

48. Anonymous, "The Hill is Alive," *Philadelphia Magazine,* February 1998.

49. Ibid., 66.

50. Pete Leffler, "Greenwood Brings Different Voice to GOP Team," *MC,* August 24, 1998.

51. Ibid.

52. Ibid.

53. See Richard Fenno, *Home Style* (Boston: Little Brown, 1978) chapter 3.

54. Theodore Kutt, "Greenwood Seeking Fourth Term in House," *Intelligencer,* February 20, 1998.

55. Rick Martinez, "Moderate Not Dirty Word for Incumbent," *BCCT,* October 15, 1998; Natalie Kostelni and Diane Gimpel, "Rep. Greenwood Reclaims the 8th," *MC,* November 4, 1998.

56. Editorial, "The Race Is On," *Intelligencer,* May 20, 1998.

57. Editorial, "Borski and Greenwood," *PI,* May 13, 1998.

58. Editorial, "Keep Greenwood in Congress," *MC,* October 18, 1998.

59. Kostelini and Gimpel, "Rep. Greenwood Reclaims the 8th."

60. He voted "yes" on two counts and "no" on two counts.

61. Micek, "Greenwood's GOP Roots Run Deep."

62. "Pennsylvania 8th District," *CQ,* January 16, 1993, 131.

63. James B. Witkin and Cassiellen Cromwell, "Senate House Bills Aim at Cleaning Up," *Legal Times,* April 21, 1997, 2.

64. James Stanton, "Out of State Trash Reduced Under Measure: Greenwood Treats Cap Trash," *BCCT,* September 11, 1994; Julie Knipe-Brown, "Trash

Limits Passed: Greenwood Bill Reduces the Waste Trucked into Bucks," *Intelligencer,* September 29, 1994; AP, "House OK's Bill to let Governor Limit Trash from Other States," *PI,* September 29, 1994; Bret Lieberman, "House OK's Interstate Trash Bill," *MC,* September 29, 1994.

65. Rick Martinez, "Moderate Not Dirty Word for Incumbent," *BCCT,* circa October 15, 1998.

66. Pete Leffler, "Greenwood Brings Different Voice."

67. Edward Levenson, "Ebullient Greenwood Wins 4th Term," *Intelligencer,* November 4, 1998.

68. Rick Martinez, "'Moderate' Greenwood Wins," *BCCT,* November 5, 1998.

69. John L. Micek, "Greenwood: A Major Political Player," *Intelligencer,* June 13, 1999.

70. Two major fights in which Greenwood played an important and losing part were human cloning and the environment. For Greenwood's activity on human cloning, see Laurie McGinley, "House Votes to Prohibit Human Cloning," *WSJ,* August 1, 2001. For Greenwood's activity on the environment, see John Bresnahan, "GOP Centrists Vent Frustration to Cheney," *RC,* May 10, 2001.

71. Ben Pershing and Lauren Whittington, "Greenwood Set to Leave House," *RC,* July 20, 2004.

72. "Viewpoint: Rep. Greenwood Ponders Future Walking Over to the Other Side," *RC,* July 22, 2004. The other main Philadelphia paper took a negative view.

6. Zoe Lofgren

1. A 2006 census study of "larger American cities" found San Jose's median income of "around $71,000" to be among "the highest" ("The Census Snapshot of America," *Wall Street Journal,* August 30, 2006).

2. Her outer office on Capitol Hill had the identical motif. Jackie Koszczuk, "Settling for Small Victories," *Congressional Quarterly,* October 28, 1995.

3. One 1996 estimate was Hispanic 38 percent, white 32 percent, Asian 23 percent, black 3 percent, (Portuguese 3 percent), *Almanac of American Politics,* ed. Michael Barone and Richard Cohen (Washington, DC: National Journal Group, 2005).

4. Jacquie McCrossin, "Incumbent Takes Nothing for Granted," *Spartan Daily,* October 10, 1996.

5. One suggested estimate was that the Portuguese community made up 3 percent of the district.

6. For information on SJSU, see: www.sjsu.edu/about_sjsu.

7. Pool-Rosenthal calculations.

8. *The Newshour with Jim Lehrer,* January 3, 1995.

9. Ibid., April 7, 1995.

10. Ibid., August 4, 1995.

11. Ibid., January 4, 1996.

12. Jackie Koszczuk, "Settling for Small Victories," *CQ,* October 28, 1995.

13. *The Newshour with Jim Lehrer,* September 26, 1996.

14. A program discussed at length in Richard Fenno, *Going Home: Black Representatives in Congress* (Chicago: University of Chicago Press, 2000).

15. On the possibility of changing committees, she said that she briefly entertained the idea of opting for the Appropriations Committee, but had visited it, found it "so boring that I'm not sure I could stand it," and given up the idea. Besides which, she said, she was enjoying her dual committee membership—on the Science Committee. There, she found the senior Democrat to be "fun," "smart," "thoughtful," and a fellow Californian.

16. Interview with Margaret Warner, *The Newshour with Jim Lehrer,* March 12, 1997.

17. Interview with Debra Dodson, March 11, 1998, Center for American Women and Politics, Rutgers, State University of New Jersey. Quotation with blanket permission to quote from pp. 1–10.

18. Encryption is a complex process for converting ordinary language into a special code. It is essential for security purposes. But economic trade may be adversely affected.

19. *Congressional Quarterly,* September 19, 1998, 2492–2493.

20. Susan Crabtree, "Centrist Democrats Hope to Flex Legislative Muscle," *Roll Call,* September 11, 2000.

21. Excerpts from debate, *New York Times,* October 10, 1998.

22. Plus, she said later, "Max Farrand's 1913 classic, *The Framing of the Constitution* and the 1974 Judiciary Committee report on the history of the impeachment clause," Zoe Lofgren, "Defending the Constitution," graduation speech at Santa Clara Law School, September 27, 1998.

23. Excerpts from debate, *NYT,* October 9, 1998.

24. "Ten Worth Watching on the Judiciary Committee," *CQ Weekly,* September 19, 1998.

25. "Considering Impeachment," *CQ Weekly,* October 10, 1998, 2763.

26. Louis Freedberg, "Rep. Lofgren Disillusioned by Hearings," *San Francisco Chronicle,* December 11, 1998.

27. "Democratic Rep. Zoe Lofgren seemed close to trapping the Independent Counsel, but let him wriggle away. . . . At least she asked questions," Fred Hiatt, "Kendall's Theatre," *Washington Post,* November 22, 1998.

28. "Meet the Players in Possible Impeachment Inquiry," *RC,* March 9, 1998.

29. Ibid.

30. "Ten Worth Watching on the Judiciary Committee," *CQ Weekly,* September 19, 1998.

31. Adam Cohen, "We Fight Like Cats and Dogs," *Time,* September 28, 1998.

32. Freedberg, "Rep. Lofgren Disillusioned."

33. "Direct Access: Zoe Lofgren," *WP,* December 15, 1998—an informative talk show interview.

34. Faye Fiore, "The Impeachment Debate," *Los Angeles Times,* December 19, 1998.

35. Ibid.

36. For example, in one national newspaper, she was called "a prime time player" and "the television savvy Democrat from Silicon Valley," Michael Powell, "Target Practice; Outside the Hearing Room," *WP,* December 9, 1998.

37. *WSJ,* August 30, 2006.

38. Ethan Wallison, "Pelosi: Wages Dot Com Bid," March 20, 2000; Erin Billings, "Diversity Defines Pelosi's Inner Circle," *RC,* November 13, 2001.

39. Ethan Wallison, "Lofgren, Clyburn Seek Caucus Pot," *RC,* January 10, 2002.

7. Constituency-Centered Scholarship

1. For example, by the author: *Congress at the Grassroot: Representational Change in the South, 1970-1998* (Chapter Hill: University of North Carolina Press, 2000); and *Congressional Travels: Places, Connections, and Authenticity* (New York: Pearson Longman, 2007).

Acknowledgments

In the time it took to complete the research, I accumulated many debts.

First and foremost, of course, are my debts to five central figures—U.S. Representatives Barber Conable, Glenn Poshard, Karen Thurman, Jim Greenwood, and Zoe Lofgren. I thank them, once again, for their willingness to open up, to share, and to explain their home-base activities and attitudes.

To the three people who translated my interview and observational notes into typescript and then into a manuscript, I owe a second—almost equal—debt. I thank Janice Brown, Rosemary Bergin, and Donna J. Smith for the professionalism and good spirit with which they completed their copy-centered tasks. Rosemary Bergin carried the largest share of the early burdens, for which she deserves special thanks. Donna J. Smith deserves special thanks for choosing and supervising both the analytic methods and the overall project flow. Maryann Hong was a talented and essential computer analyst.

My contacts in the five far-flung constituencies were, of course, central to the logistics of the study—in preparation for my district visits and during my activity in those very different places. I owe a special debt, therefore, to the four sets of constituency-based staffers for the cordiality of their welcome and for the professionalism of their support during my time in their respective baliwicks.

New Yorker Barber Conable was, for all intents and purposes, his own district manager. But I wish to thank his top Washington aide, Harry Nicholas, for his all-around assistance during Washington visits. In Illinois, Professor Joe Foote of Southern Illinois University suggested I seek out Representative Glenn Poshard. And he, along with Political Science colleague John Jackson, provided insightful perspectives on the congressman and his district. Representative Poshard's wife Jo added her openness and insight. Staffers Judy Hamilton and Jimmy Williams specialized in cordiality and document retrieval in the congressman's Marion office. During my Florida travels with Karen Thurman, I was routinely educated—usually in the car—by Ann Morgan, the congresswoman's informed and trusted district aide. Staff member Patricia Ortalano tutored me in district data. Debra Dobson, Political Science Professor at Rutgers, generously offered, and lent me, her own interview with Representative Thurman. I thank them all. Traveling with Jim Greenwood in Pennsylvania, we were often joined by one or two campaign aides traveling to events. On such occasions—and at headquarters or at mealtime—I learned about local politics. In this respect, Mike Walsh was uniquely informed, helpful, and engaged. His assistant Stephanie Fischer was equally welcoming. Staffers Bob Loughery and Tim LaPira also earned my thanks. In my California explorations, I owe special thanks for the guidance—in getting me to San Jose, and in organizing my life while there—of Doris Barnes, Kathleen Colling, and Sandra Soto.

During the years spent in these endeavors and in these places, I was lucky in the interest, contributions, and support of numerous colleagues. Too many colleagues, indeed, to recall—given the passage of time. But I want to remind myself of the interest and reassurance I received from like-minded political scientists while I was engaged. Realizing that my recall may be incomplete, I nevertheless want to acknowledge, with warm collegial thanks, the nurturing contributions of Doug Arnold, Larry Evans, Mo Fiorina, Gerald Gamm, Burdett Loomis, Gary Jacobson, Bruce Oppenheimer, David Rohde, Bryon Shafer, and Harold Stanley. Plus the unique support of fellow Red Sox fan David Castle.

Index

255